# OUT OF BRAINS

# OUT OF BRAINS

## CRITICAL DETAILS THAT CAN MAKE OR BREAK YOUR SMALL BUSINESS

**Farrell F. Neeley, PhD**

ISBN-13: 9780990625612
ISBN-10: 0990625613

# TABLE OF CONTENTS

# DEDICATION

*In thinking about all the people I've known in business, whether they stayed for decades or just passed through my life briefly, the two that stand out for me as excellent examples of small business owners are an Oregon husband and wife that I don't really think ever wanted to be in the business they ended up in. The wife was already a respected schoolteacher and the husband was a partner in a successful logging company. Then one day the logging industry in their part of the world came to a screeching halt; the Spotted Owl was found to be endangered by logging. It soon became apparent that new career opportunities for an aging logger were going to be limited, extremely limited.*

*Over the next months the husband tried other fields while his wife supported them by continuing to teach school. None of those jobs worked out for him and even if they had, they were going to be at or near minimum wage forever. In the midst of all this a member of the immediate family suggested they look at a brand new business idea involving drive through coffee kiosks. The husband reminded anyone that would listen that he wasn't a coffee drinker and didn't see how this was ever going to fit into his future. Regardless of his misgivings, he made a trip to Medford, Oregon to see one of these kiosks and eventually they sunk their lifesavings into a land-lease and a kiosk to locate on CA Highway 101 in Brookings, Oregon. Espresso 101 was born.*

*The husband and wife went on to operate that business successfully for many, many years. During those years they experienced the normal ups and downs that I talk about in this book. They prevailed and eventually sold that business to a major regional coffee kiosk chain. I've known this man and woman since 1985, when they befriended my family during the most trying period of our lives. My oldest daughter would eventually marry their youngest son. Today we share friendship, grandchildren, and memories. For me, they epitomize good, solid, god-fearing, hardworking people who started a small business and eventually realized the American dream of successful business ownership.*

*With love and respect, I dedicate this book to Cecil and Glenda Wilber.*

# AUTHOR'S PREFACE

Writers always have a wealth of ideas for books running through their heads, at least this writer does. In each case there is an emotional attachment to the topic and in my life and writings there are long periods of gestation over the materials before I finally decide which one of them will be the next topic. Some of these gestations have taken a decade or more. This one has taken a lifetime.

In the past I've published works focused on healthcare, life and business philosophy, and even good Samaritanism. I wanted to share those topics first so that if my time here on earth should run out, my children and my children's children would at least have some sense of what I believed and what I cared about. I've no guarantee they'd care, but I wrote them down just in case.

Owning and managing businesses has been a major part of my life for more than forty years now. In addition to all that hands on experience, I have earned bachelors, masters, and doctoral degrees in the field of business. I know now that I know too much to ever get into one book. Previously, I took it for granted that everybody knew what I know about business. Sadly, I've learned that where I over estimated people's business knowledge, it left them in water over their heads.

I originally thought about writing or co-writing a classic business text, but if I had written a classic business textbook, it would be twice as long and the only people who would ever pick it up are people who are being forced to do so because it's on their required reading list in their degree program. Unfortunately, the people who need this kind of information the most are unlikely to be pursuing degrees in business. They are instead pursuing their dream.

Like my last two books, this one is a series of short essays and is intended to aid you in surviving in a small business. It is not an exhaustive treatise on every facet of business. None of the essays should take you more than five minutes to read. It can be started or stopped anywhere and should eventually result in your having a better understanding of some of the nuts and bolts, blood and guts, and sweat and tears of business ownership and business management. That knowledge is power and leverage to you who read AND apply it.

Why did I want to write this book? I find that in looking back over my life, that I love business, I love being in business, and I especially love the life that business has afforded me. I hope you too can love business and be an enormous success at it. My sincerest hope in this writing is that it will help you succeed in business, or give you enough information in advance of a startup that you turn away and don't waste your resources or life in a place you don't want to be or don't belong.

Farrell F. Neeley, PhD
October 28, 2016

# CHAPTER 1

## AN OWNER'S MINDSET

### The First Time

The first time I "went into business" I was eighteen years old, and my employer asked if I was interested in "partnering" with him for a share of the profits instead of an hourly wage. I was already managing his small old-time drive-in restaurant and its five other employees. That came about because I was single, didn't have a social life, and had shown my willingness to work sixteen16-hour shifts when others failed to show up for theirs. For me it appeared a great opportunity, though in retrospect I think the owner saw it as a way to get out from under the day-to-day of a business that he said had given him ulcers. The other possibility is that the business had experienced some decline, and if it didn't do any better, he'd be able to pay me less and not guarantee any hourly wage, meager as it was forty-four years ago.

So on the appointed day he came by and brought me additional business records, showed me how to prepare a payroll, deduct the requisite taxes, and get all that information routinely to the bookkeeper. We paid the bills directly out of daily receipts when supplies were delivered to the back door. From the months I'd already spent there I knew the menu, what to buy to prepare the items, how to prepare everything on the menu, and how to keep the place clean so we could pass routine health inspections. I was somewhat surprised when he said, "I'll see you around" and promptly drove away. I received a phone call from him once a week, and after a while that even grew less. I figured he trusted me and knew I'd call if I got into trouble. I took to managing that little business like a duck takes to water.

I decided that since I was now in charge, I'd make some changes. We thinned out a sixty-item menu and added in two new signature sandwiches. Our pricing was competitive, even though McDonald's® was just down the block. We specialized in roast beef, pastrami, and other items you couldn't get in the national hamburger chains. Looking back, I now know we occupied a niche that left us without any head-on competitors nearby; this definitely worked to our advantage, as did the fact that we were open from 10 a.m. until 2 a.m., seven days a week. Being open that late wasn't a common thing back then, and we had people drive from all over town after 11 p.m. for fast food. From about 1 a.m. until 3 a.m., we picked up the bar crowd on their way home. Business began to grow.

That first month I managed to earn as much as I had the month before. The second month, I earned about half as much again. By the third month, business was starting to boom. The new menu seemed to be working, the employee situation was stable, and word was getting around that we were a good place to get a great meal. About the sixth month, an event occurred that is telling of my character and sense of fairness. We'd always had a policy that law enforcement officers ate for half price. It was a good policy because we were in a tough neighborhood, and having a near-constant police presence helped to keep us all safe on those late nights. We also had a policy that the owner's family ate for free. I knew this and wasn't troubled by it in the least. I was grateful for the chance to be in business, to learn business, and to make better money.

My partner's teenage nephew attended a nearby high school and one day came by for food. He insisted that the girl taking the order provide free food for three of his friends. She asked me, and I figured it was a one-time thing and complied. After that, it became an everyday event, and when the following week rolled around, I told him that I had been told to give him free food, but I hadn't been told to give free food to all his friends. I'm sure it embarrassed him, and he left with the comment, "Just wait until my uncle hears about this." The following day, his uncle showed up and questioned me about my refusal to feed his nephew. He was clearly upset and getting loud. As I explained the situation about the group of friends now showing up every day, I could tell he was embarrassed, but he'd already blown up on me. "I think you need to go back on an hourly wage" were the next words out of his mouth.

There were a lot of emotions that went through me at the time. I knew the business was grossing nearly three times what it had been just months before; I knew we had a reliable and stable workforce for the first time since I'd been there; and I knew that I was no longer willing to work for minimum wage after sweating blood and working many sixteen-hour days to build the business I reasoned he now saw as a cash cow. The next words out of my mouth were, "I appreciate the opportunity you've given… and please consider this my two weeks' notice." I could tell he was stunned and hadn't figured I'd do anything, that I'd be a "good boy" and return to the way things had been before. The problem was that I'd seen I could manage a business, and in doing so, I could make a lot more money than minimum wage.

As I'm working my way into my seventh decade, I think back on that first time frequently because of the many valuable lessons I learned there about business, people, partnerships, and owner-ship. The things I learned there paved the way for me to own and/ or operate other businesses over the years. I've certainly had fat years and lean years, but I've never worked for minimum wage again since that day; I'd learned I had more potential and more value than that. The owner resumed management, and the business in question went back into decline. After a couple more years, he sold it. In time, those owners too floundered, and the doors eventually closed forever, a victim of bad choices and the growing string of national burger chains cropping up nearby in the 70s.

I really liked that man a lot, and his betrayal hurt me. I still recall the day, years later, when I saw his obituary in the newspaper. It saddened me as I thought of what might have been. At the same time, what had transpired between us taught me what a brutal and cold-blooded world business can be. Business is tough, blood is thicker than water, and family members can and do destroy business relationships; I've seen it many times now in the nearly five decades since. You're going to pay some sort of price for your business knowledge; nobody gets that for free. But without that hard-won business knowledge, you'll never succeed in business. Business still pretty much operates on the master-apprentice system. Knowledge about lines of business is passed on firsthand. No textbook I ever saw or lecture I ever delivered could possibly replace that.

## Thinking About Going Into Business

The best time to think hard about how to handle going out of business is when you're thinking softly about going into business. Many people who dream of owning their own business won't even consider the possibility that they could struggle or outright fail in a new business; the failure rate for new businesses is as high as 65% when examined over the most recent five-year period. I know this to be a fact from trying to counsel clients to consider failure and having them react as if I'm the one who's lost his mind.

I suggest this because when the struggle begins or the business falters altogether, business owners are often in full-blown panic mode and no longer able to think calmly and clearly. Even if your business fails, your ability to rationally strategize your shutdown in advance can definitely limit the damage to your finances later. You owe it to yourself, your family, and your future employees to take a hard look at this possibility in the cold light of day. The effects of the Chardonnay last night and the euphoric plans you scratched out on the yellow legal pad need to be ignored in all this.

Over the past twenty-five years, I've routinely tried to talk people out of going into business, even when they want to pay me to write their business plan and help set things up. Then when we finally sit down and go over their business plan, no matter how rosy the projections, I try to talk them out of it once again. The pity is that more than 90% of the people I've counseled not to go into business ignored me and launched their dream anyway. At least 65% of those failed in their business within a year; another 25% failed within five years. This mortality rate isn't unusual.

Business is a blood-and-knuckles reality, and the marketplace doesn't care if you lose your life savings, your retirement, your insurance settlement, your divorce settlement, or your children's college fund. It also doesn't care how much money you borrowed from banks, credit cards, friends, or relatives. In short, it's a place where you pay to learn, and sometimes the lessons are costly and painful. Four people I've worked with committed suicide over startup failures; others I knew who went into business and were successful for some period of time committed suicide when they came on business hard-times in later years.

So before you decide to open your own business in the coming year, analyze what forces could cause you to fail and how you'd deal with them as they arise. I know this sounds like I'm taking a terribly negative approach to matters, and I am. But I've done protracted SWOT (strengths, weaknesses, opportunities, threats) analyses over the years for businesses big and small, and I can tell you that knowing the obstacles going in is far better than a sudden blind stumble or catastrophic fall.

## Buying An Existing Business

One of the ways to get into business quickly or for the first time is to buy an existing business that is already underway. I've been involved in advising people on this approach, and I've also bought a couple of businesses that were already underway. Just as with every means there is possible to get into business, buying a business will have its proponents and its opponents. I take a neutral approach because my education and experience have taught me that whether it's a good experience or a learning experience all depends on how seriously the buyer takes his or her role in conducting their own due diligence. Due diligence might best be defined for our purposes as it is in Black's Law Dictionary as "a comprehensive appraisal of an existing business undertaken by a prospective buyer, especially to establish its assets and liabilities and evaluate its commercial potential."

Allow me extrapolate the rules of law I see raised in the brief definition above. It's 1) a comprehensive appraisal; 2) of an existing business; 3) undertaken by a prospective buyer; 4) to establish its assets and liabilities; and 5) to evaluate its commercial potential. That seems fairly straightforward when viewed in bite-sized pieces like that. But I can assure you that to be conducted properly, due diligence is anything but straightforward. The reason for this is quite simple: there's money to be made and money to be lost in the sale and/or purchase of an existing business. Any time money is involved, it is true that the more money there is at stake, the more adversarial the dance between buyer and seller becomes. You have a business and I want to give you money for it, or you have money and I want to sell you a business for that money. Both parties have an interest in getting the best deal they can; each want what they perceive to be a fair return on investment.

**Rule 1** The burden in this transaction falls heavily on the buyer. It is the buyer who must conduct a comprehensive appraisal, and this is where the trouble starts. It presumes the buyer will know what a comprehensive appraisal entails and either knows how to carry one out or knows someone who can. This is often a case where pride goes before a fall as a buyer decides he or she will become his or her own brain surgeon. Most people don't even know where to start in conducting any kind of appraisal, much less one involving a running business. Caught up in the moment, they simply take the words or the documents provided by the seller as immutable truth. The outcomes in the vast majority of these instances are disastrous. A comprehensive appraisal looks at every aspect of the business in question (e.g., property, revenue, business model, employees, etc.) and then has to ask some pointed and embarrassing questions of the seller about a dozen areas within each of those examples offered. Any one of them can be a deal killer.

**Rule 2** talks about the business in question being an existing business. That seems to be quite straightforward again. But it may not be as straightforward as you think. Is the person selling you this business the founder or the fifth guy in the last four years to own this business? Was the business launched a decade ago, a year ago, or six months ago? When I think of existing, I like to know more about its operating history. Has it been open 24/7/365 for a decade, or has it been run as a hobby and only opened on weekends, holidays, and other days when the owner(s) felt excited about the possibilities? I'd even suggest that whether or not the public saw it as an existing business and not just a whimsical on-again/off-again effort will impact the future

prospects of that business. Bad experiences and the negative perceptions they've created with existing customers carry over to
new owners and can impact the bottom line for months or years
to come. Some can be easily overcome...some cannot.

**Rule 3** says that due diligence will be undertaken by the
buyer. Now once again that seems to be absolutely straightforward, doesn't it? For the sake of argument, let's agree that the
buyer is going to take this on or hire someone to act as his or her
representative in the effort. The place I've seen this break down
most often is along the lines of rigor and competence. A couple
of years back, I looked at a business for one of my daughters and
her husband. Based on the documentation the owners offered,
it appeared a payoff period of less than two years was possible,
and that a wheelbarrow load of money would be made every year
thereafter. Of course their first mistake was to trust the sellers'
documentation. My gut churned at this rapid payoff...and even
more so when I realized one of the sellers was a lawyer. When I
insisted they demand more and better records of the business,
more third-rate documentation arrived. They eventually passed
on the deal and the ultimate buyers took a financial hit.

Don't be shy about asking for and then questioning the
information offered by a seller. In many cases I've been involved
with, the details only fill a single-spaced type-written page. In others, the sellers offered nearly a hundred pages of words, charts,
figures, and photographs. The truth is that in both of these
kinds of data dumps, the deals can be rotten and the dealers
can be searching for a sucker to take over their business alba-
tross, thus reimbursing them for their own foolish business decisions. If you've bought or sold businesses before, then you know
that nothing I'm telling you here is new information. But if this
is your first time buying a business, then you need to listen up
and wise up very quickly. The business world has some wonderful people in it. Just as certainly, there are crooked people, evil

people, desperate people, and ignorant people who will do their best to sell you a questionable business. Their means and motivations would fill entire books; suffice it to say you need to be skeptical, bordering on rude if necessary, to conduct your due diligence and protect your interests.

**Rule 4** of our definition deals with establishing the assets and liabilities of the business you're considering purchasing. People will invariably read this part of the definition and think about an accountant. To them I'd say that's an excellent starting point, but it's only a starting point. A reliable accountant will be able to quickly glance through the books and get a gut feeling about the business. That first gut feeling will be about whether or not it seems legitimate. Any more than that will come about as the accountant pours over the numbers provided in conjunction with bank statements, invoices, wage and hour documents, tax bills, licenses, and so forth. If all you can get is a report from the owner and you can't see actual documentation in support of the owner's documents, you've got more faith than a firewalker. Even then you'll have to be certain the data hasn't been manufactured to give the potential buyers a warm and fuzzy feeling about the business's potential. Sellers, especially crooked or desperate sellers, may resort to cooking their books to make the cake you're buying look more palatable.

Using an accountant as your starting point helps determine quickly the validity and soundness of the assets and liabilities you've been assured exist, but it's only a start. Let's say you want to buy a pizza parlor. Let's say it features a full kitchen and dining room. Let's further say that a great deal of the value the seller is placing on his or her assets or liabilities is based on that equipment and other business furnishings. Who is going to determine what condition those are in to help you justify spending the money requested to buy them? I used to watch a program on television from time to time called *Pawn Stars*. The owner's name was Rick, and when he was appraising something he had no expertise in, he'd tell the potential seller, "I've got a friend." The friend was invariably a person with specific expertise in whatever it was the seller had trotted out to pawn or sell to Rick. Buyers need a friend whether they're buying a pizza parlor, a nuclear reactor, or anything in between.

I don't like to belabor a point too much, but I'd feel remiss if I didn't hit on "goodwill" here before I move to rule five. I'm going to borrow this definition from Wikipedia® and hope it makes sense to you: "goodwill in accounting is an intangible asset that arises when a buyer acquires an existing business.... The goodwill amounts to the excess of the 'purchase consideration' (the money paid to purchase the asset or business) over the total value of the assets and liabilities." This is a very tricky evaluation, and one on which many new business buyers get burned. In essence, you're not just buying furniture and location, you're buying that business's ability to generate revenue at a certain rate, and all the intangibles (e.g., name, faithful customer base, good employees, history, patents, processes, proprietary formulas, etc.). I conducted an evaluation where the range was $15,000,000 to $64,000,000 depending on how you presented and valued the goodwill. Goodwill is nothing to be taken lightly...by either party.

**Rule 5** speaks of evaluating commercial potential. Commercial potential is another one of those intangibles that usually falls under goodwill, but it is so critical it needs to be evaluated on its own here. So we'll expand on some of its aspects in these final paragraphs. Commercial potential involves looking into the future and trying to see where the business you're considering buying will go. Now, if you're gifted in this area, you should consider just stopping whatever you're doing right now and go buy lottery tickets or bet on race horses or greyhounds. Assessing commercial potential is predicting the future with training wheels. By that I mean that one studies all the aspects of a business (its present business environment, its future business environment, and regulations in the pipeline), throws in a dash of insight or knowledge of potentially enhancing patents or processes in existence, and then makes a highly educated guess. In business school, we studied the Rollerblade® company and its sale for $30,000,000. The buyers recognized untapped commercial potential and later turned it into a $300,000,000 business. Can that pizza parlor you're considering buying grow, and if so, how much? Can it become two pizza parlors or ten pizza parlors? Can that pizza parlor concept you're considering buying be turned into a franchise opportunity à la Papa John's®, Domino's®, or Little Caesars®? How about the plumbing business you're thinking about buying after all those years working for another plumbing company? Can you keep the customer base they had and add to it, or will they desert you? Will the employees who've made the company what it is find other employment, or will they come to you with an idea that will make the company grow explosively? Will you find out on day one that all your plumbers are angry because they haven't had a raise in three years and are ready to leave? Do you know of a new plumbing innovation that will cut your labor costs by 20%? How about that little dress boutique you're looking at? Can you take that tired little shop and grow it from brick and mortar to an online juggernaut grossing/netting far more than the seller was ever able to? These are all part of the process of evaluating commercial potential; take it seriously or suffer serious consequences.

My hope in this book is always that it will inspire you to think and question. Someone asked me in a recent conversation how many graduate-level business classes I've taken at this point. I hadn't previously given it any thought and suggested thirty or more. I later looked at old transcripts and realized it was in excess of forty. In my lifetime I'm going to convey bits and pieces of what I know about business and its various aspects, but I cannot convey all that I know in this kind of format and neither could anyone else. What I can do is inform you, inspire you, and alert you so that you can begin to read, think, and learn along the pathways your life is leading you. Buying a business, a piece of property, or world-class painting all require due diligence. If you make the right choices, you end up wealthy, warm, and cozy. Make uninformed or poorly informed choices and you end up living under a bridge.

## Buying A Business Franchise

As I was writing this book, someone I know asked me if I was going to write anything about buying a business franchise. I've already written about buying an existing business. I don't want to belabor this point too much since buying a business is buying a business in many aspects, but truth be told there are some unique aspects to franchises, and in order to be somewhat helpful, I'll hit a few of the high points here. The only franchises I ever tried to buy (restaurants) turned out to be too rich for my blood. Plunking down six figures for the franchise right and another six figures to get the actual physical location and operation going were too tall a hurdle to entry for me and my wife. I'm told today most franchises sell for less than $35,000 and locations run the gamut; the best ones are considerably more.

Now the folks selling you the franchise will say things like 1) this is an all-inclusive package and you won't need to search around for parts and pieces, 2) we'll set everything up for you and all you'll need to do is follow our blue-print, 3) we're going to be your expert advisors so you don't need to know anything about this line of business, 4) we've already worked out all the bugs and developed the tools and products you need to succeed, 5) we'll train you how to run this franchise even if you have no business experience, and 6) if you buy our proven concept, it will eliminate the risk that goes with starting from scratch. We can almost guarantee your store will be successful from the word go. Now if that sounded like a hustle, it was. Some franchisors hustle harder than others, but they're all selling something.

I can easily name some other positives that franchises can aid you with that would in fact be great resources for any new business owner: 1) they're going to have a full marketing plan with a plethora of advertising and brand-building options (that could take years and cost a fortune to get in place otherwise); 2) they're going to have in-house property experts who know the market you want to go into, and they may even have property rights to a killer location; and 3) they can hook you up with other franchisees in your state and around the nation who can mentor you through your tough times and give you the inside story on owning your franchise and not giving all your profits away in taxes and lawsuits.

Now just as surely as there are positives to buying a franchise, there are negatives that you need to think about before you rush out and hand off your retirement fund to a franchisor. The first one is that franchise fee I mentioned above. You might get a franchise to a "Dusty's Donuts" for $35,000 and find yourself a cheap location, but you're not going to get a McDonald's for that. Some franchises can cost ten times that much. You get what you pay for, and there are very few iron-clad guarantees for you in the fine print to these contracts. Secondly, you're going to pay some sort of royalty; they can range from 5% for a fast food joint to 15% in professional franchises in various forms of consulting. That can mean a hefty payout every month; 5% of $30,000 is $1,500 and 15% of $30,000 is $4,500.

Did I mention that franchisors have an obligation to protect their brand for themselves and their fellow franchisees? To do this, you're going to sign an agreement to abide by certain rules and covenants that will cover everything from the outside paint scheme to the types of toilet paper and napkins you use inside. There are stiff penalties involved, up to being sued for damages and forfeiting your franchise. In a franchise you will not be able to wing it, as some free spirits want to do. You'll buy the franchisor's products and you won't be able to play around with anything. You can't change the color-scheme, you can't improve the secret sauce, and you can't go buy cheaper items at the local Cash & Carry. If you're good at following rules, this will be okay. If you're not good at following rules, it may be a very bumpy relationship.

I recall the first time I ever heard about co-marketing or cooperative marketing. My wife and I had a small non-franchised sporting goods store, which she operated with the help of a couple of part-time clerks while I worked an outside job. We'd bought the right to sell a couple of exclusive lines of high-end clothing. What neither of us fully appreciated was that we'd also bought the right to help pay for a cooperative national television, radio, and print advertising campaign; it was an expensive education. Now frequently when you buy a franchise, you also agree to help keep the brand strong. This comes about by adhering to the franchise rules, and it also comes about as you pay either a flat fee or a percentage of your gross receipts to an annual cooperative advertising campaign.

There's one final note I'd like to sound here: What happens if you decide you want to retire or you discover after a while you hate the Dusty's Donut world and everything in it and you want to get out? I have some experience in buying un-franchised businesses, and it's pertinent here. Existing businesses often operate out of leased space, and in order to buy a business, you must get the landlord to allow you to assume the lease; they don't have to let you. In those cases, the business is yours only if you want to leave the location that makes it worth having the franchise in the first place. Similarly, the franchisor doesn't have to allow you to sell the franchise to just anyone who comes along with a handful of money. Check out the fine print in that franchise agreement before you start looking for buyers.

As negative as I may have made that sound, I think franchises are a great option for someone wanting to start a business if they've got the money and the brains to work within the franchisor's system. They don't seem to work out for 1) folks who are new to business, 2) have strong anger or persecution complex issues, 3) want to always be the person shaking things up, or 4) have a hard time following rules. Realistically, when you buy any business, you're buying earnings potential. This is why your accountant will talk to you about return on investment and the business being worth some multiple of its proven annual earnings. If items one through four above doesn't apply to you, franchising might be the way to go. If you're a "joiner," you like to work with other people, and you don't mind someone else having the final word, it's a great way to get in a solid business quickly.

## Business Ownership Is Disruptive To Your Life

One of the ugly surprises for people who enter the world of business ownership or business management for the first time is that it's so disruptive to their perhaps formerly stable lives. Your life will be unpredictable because people and events are unpredictable. Unexpected things will happen regularly in business, challenging the idea of a firmly established living routine. If you truly need a fixed routine to be happy, I don't recommend business ownership or management at all.

If you're new to business ownership or management, you're going to find you have to show up earlier and stay later than anyone else in the place. You're the person who gets called when something malfunctions or stops working entirely. You're the person who gets called when the toilet plugs, the hot water heater fails to heat, or the coffee is cold in the break room. You're the star player of the team, and your teammates look to you for ALL the answers.

If and when you finally plan a day off, one of your key employees will call in sick or from the county jail. The special anniversary or birthday dinner gets postponed or delayed entirely because the burglar alarm won't set at closing time, the credit card machine won't send in the daily totals, or your newest employee suddenly doesn't feel safe to walk to their car alone in a lighted parking lot after dark. Time to yourself without an employee or customer needing five minutes will be exceedingly rare.

I could go on in this vein for ten thousand more words, but you get the picture of what's in store for you as an owner or manager. The old television images of energetic business owners coming home at five p.m. to their martini and their picture-perfect lives and evenings is just that, television. In the real world, more often than not, they arrive home tired and late to a disheveled house, the demands of their family life, leftovers, crockpot fare, or take-out food.

Even after the evening meal is done and whatever routine interactions they have with their family are complete, there may still be an hour or more of paperwork or research that they need to deal with before they can slow to a stop for the day. If they have clients in other time zones, they may have to stay up very late or get up very early to conduct their business. Younger people may indeed thrive on this schedule, but many older business owners and managers either sell out or retire early due to the strain.

## Hard Work And Lots Of It

When I talk with people who are thinking about starting their own business, or people who are up for a promotion at their job where they will manage a business, I frequently encounter what I term "magical thinking." In psychology, magical thinking is the term used to define people's behavior when they believe that by thinking or wishing something, it will occur. This mindset and those who hold it are doomed to fail as either business owners or managers. Success in business or management involves many things, but most of all it involves hard word and lots of it.

## Holiday Season Euphoria, The New Year, And Going Into Business

It happened again, just as it does every year about Christmastime. I start to get phone calls from people wanting to create a business plan; I see people out and about peering intently into vacant storefronts and other vacant properties, and the hucksters who know well of this annual drill start to redouble their "go into business for yourself" offerings of their latest get-rich-quick scheme. Welcome to the year-end madness of people deciding their New Year's resolution is to launch their very own business.

Of course people are considering launching new businesses throughout the year, but as the year draws to a close and the New Year beckons, the pace seems to quicken. Sometimes this occurs because people have finally resolved all the thorny details they were working their way through regarding a business and a business plan. Sometimes this occurs because people have started to gather with family and friends they've now successfully tapped for partnerships or loans. Other times it was an ill-advised business idea that came together on a bar napkin over too many holiday drinks with friends or family.

Regardless of what compels the decision, the result is a rush by people to launch their latest idea for how they'll become their own employer and a financially independent entrepreneur. I know something about this because I've done this more than once myself and have had mixed outcomes. The whimsical year-end efforts, such as the time I rushed into business with two old friends after we'd decided we needed to be free from our then current employer, didn't pan out so well. The more serious and deliberate efforts where I'd researched thoroughly, planned diligently, and lined up adequate financing did better.

Just because you're in the holiday season and perhaps experiencing some holiday euphoria, that doesn't alter the rules of business; only our perceptions of the current reality are altered at these times of year. While there may be tax implications for some by making investments during the current calendar year, for most people who are launching their first business, this isn't the case. Most lines of business could launch just as well in March, July, or next October. Let's consider the words ministers use at a marriage. Business isn't something "...to be entered into lightly or ill-advisedly."

Having said all that, if you've done your homework to learn all you can about the business from the outside (even better if you were able to experience the inside), you've put together a solid business plan you've either ran past a professional business advisor or your banker, and you've re-arranged your life and the lives of your family to accommodate the drastic changes that will be coming, I'd say, have at it. You see, there's also nothing inherently wrong with launching a business set to take off in the New Year. The basics of solid business planning aren't really seasonal.

## In Business For All The Wrong Reasons
People have come to me over the years who told me they wanted to start a business. Frequently, they were the spouse, lover, child, or grandchild of some person who was affluent enough to support them in their effort to start said business. This is in contrast to those dedicated people with a dream who'd saved for years

and bled and sweated to earn the money to launch it. Over time it became obvious to me that what many who had no personal skin in the game actually wanted to do was avoid getting a real job commensurate with their skill set and showing up every day to work at it. The first problem with this dilettante approach is that owning and operating a business turns out to be incredibly hard work, lots of it, and very tedious at times. After a while, showing up every day to face hard work at your latest dream can be off-putting to those who have low or zero personal financial commitment.

In some cases, I've had these same low-commitment entrepreneurs approach me two or three times over the years needing a business plan for another surefire idea for a business they wanted to try. Predictably, their "financier" was willing to go all in again. You see, somehow the last surefire idea floundered after losing all that earlier investment. Whereas this new idea is guaranteed to make them millionaires or at least assure they can hold their head up at country club soirees as they share with their friends about their latest business venture. Candidly, there are parents, grandparents, spouses, and lovers who are an unending fount of money for dilettante husbands, wives, lovers, children, or grandchildren who are never going to actually create and sustain an enterprise. They know this, I know this, and they know I know they know this. It's an expensive game that in some cases leads to broken relationships and fortunes.

This mindset seems to evolve most often when the financier has made their money in a mundane line of business the spouse, lover, or offspring hates. It doesn't matter that these are businesses that actually make money; they want no part in them. I've seen it in oil, gas, mining, farming, manufacturing, wholesale, retail, and service businesses. The founding generation went out and made a success of themselves without the benefit of higher education, social connections, good manners, or proper elocution. Their entrepreneurial spouse, lover, or offspring, all in possession of the social niceties the founder lacked, have no desire to till the soil, drill for oil, manufacture widgets, or service air conditioners. They want to open a dress boutique, an art gallery, a trendy vegetarian café, an avant-garde oxygen bar, or a bookstore/espresso house dedicated to the writings of seventeenth-century French philosophers.

My first wife said I was a "dream killer" because of my work in carefully examining these outlandish and ill-conceived ideas to determine if they could succeed. If I found no indication they were workable, I said so. I then encouraged the low-commitment entrepreneur to either rework their idea or abandon it altogether before they or their benefactor took another financial bleeding. I've seen their tears, heard their threats, recoiled at their recriminations, and been damaged by their claims that I was committed to a practice of quackery. The fact was they had a terrible idea for a business as they conceived it, and without a major revamp, there was no way their dodo was ever possibly going to fly. People don't want to hear that! When people get into that manic stage I associate with launching dreams, they're often as mad as the proverbial hatter; no amount of reason will dissuade them. Besides, if it's someone else's money, what difference does it make?

## Business Ownership Is A Lot Like Marriage

For fourteen years, between the ages of twenty-one and thirty-five, I was a pastor in an Assembly of God church. In that role, I counseled a lot of young and not-so-young couples who were contemplating marriage. I took the attitude that if I could talk them out of getting married, I'd have done them a favor. I figured that if they could be easily convinced to back off from the great love of their life, it probably wasn't the great love of their life. My major regret was that there were a lot of couples I failed to talk out of marriage. Their divorces were expensive and painful for all parties.

I've felt much the same way when I've worked with people who were considering starting or buying a business over the past twenty years. Business ownership is a marriage, whether or not you recognize that going in. If you've ever been married and started or bought a business, you know what I'm saying is true.

If you're to remain in this less-than-perfect union, there'll be arguments, tears, anger, recriminations, sleepless nights, disappointment, and disillusionment. You'll wistfully consider walking away and just disappearing more than once. I have to report that I've known more than one business owner who broke down mentally over a failing or failed business. I must also share with you that I've known other business owners who, when their business failed, couldn't accept the financial losses, the social embarrassment, and the sense of failure, and they chose to end their own life.

There are solid studies that show a high correlation between the rigor and length of pre-marital counselling and a successful marriage. I suspect the same is true of solid business plans and rigorous research before entering business. Now let me say emphatically that business ownership, just like a successful marriage, can be a beautiful thing and a great way to make a life for yourself and the ones you love. I always wanted prospective brides and grooms to have a long and happy marriage. I feel the same about people entering business.

Your expectations about a business need to be realistic. Just like your marriage didn't make your life perfect, entering business won't either. Just like your marriage turned out to need work, and lots of it, a willingness to accept that there will be problems and the attitude that you'll work through those problems is at the heart of every successful business. Marriages aren't magic, but there are magical moments that keep them interesting, fulfilling, and vital. Business ownership isn't magic either, but there are times you'll realize you wouldn't choose to live your life any other way.

## There's A Lot To Consider

I was explaining to a teenager recently why simply buying something for a dollar and planning to sell it for two dollars wouldn't necessarily make you rich over time. You have to take into account how long it's going to take to sell it. You have to take into account where you're going to store it in the meantime. You have to take into account what inflation will do to its value. You have to take into account the cost to protect it from thieves and the elements. You have to take into account the cost of insurance against thieves and the elements. You have to take into account licenses and permits. You have to take into account taxes. The teenager nodded as he started to get the picture.

When we were kids with our first lemonade stand, it looked pretty simple. And besides, we were using Mom and Dad's supplies. But whether you've owned a business in the years since your youth or you work for a business, by now you should know it's far more complex than the old lemonade stand. Over the past few years, I've seen businesses of all sorts that had existed in my local area for my entire lifetime close their doors and be auctioned off in bankruptcy. In some cases, it was bad management or a bad economy, but in others it just got to where there were too many things to take into account, and the profits dried up completely.

## Are You Just In Love With The Idea Of Being In Business?

As a child we often imagine what it would be like to have a life like our favorite heroes and heroines. We fantasize about the great adventures we'd have and the mighty and wonderful things we'd do if we were them. We wonder about what beautiful places we'd travel to, what amazing sights we'd see, and what exotic and interesting people we'd meet. As childhood passes, our imaginations, fantasies, and wonder is tempered by the realities of the true knowledge we learn about people, life, and how things work. I hope as you read this you're a grownup in all the best ways and that life has been able to teach you important lessons without robbing you of your dreams.

Anyone who's worked with me, worked for me, or been a client of mine knows that when it comes to owning or managing a business, I'm all about facing the harsh realities head-on and not pretending that life is fair, business is easy, or the check is in the mail. Look back at the first paragraph for a moment because I want to touch on particular problematic individuals who dream of owning or managing a business. I say problematic because frequently they're long on dream and short on realistic concepts of how life unfolds and business works. As a boy I swept sidewalks for a quarter at small businesses in my hometown. I peered through their windows with rose-colored glasses.

In the mind of that ten-year old boy, they all lived grand lives, were their own bosses, had lots of money, were respected by their peers, and were welcomed like conquering Caesars at the local branch of the Community National Bank. Looking back fifty-plus years, I laugh at my childish naiveté regarding what it must have been like to own or manage a small business in the early 1960s. There were barbers, beauty salons, a small pharmacy, a book-keeper, a furniture store, and other similar one-or-two person operations. In retrospect, most of them were likely just surviving, and over time, some of them closed shop and moved on as their businesses floundered or market innovators squeezed them out. The irony for me is that many I meet today who want to own or manage a business are as naïve as that ten-year-old boy was.

As the years have gone by, I've worked for many companies, managed several companies, and owned a few companies of my own. The overarching thing I've learned is that successful business owners and managers put out an inordinate amount of time, heart, and physical and emotional energy to make a business go. Even then, there's no guarantee that this level of sacrifice and investment will result in success for the business or them. It's also at this point that clients begin to express surprise, disillusion, and even anger to me about what being a business owner or manager has really turned out to be. They didn't expect the long hours; they didn't expect the red tape; they didn't expect employee problems; and they didn't expect that riches weren't going to pile up early on.

I've concluded from many of these types of encounters that people see being in business as a great way to be their own boss, a great way to meet lots of interesting folks, a great way to have the respect/envy of others, a great way to put the heavy lifting in life off onto someone else, and a great way to build personal wealth. It can certainly be all those things. But it could easily take from three to twenty years to experience all of that, and there will be considerable unpleasantness long before the end of the first year. If you sincerely want to get into business ownership or business management, you should first really ask yourself the hard question: "Am I in love with the idea of a fantasized life of a business owner or manager, or am I realistic about whether or not I want to handle it all and clean the bathrooms?"

My standard advice always is that before you invest a dime, if at all possible, work in the industry you want to get into so you see firsthand what level of commitment, blood, sweat, tears, and cash it's going to take. If you can arrange it or get promoted to it, then manage a business in the industry you want to get into. The more you understand the reality of the business you're targeting, the greater your chances of survival if and when you own or manage a similar business. I've encountered owners and managers who didn't think they'd have to handle every menial task in the business, only to discover that at some time or another it fell to them to do just that. They weren't envied or respected, they didn't build great personal wealth, and they hadn't had a real vacation in years.

For people who can thrive in that kind of environment, and there are millions, then no other life would ever be as satisfying. For those who want to avoid the heavy lifting, want respect/envy without sacrificing their entire being to have it, want great personal wealth without giving up every waking minute, and want to constantly be meeting interesting and friendly people, there are hundreds of careers which don't involve business ownership and don't involve business management that they should go into. There's no shame in owning a business or being a business manager. But there's certainly nothing wrong with looking at the prospects there and saying, "You know what? I don't think that's the life for me." If you can do that with lucidity while standing on the outside looking in, you'll save yourself heartache and treasure.

## Working Part-Time Or Full-Time In Your New Business

Most first-time business owners plan to work either part-time or full-time in their new venture. This raises the issue of how you'll offset the loss of your previous income. It also raises the issue of what you will do for healthcare coverage and a host of related perquisites provided by your previous employer. If you planned for these issues in your capitalization, there'll be no problem. If you didn't make provision for these issues in your capitalization, there'll be big problems.

## Business Creation

There are distinct differences between creating an entirely new industry, starting an identical business within an existing industry, and innovating within an existing business industry. National business worlds have each of these types, and each plays a role in establishing, sustaining, and revitalizing the economy of a nation. What they all have in common is the need for capital and the need to take a risk.

What people outside of business often miss is that the capital requirements and the risk involved are not the same. In the field of business, we talk with clients about entry costs, which refers to the amount of money, effort, brains/skills/talents, and emotional energy they'll have to invest to be successful. Opening up your first lemonade stand has very low entry costs. Opening up a four-star restaurant has very high entry costs. There are many entry points in between those extremes.

The person creating an entirely new industry may be a college kid working out of a garage, dorm room, or business incubator. On the other hand, they may be a physics startup by a handful of PhDs that raised $30,000,000 for research and development and the building of prototypes. They then take the prototypes to investors and ask for the $300,000,000 they need to make a go of their idea in order to get it into the marketplace.

The person creating an identical business within an existing industry is more often than not someone already working in that industry who wants to hang out their own shingle. They may already own everything they need (e.g., vehicles, tools, pots and pans, accounting software, etc.) to launch off, thus requiring only that they find office or showroom space. Or perhaps they'll just work from home and let potential customers know they're in business.

The person creating a business through innovation within an existing industry is likely more similar to example number two than example number one. They already exist as a business entity within their industry and have decided they can build a better mousetrap. They may in fact be working on that better mousetrap with existing capacity (i.e., facilities, labor, and capital they already own). They may also already be a known force within their respective industry.

Each of these businesses can potentially create anywhere from one to 100,000+ jobs; each of these businesses takes on varying degrees of risk; each of these businesses is looking at varying degrees of potential reward; each of these businesses can be wiped out by a single unforeseen stumble. Within pure capitalism, all the risks and the rewards are on the capitalist alone. Under a pure capitalistic system, winners, losers, and perpetual also-rans are selected by the marketplace.

## Your Business Ignorance Will Be Expensive

My children learned at an early age that I saw a distinct difference between ignorance and stupidity. Ignorance meaning you don't know about something or haven't been informed yet. Stupidity being the condition that occurs once you have been informed about something and yet you continue to act as if you haven't received the necessary information. In this context, we're all ignorant on a regular basis, but if we're stupid, it's usually by our own choice or some inherent inability to retain what we've been informed of.

You'd be amazed at the number of otherwise intelligent people I've worked with who dumped small fortunes into starting or buying businesses they hadn't researched to even a minor degree. Prior to jumping in, they hadn't even done the minimal amount of research you might expect one to conduct in order to buy a refrigerator, much less buy or start a business. In all but a few cases, the experience ended badly for them, and their small fortune diminished greatly or was vaporized entirely.

There will be the tendency on the part of novice entrepreneurs to overestimate their understanding of how a line of business works and to underestimate their challenges upon entering a new line of business. Old business hands know that money and time invested in gaining a complete understanding of your business is money and time well spent. Eager new entrepreneurs are sure their spirit and enthusiasm alone will suffice. On the rarest of rare occasions, it does.

If you're thinking about starting a business or buying an existing business, why not take a deep breathe, slow down, and vow to spend whatever time and money is necessary to learn more about the new business you've decided you just have to get into? I understand how compelling it is to think, "If I don't do this now I'm going to miss the opportunity of a lifetime." But I also know this feeling comes from the same family of "brain drugs" that lead to bad relationships, hairstyles you wish you'd never tried, and timeshares in Maracaibo, Venezuela.

## Launching A Luxury Business

When people first read this title "Launching A Luxury Business," it will likely confuse folks who never really gave the concept of what a luxury business consists of much thought. The pity is that many of those who will become confused and never previously gave the concept much thought are the same people who are actively thinking about entering into just such a business venture. Let me offer my definition of a luxury business to bring this into clearer context. A luxury business is a business that relies to great degree on wealthy clientele and/or clientele currently having access to disposable income that can be spent on non-essential goods or services. Examples might include opening a Lamborghini dealership, a high-end clothing boutique, an antique store, working as a personal chef/dietitian, opening a boutique sporting goods business, a specialty food restaurant, or becoming a business consultant. In other words, goods or services people could survive without if their personal wealth suddenly disappeared or their current high-paying job was offshored or taken over by a robot.

Experience in this area was hard-earned on my part; in addition to being a business consultant for years now, I once owned a small boutique sporting goods business that specialized in mostly high-end items you couldn't find at Big 5®, Walmart®, or Sport Chalet®. It was one of those hobby-turned-business ideas I now routinely warn folks about, except it had finally hit the break-even point when life forces and a souring economy caught up with us. You learn very quickly that people don't need a $500 down jacket, a $750 fly rod, or a $200-a-day guide for the wilderness weekend they can no longer afford. Understand that the wealthy usually have wealth even when the economy goes to pieces; disposable income is a constant in their lives. The problem lies more in the area of economic collapse for people who are splurging to purchase a good or service that is a reach for them, but due to their present economic circumstances they feel they can afford it. Then the oil business dies, the mine closes down, the widget factory goes under, or there's a layoff for one wage earner in a two-wage earner family, and the belt must be tightened.

Your former customers don't hate your business when this happens; they just don't show up anymore. They're there in their homes (I used all three forms correctly), struggling to make ends meet and perhaps even selling off some of those very expensive non-essential items you sold them so they can pay the rent, the utilities, and feed themselves and their children. Look at Craigslist® any time after the crash in 2008 and notice what was and is being sold. Now if you're in a large enough population area, there may be sufficient demand for your goods or services to survive such an unfortunate eventuality, and you can make it through to the other side, where brighter days and a rising tide again raises all ships. However, if you live in a small- to medium-sized town, there may just not be enough billionaires, millionaires, and trust-fund babies to carry you through. This is not to say that you couldn't own a business and offer a few high-end goods and services in a healthy pricing mix. But if you dream of rubbing elbows with only the upper crust and don't want to sell low or moderately priced goods or services, you could be investing in a shipwreck.

Now that I've completely depressed you and nearly killed your dream, let me relent a little bit here. I know several very successful luxury businesses that are doing great and have weathered the various economic storms for thirty years or more. What I attribute this to is owners who were not only committed to their dreams but knew their line of business, had planned for the inevitable downturns in the business cycle, and had adequate cash reserves or lines of credit that could carry them through. In other words, they were men and women who had dreams but kept their dreams rooted in the brutal reality of the marketplace. You as a business owner must not only have a business plan that details how you'll expand, you need a business plan that can contract without collapsing. If your market falls in half, how will you staff for it? If your cash flow suddenly acts like the roller coaster at an old-time amusement park, how will you hang on, pay the bills, and not be thrown over the side? The success stories are people who've figured this out. They may have endured some hard knocks, but they figured this out before it crushed them.

I would love to see everybody have their dream come true. But some dreams are so unrealistic that they're truly fantasies divorced from any shadow of reality. I think it's a good thing when people can get their noses bloodied a bit in business without losing their health, their family, or their life. You learn from those kinds of experiences, you modify your thinking, you update your dream, and you move on. Business lives pass through iterations just as building designs, writing books, and medical experimentations do. Each iteration we try teaches us to either give up entirely or modify the last iteration before we try again. If you'd been able to sit with as many old, experienced, highly successful business people as I have, you'd soon begin to hear war stories of their own short-sightedness and what it had cost them along the way. A luxury business is a hard row to hoe. I don't feel it's for the faint of heart, I don't feel it suits the shallow pocket, and I don't feel it suits folks prone to wide swings in their emotions. For those who can figure it out and persevere, it can be a fabulous life.

## Know Your Market, Know Your Offering
Whether you're selling widgets or rocket ships, it's important to know your product or invention and to know your market for those things. Getting the correct product or invention in front of the appropriate sets of eyes and ears is a matter of business life or death. You'll encounter organizations that have a great product and/or inventive minds and yet absolutely flounder or die if they can't figure out which market they need to be pitching it to. This is frustrating and sad to encounter in any type of enterprise. Yet every day there are businesses closing because they were never able to fully figure out who the market for their product or invention was. If you are in business now or plan to be in business soon, this is a critical fundamental that can't be overlooked.

Anyone can offer their products or inventions to the market of their choice. However, that doesn't mean that the market of their choice will in turn choose their offering. It's not enough to wish and hope for success here. You'll also have to align your product offerings and your inventions to market needs that exist today or will soon; otherwise you end up with a great offering that has no place to call home. For instance, it does you little good to produce a fantastic typewriter if the typewriter's day is over. It does even less good to produce an inventive solution to a problem that never existed in any place other than your mind; business people are guilty of those kinds of errors more often than you'd think.

I've been inventive my whole life and was fortunate to get to work on patent projects and proprietary projects that even today remain trade secrets. I've always prided myself on practicality of products and invention. Items you invent or products you develop have to fill a real-world need, or they need to anticipate a real-world need that you see coming shortly. If you have product development or inventive abilities, remember that just because you thought it up, and just because you think it's the greatest idea since sliced bread, that doesn't mean much if it serves a need that other people don't perceive or are unwilling to pay for. Throughout your business career, you're going to see products that didn't sell and inventors who died broke.

Now dying broke in these instances isn't the worst of it. What adds insult to injury here is when someone comes along after an idea or a product's originator has given up and realizes a place the invention or the product could be utilized. They then proceed to make a fortune off the old idea. Now, if the originator had locked the idea up with a secret recipe, a patent, or protected it in some other manner, then at least his or her heirs might get some benefit. If on the other hand the originator gave up out of frustration without patenting or otherwise protecting the idea, the heirs won't see a nickel out of the product or invention. There were a lot of geniuses early in the last century who fell into this category of "dead too soon" due to being too far ahead of their time. Some of those ideas have gone on to make billions.

I want you to take a look at this matter from both lenses. If you're trying to push an existing product offering out into commerce, you better know where it fits. If you're trying to develop a new invention that hasn't seen the light of day before, you must work diligently to figure out its inherent uses before you spring it on the world. If you don't, someone else will figure them out, and unless you were smart enough to protect your idea for the long-term, some other person or family will reap the benefits of your efforts. The Japanese have done a tremendous job of data mining old patent ideas, seeing some new aspect the originator missed, patenting that new aspect, and making money from it. Finally, keep your mouth shut! Far too many bright people want other people to know just how bright they are, and they give away all their valuable ideas, recipes, and inventions out of ego needs.

## Overly Optimistic Projections

In working on business plans for both startup companies and business expansion plans for existing companies, I find there's always a danger of the principal parties being overly optimistic about how well their new endeavor will perform. There is a tendency to downplay the potential negatives and overemphasize the hoped-for positives. This plays out when they're asked to estimate things like daily cash flow, the number of healthy births of their livestock, or how many people they expect will call wanting to purchase their new service. The numbers given to me by the principals are often best guesstimates and only offer an approximation of future realities unless a lot of effort has gone into getting real-world numbers. Invariably I have to caution all but the most seasoned business hands not to go with the very best numbers they can find. Instead, I suggest they see if there is data that offers highs, lows, and in-betweens, and then find some moderate answer. We don't want to project a future on every day being either the worst day ever or the best day ever; we're looking for an average number on which to build an operating model.

Now let's get a little deeper. Once we have a reliable average, I also recommend building a mathematical model that utilizes a slow start. A slow start means that your first day, week, month, and year in a new venture will likely be slower than those same subsets in each successive year. Either that or you'll already be broke and the successive years won't ever matter. I once built a medical model for a new venture that showed the business could actually be making money after the first year. I was concerned that it was overly optimistic, and I'd built it. Imagine my surprise when they were making money after eight months. The principals jokingly chided me for being overly pessimistic, but they were thrilled that the venture was going to be a major cash cow for their group. The model I built for them showed the business growing at a modest rate each month. I like this modest-growth approach because I've rarely seen a business grow explosively right from the start. I have seen it, and it's exciting when it happens because your client is likely going to get rich, but it's rare.

The axiom "If it's too good to be true, it probably is" may be one of the most valuable tools that exist when you're evaluating an existing business or building models for a new business. When a potential business owner or an existing business owner comes to me with numbers that suggest growth beyond anything similar in the same market, I always have this gut-level feeling that something is off, perhaps way off. When you tell me you can take your $10,000 investment and turn it into $1,000,000 in a year…call me skeptical. Now occasionally someone comes along who really has built a better mousetrap and really does have an idea with explosive growth and profit potential. It's for that reason that I never reject one of these meetings outright; you never know when someone's going to come up with the next equivalent of the frozen yogurt, health spa, Instant Pot®, or Facebook® craze. However, unless they have one of those in their pocket and the math bears it out, I tend to slow roll their enthusiasm. This isn't because I want to kill their dream, it's because I don't want to be part of encouraging them to lose their $10,000.

Here I want to talk about "mania" for a moment and how it impacts business ventures. I'd wager that the majority of people reading this know there are people who are manic, depressed, and in some cases bipolar. These are mental health issues that can range from mild to severe. What most people seem unaware of is that certain circumstances can foster both depression and mania in otherwise apparently mentally healthy people. I've encountered dozens of successful businesspeople who actually seem to get "high" or manic off their newest idea. This can manifest itself as abandoning a current successful business to chase an entirely new line of business; working for hours or even days straight on a new idea; ignoring any constructive criticism of the new idea, even when it comes from their family or friends; and sinking large sums of money into a new venture before having even the most rudimentary information in place. In these cases, it seems to be a temporary form of insanity that only subsides as the technical and financial realities unfold. At its best, there's the loss of money...at its worst, I've seen it end in suicide.

## Bad Business Decisions

As a small business owner you can only squeeze margins so long before they disappear. When the gross profit margin disappears, your business will not be far behind. You are better off to raise your prices modestly and see what the market will bear than to engage in behavior that alienates your customer base. As a rule of thumb, if your customers find you gouging or stealing from them, they're not likely to continue doing business with you. Scamming existing customers always ends badly.

Two small businesses I've competed with at times have recently folded. The story I'm hearing from their former customers now coming to me is that prices were cheap; neither company raised their prices for nearly three years. Instead, they started padding invoices with items they didn't actually sell and services they didn't actually provide. Their clientele, upon realizing they were being robbed with bad paper, voted with their feet and took their business elsewhere.

## Escaping With Your Business Life

On occasion I've encountered situations where a person who is seriously mentally ill achieves a position of extremely high stature within a business and is then given free rein to impose their "vision" of how things ought to be on the entire business and all its lines. In the past forty years, I have yet to see it end well. At best the business escapes with its life. At worst the business faces the time and expense devoted to picking up the pieces before the seeds of death sprout, grow, and eviscerate the struggling host.

Be very cautious in your business life of those you hire or consider for management of your business who seem somehow anointed to lead. Occasionally you'll find that diamond you've been looking for in the coal pile, but that happenstance is exceedingly rare, and the men and women tagged (often by themselves) as "great natural leaders" often are neither great or natural leaders. The best talkers, glad-handers, and hail-fellows-well-met have their place in business (usually in sales). But at the same time, remember that some of history's worst sociopaths were uncannily gifted with the same set of skills just enumerated.

## Business Alliances

I suppose business alliances go all the way back to ancient times as we encounter some early crude equivalents in the Old Testament. Admittedly, the earliest seem to have been among families, or as they called them in those days, "near kinsmen." We also see alliances between neighboring herdsmen, farmers, craftsmen, and the smattering of professionals active in those days. At first they were likely about self-defense against common enemies (e.g., weather, pestilence, marauders, grifters, etc.), but in time they no doubt shared information about their lifestyle, which was their business, and other casual observations about nature, geography, and politics. This collective of information was extremely valuable because it allowed non-family knowledge to pollinate within a closed community and assured that a hothouse mentality didn't so limit the business view that an enterprise might die from a single bit of ignorance. The benefits were obvious to the keen among them, and though at those stages things were less legal and formal, they no doubt were held together by that perceived mutual benefit.

Many of the same things can be said today about business alliances in modern times. Yes, there are thousands of books, podcasts, videos, television programs, and public training available about whatever line of business it is that one wishes to enter. But I submit to you that none of those alone are a good substitute for having contacts or outright friends within the line of business you wish to pursue. Alliances aren't partnerships, which I address elsewhere in this book. Alliances are more casual, flexible, based on some degree of mutual respect or outright friendship, and (unless formalized) far less legally binding than a partnership. They spring up more often than not as some sort of casual encounter where two or more people discover they have a common interest or at least a tangentially related interest. Perhaps they decide to meet again more formally to discuss this common interest or perhaps one simply calls the other and places an order for a product he wishes to use or sell. The alliance has begun whether either of the two recognizes it as such at the time.

I want to move to the potential benefits of such an alliance. It would be instructive at this point to say that mutual benefit is at the core of each successful business alliance. Let that stand both as an encouragement and a warning about entering into alliances. If both parties benefit to an equal or nearly equal degree, they can be a powerful means to leverage a business and help it grow. Alliances can provide current information, business history, political insight, regulatory guidance, industry contacts, sales leads, references, and at times short-term loans of people, equipment, or even working capital. I've had a fair number of alliances over the years that remained intact decades after they first began. I value those relationships and strive to continue to be someone that those allies want to keep seeing, communicating with, and relying on as they go about their own businesses. I cannot overemphasize the value of mutually beneficial alliances.

Conversely, I cannot overemphasize the danger of entering into and remaining in alliances where one party is always the beneficiary and the other party is always the one giving something away. These relationships are at best one-sided and at worst deliberately abusive. Even if you've never been in business before, you've had previous relationships with family or friends that were in part alliances. You can look back now with the benefit of twenty-twenty hindsight and see where some of those relationships began to derail. I don't even need to go off into specifics here because every one of us has had an abusive relationship with some of these same characteristics. What we should've learned from them is that if we're the abused party and wise enough to realize that we're just being used, then we'll begin to work our way out of such a relationship. But if as the abused party we aren't wise enough to see what's happening, the beneficiary will continue to take forever without reciprocity. Bad business alliances are no different, so beware.

In concluding these thoughts, let me encourage you to keep your feelers out for potentially mutually beneficial alliances. Please note I used the term *feelers* and not *feelings*. There has to be some note of deliberateness involved in any business relationship we want to enter into; emotions will fail us here if we're lonely and actually just looking for friends. It's been my experience that trying to manufacture alliances just because we're in similar or connected business lines doesn't work. More than twenty-five years ago, the idea that we could craft alliances out of whole cloth was all the rage in corporate America; I was a regional manager for a publicly traded company at the time. Our leadership tried their best to cobble together alliances with other companies who were similarly trying to cobble together alliances with other companies. They all failed; some with a whimper and some with a legal explosion. Early in business, you're bright-eyed and bushy-tailed in your search for allies. IF you survive, it will be because you moved along cautiously and didn't just jump in.

## Your Word Matters Every Day

I received a phone call earlier today from a contractor who did some work for me fifteen months ago but left the job with only seventy percent of the task completed. At the time he told me he had another job he needed to get started on and he'd be back within a month. Having been in the same position when I was a young contractor, and fully expecting him to keep his word, I paid him for the work he'd finished so he'd have money for the next job and expected he'd get back to me as promised.

When he finally called, I was not only surprised to hear from him, I was even more surprised at his statement and question:

"Things have been kind of slow lately, and I was wondering when I could come by and finish up the work I was doing on that expansion project?" "You can't," I replied. "I got another contractor to finish it thirteen months ago." Even in this crazy world, your word in business still matters. It may not matter today, but it will at some point.

## Long-Term Business Is Built On Mutual Trust

It's troubling to find so many people willing to cheat other people to make a buck. I hope it is and remains troubling to you as well. Over the years, I've been involved in hundreds of millions of dollars' worth of purchasing in businesses I worked for or owned. On one hand, we hear more and more lip service given to the ideas of fair dealing, value, and customer service, while simultaneously experiencing poor value, unscrupulous deals, and little to no customer service. Recently I bought an item online from a Bay Area merchant who showed pictures on eBay® of the item, along with the model number and a manufacturer's description. My cost delivered was $400. The package arrived "factory sealed." We sat it on the shelf for use in a project due to happen about ninety days hence.

Now when time to use the item came around, we checked the contents and discovered that there had been a bait and switch. The item inside the factory sealed package was of a different style and type than the item ordered. The item inside the package was worth less than half of what the item ordered would be. By then, ninety days had passed, it was too late to go back and do anything about it through eBay® other than chalk it up to bad experience on my part for not checking sooner. When I started to recheck the original listing and the seller's overall ratings (99.3%), I noticed that on each of the three complaints he'd received in the past year, they accused him of a bait and switch of factory sealed items and his then refusing to take the merchandise back. There were of course a hundred others saying what a great deal they'd gotten. In checking forums outside eBay, I found he'd done this bait and switch routine to others as well; a pattern was emerging.

Now I'm a big boy and I'll get my money back out of this item at some point, but I won't be able to make the profit on it that I'd expected. Of course I won't ever deal with this merchant again, and I've also sent his name and his eBay identity to my business associates who also buy and sell similar items. Yet for me, the more troubling aspect here is that much mercantilism is based on the course of dealing and ongoing relationships between merchants over a period of years, perhaps even decades. People like this fellow take a very shortsighted view of the road ahead. I figure he came out ahead $100, but he lost my goodwill, all future purchases from me, and his name is now circulating among reputable merchants as someone not to be trusted.

Candidly, I see this kind of behavior as every bit as objectionable as any other form of thievery. But it is the loss of a little bit more of my faith in my fellow man that troubles me most of all. It's a beautiful world, and there's no reason we shouldn't all cooperate and prosper. Unfortunately, there are always those people who would rather steal a dollar from their fellow man than make $100 in a fair deal with the same trading partner. Call it sociopathy or just being a thief, but at the end of the day it makes the world a little darker place in which to reside. That the behavior of one can have an impact on many can be both a blessing and a curse. The upside for me and my fellows is that a con man has been exposed. However, our cynicism grew as well.

### Racing To The Bottom

In their race to the bottom line, many businesses forget there's a point at which customer service becomes so poor that customers get fed up and walk away with their dollars. The business soon finds that their race to the bottom line became a race to the bottom of the barrel.

Case in point, my preferred medium-sized drug store chain was sold to a giant drug store chain. Since then, it seems to me things have gone downhill. You can give customers all the in-store coupons on the planet, but if your employees are brusque, poorly trained, or downright rude, many customers will move along.

The reason so many mom-and-pop drug stores manage to survive in the age of the big box drugs store is because of their relationships with their customers and the service they provide. The little guy has to charge more money to survive, and yet people keep flocking in. I believe that relationships and good service are the main reasons.

# CHAPTER 2

## An Owner's Pitfalls

### Does Your Manager's Cousin Own That Business?

Periodically I'm asked by clients to check out their vendors to find out who actually owns the businesses they're dealing with and who they might be connected with inside the client company. We've found employees doing major business in their employer's name with the employee's uncle, brother, sister, father, best friends, etc. It's good to trust your people because businesses run on trust; it's even better to verify that trustworthiness once in a while. You need to keep the money you make and be certain it isn't being finagled out the side door while you're not looking.

### A Thief At Your Side

I was listening to a certified public accountant last night detail some financial security measures he was recommending to the board of trustees that I serve on for our local cemetery district. Having been a senior manager for more than thirty years, I've encountered my share of embezzlers and in at least one case helped prosecute two of them and send them to federal prison.

The accountant was sharing with us a money-skimming scam he'd recently encountered that pulled $30,000 out of one small company in about eighteen months. The details are too long and convoluted to go into here even if I were at liberty to share them. I continue to marvel at how clever people are and how quickly they can spot a weakness in a financial system that they can exploit.

If you are now or ever become a business owner, I have some serious advice that comes from life experience. In every case that I've ran across where someone seriously damaged an organization financially by embezzling, it was a key employee or family member regarded as "The most trusted we have." It wasn't some seedy character that had somehow gotten hired; it was a most-trusted associate.

In the case of family members, keep your eyes open and your mind open to the possibility that your brother, sister, child, grandchild, nephew or niece might steal from you. In two of the worst cases I've encountered of that sort, the family members had been trusted employees for years. One became addicted to drugs, the other to gambling. Both had stung the family businesses for around $750,000.

So, when you start watching for potential embezzlers, look for a thief at your side before you start looking too far off in the distance.

## Critical Incidents

You're going to discover in your business life that there are times when a single missed opportunity, failure to act timely, or negligence on your part or the part of one of your employees will either cost you a sale, a client, or your business. One of the toughest parts of being the owner or manager of a business is staying on top of what your direct reports are doing and if they're doing it diligently and correctly. You have to be able to trust your employees, but you can't trust them so much that you allow yourself to be blindsided by an oversight on the part of someone you trusted.

The business world today moves at the speed of the Internet, which is to say very broadly that it moves at the speed of electricity and its various resultant signals. The term "time is of the essence" was never more meaningful than it is in today's business world. It's no longer a phrase relegated merely to business law and business contracts; now it's the way everything is handled, from the stocking of bolts and nuts in a garage to how long a restauranteur can have swordfish in the walk-in refrigerator before it has to be tossed to the cats. Just In Time (JIT) was once a novelty in business, now its standard operating procedure.

These time criticality issues have made it easier than ever to miss a critical piece of information, which leads to a critical incident, which can lead to critical outcomes. In the days when business moved along at a leisurely pace, a mistake anywhere along the way was likely to occur so far in time and space from the end result that there was usually time to recover. But when you're virtually moving near the speed of light, it's the difference between driving go-carts at a local race track and piloting a 200-mile per-hour race car in the Indianapolis 500. The time between recognizing there's a problems and reacting to the problem in a way that avoids calamity has been reduced to near zero.

Over the years I've received a lot of calls from businesses who are already in some sort of trouble (e.g., financial, regulatory, health and safety, personnel, etc.). This happens because being a business consultant is a lot like being a physician; for the most part people don't go to their physician until they're sick, and people don't call business practitioners until their business is in trouble. I think you'd have to agree that taking preventive measures, like regular check-ups, is much more preferable to hearing that your condition has gone from serious to deadly while you avoided the experts who might have helped. As simple as that seems, physicians and business consultants are often the last people called...literally, the last people called.

I was reminded this week of how important it is not to let one's employees or contractors have too much free rein in making critical decisions. A client I work with had given free rein on a project to a trusted employee and a group of contractors. At some point in all that effort, the trusted employee and the contractors went off the rails. Now whether this happened through malfeasance or just incompetence, the result was the same. The client, a small business, had made a capital investment of nearly a million dollars in an effort to expand their operational efficiency and effectiveness. The idea was a sound one. But at the time things began to go wrong, the trusted employee and the contractors worked diligently to keep the information to themselves.

When the dust all settled and the growing catastrophe began to become evident, the finger-pointing began in earnest. Unfortunately there is a point in time where it's too late to point fingers for any reason other than to assign blame; the damage is done, the money is gone, and the project is in full-blown failure mode. Inevitably, this is the point where voices get loud, people are fired, people quit, hands are wrung, and a widespread wailing and gnashing of teeth takes place by the owner or owners. Sometimes these problems can be rectified; usually by a large infusion of new capital. Sometimes these problems can't be rectified, even with capital, and the business is forced to reduce in size or wither up and die on its own.

Wait just a moment. There's that critical incident and JIT issue I mentioned earlier in this treatise, which now needs to be taken into account. In a business atmosphere where every action has consequences, the initial catastrophe is frequently followed by a cascade of negative consequences and further lesser or greater catastrophes. In this instance, in the interim, a host of regulatory deadlines came and went. Along with those regulatory deadlines came new regulations, which impacted the project and how it could be accomplished. In the regulatory world, there are windows of opportunity which once closed cannot be reopened. Missing them is always expensive.

In the matter at hand, the regulatory change brought about rules that added tens of thousands of dollars in new expenses associated with revised engineering, demolition, and reconstruction of some portions and a significant boost in cost due to new requirements for the business to add hundreds of thousands of dollars in "givmees" that government agencies demanded. These were to be done to fit in with an area-wide improvement plan they'd adopted while the project was being mangled. Once the dust settled, the cost of the project ended up being about 30% greater than it would have been without the train wreck it had become.

Could you afford to have huge tail-end expenditures to try and save your business once a bad decision or a series of bad decisions have already taken place? Even small businesses with budgets of a million dollars a month often live paycheck to paycheck. Do you have an extra $5,000, $50,000, or $500,000 lying around to save your company? Is your credit in such good shape and your financials in such solid condition that you could run to the bank and quickly get a loan to tide you over and avoid insolvency? Do you have rich family members you could go to for those kinds of monies? If the answer to all those questions is no, then you need to begin to consider how you might avoid such a need.

Small businesses, especially in their early and formative years, typically require that someone be on top of the day-to-day and every critical aspect associated with them; catastrophe can arise in a single day. Usually this is either the owner or a key employee. As the years go by and the business becomes more stable and perhaps has some cash put away for a rainy day or a great line of credit down at the bank, then the grip can be loosened. But even then, it can be loosened only slightly. If an owner destroys their own business and it was entirely their assets, that's one matter. But if there are investors or the failure is the responsibility of a hireling, the pill becomes extremely bitter to swallow. Investors want their investment back and owners want their business back—and perhaps some blood.

I've been asked frequently when speaking on this subject how something like this ever happens in the first place. There are several different versions but only a handful of reasons. My momma taught my siblings and me that the road to Hell is paved with good intentions. I always took this to mean that none of us start out to botch a task. Those we trust start out bright-eyed and bushy-tailed and assure us of their competence, diligence, and trustworthiness. Over the years I've developed a well-deserved reputation for cynicism. This came about from encountering so many employees in management slots who were not competent, diligent, or trustworthy. And even the well-intentioned ones don't want to share their shortcomings with their employer.

Businesses fail when important players lack professional or technical competencies and have either hidden it from their employer or their employer assumed far too much professional or technical competence. Businesses experience critical incidents when the owner or manager assumes that in their absence, every employee has their nose to the grindstone and their shoulder to the wheel. Businesses implode when employees in key roles, overwhelmed by their own money problems or greed while seeing the business taking in steady money, are corrupted by an inducement for kickbacks. From these areas flow most of the problems of this sort I've encountered through the years. Likely you can easily extrapolate on them and connect the dots using your own life experiences.

The answers here are simple and some I routinely hammer into the managers and owners I've worked with. You must determine the levels of professional and technical competencies of all your players, but especially those of the men or women at the helm. Businesses that don't have controls in place to assure that people are competent, faithful, and diligent in carrying on the company's business invite abuses and assure major goals are never met. Trust your employees, but never hesitate to check up on them or to confirm that they do indeed have all the skills they claim. Finally, you have to keep an eye on ALL the people who handle the business money or its equivalents. A biller having a nervous breakdown and failing to bill for a month is nearly as deadly to cash flow as having an embezzler steal a month's worth of receipts.

## Keep An Eye On The Mice

I've been having my oil changed in my car and truck at the same locations for some years now. I've recommended them to my friends and to my customers. I got to know the owner when he first bought the place about five years back, and he took it from a struggling enterprise ready to close its doors to a bustling business on a major thoroughfare. I noticed at the start of the new year he was no longer on site when I drove past, and in the first six months of the year (I drive about three thousand miles a month), the three times I came in, he was only present once. The last time I was there I asked the new manager what was going on, and he said the boss had semi-retired. Now let me say right here that being semi-retired is a great thing to be able to engage in as you age. You get the best of both worlds as you get to enjoy the fruits of your labors before you're in a wheelchair or a hospital bed.

So, what's wrong with this rosy scenario? Only this: last week I brought my truck by for an oil change, new air and cabin filters, and a transmission service. I figured to plunk down about $250.

Now in the oil change business, that's a big deal, as your average invoice is $70 or less. When I pulled up, I noticed the new manager and his helper had a car on pit one, and the second pit had a barricade in front of it. I sat there for about five minutes until the manager came over and told me, "We have a car that we're making a repair on, and we'll be tied up for an hour. Can you come back in an hour?" He knew I was a regular, and I told him, "sure." I ran an errand or two and came back in ninety minutes, and the repairs were still underway.

I don't know how much you know about the quick oil change business, but it's based on volume and add-on sales of filters and other more expensive items, like wiper blade refills, radiator flushes, and headlight lens resurfacing. Quick lube places are not known for their tremendous auto repair abilities. So, when I saw the same car still being worked on, I walked up unannounced to see what was happening. The conversation reminded me of when I was younger, when a couple of buddies and I were working on one of our cars to make a cheap repair that we couldn't afford to have done at a garage. It was obvious within thirty seconds that they were working on a friend's car on company time. When the manager saw me, he again said they were still tied up and maybe I should come back the next day.

I went to another quick lube; they're all pretty much the same, aren't they? I didn't have any more time to waste on a place where the boss had vacated the premises and the employees lacked the personal integrity to carry on business in a businesslike manner. After that, I figured I'd give them one more shot and came in near the end of the day with my wife's Camry. Now here it's important that I point out that it was twenty minutes until closing time, and both pits had barriers up. The manager came out and began to explain to me that they were already closed for the day and I'd need to bring back the Camry in the morning. I didn't fuss or fume, but in the morning I took the

Camry to the new place I was having oil changes on my other vehicles.

I will make direct contact with the owner. I feel that as a fellow businessman, former customer, and management consulting professional, I owe him that. My suspicion is that he's over at the beach (this is California after all), and he figures these two employees are over here hard at it. He sees himself raking in the revenue hour by hour. My assessment is that he's abandoned his business to such a degree that these two feel free to do as they wish. His books will take weeks or even months for him to see that his business is in decline. The damage these two malfeasants are wreaking on his business can take a year or two to correct. Why? A lot of folks will encounter circumstances here similar to my own and just say, "Never again."

"When the cat's away the mice will play" is an old adage my momma shared with me. Keep an eye on the mice.

## It's Your Hire

Over the years, I've conducted employee testing on more than a thousand potential employees. This was undertaken to assist potential employers in determining applicants' levels of aptitude relative to the task they were seeking to be hired to perform. Some companies do this routinely and others not at all. If you have only two or three employees, getting the right hire becomes a matter of life and death to your organization. There won't be a lot of forgiveness in such a tight system.

Sadly, it's not uncommon to test a candidate or existing employee with a high school diploma who reads, writes, and performs math at a seventh-, sixth-, or even a fifth-grade level. Neither is it uncommon to test a college graduate and find that their sheepskin hides a deficit of high school level skills. I've seen the same can be true at masters and doctoral levels as well. Diplomas and degrees indicate the ability to navigate the educational system; they don't guarantee intelligence or career aptitude

It's not my place or purpose here to discuss the why of all this or how people got their degrees. I'll leave that to parents, politicians, and educators to debate. In those instances, my job is to help an organization find the diamond in that pile of coal that sits on their HR desk as a jumble of resumes. The debate about devalued degrees will go on long after I'm dead and your organization closes its doors.

A competitive world dictates that those most fit to compete in a given arena will survive and thrive, while those least fit to compete will perhaps survive at some level, but thriving is rarely in their picture. It's your organization! You have to decide how you'll make employee selections. Today, hiring an attractive, hail-fellow-well-met, is not nearly enough and may spell disaster for you and your next venture.

## It's Still Your Hire

I learned years ago that when interviewing potential employees, the ones who are most verbally engaging (good talkers) scored better with me than the ones who were not good talkers. However, when I tested the skills and aptitude of the two groups, I often found the good talkers were not nearly as good a fit for the task as I'd initially believed them to be. I'd unwittingly fallen victim to an old and well-documented bias.

Research has shown repeatedly that we all have a bias that favors good talkers, good lookers, and good schmoozers when we're conducting job interviews (and in life in general). Now in some job categories, those qualities are highly important (e.g., sales, presentations, management, etc.) and highly sought after, but where we get into trouble is when these biases kick in on the wrong hiring situation.

Bad hires come in all shapes and sizes, but often they come aboard because the people doing the hiring were taken in by a great personality. Employer, ask yourself: does your machinist, janitor, assembler, clerk, cook, or grounds person really need to be a good talker, good looker, or a good schmoozer? What exactly are you hiring them to do? You may simply be hiring incompetent trouble in an attractive package.

Are you spending your time trying to get your new hire to shut up, move away from their coworkers, and go do the job you hired them for? If you are, then they're not a good fit for the job you have, and it's likely your fault for placing them there. Or, are you spending all your time trying to get your new hire to engage? Some people are naturally standoffish and work well alone; some people need to be with other people and work well in a group. Figure out which one you need for the job or go broke for failing to learn the difference.

Over the forty years I've been in some form of management, I've seen employees from both groups turn out to do excellent jobs and become valued employees within their respective organizations. This happened because those people were placed in jobs that fit the entire skill set they brought to the table, and not just the superficial social ones. If you are to survive, you'll have to stop making bad hires based on superficial qualities and start to look a little deeper in the future.

## Managing Like Momma And Daddy

During my career, I've been privileged to manage a lot of people. Moreover, I've been able to work with a lot of managers and to train and mentor a lot of managers. As I rose through the ranks, I went from my direct reports being line level workers to managing forepersons, then managers, then regional managers, and finally executives, from vice presidents of various types and configurations to C-level personnel of various titles (e.g., COO, CFO, CTO, etc.). Now, I tossed all my history and all those acronyms at you to let you know that I've had the opportunity to watch managers at every level that exists in business. That means I've worked with high school drop-outs who owned businesses or managed other people's companies, and I've worked with people who have MBAs from some of America's most prestigious business schools. So I'm going to share with you a secret about a management style that I've spent hundreds of hours over the years trying to train new owners and managers out of. I began to notice years back that if I worked for a company that was family-owned, all the employees and I eventually got caught up in the family's dynamic and ongoing drama. We knew way more about the family and how the parents treated their kids and how the kids treated their parents than we ever wanted to.

Now you're saying to yourself, "So what? Why do we care about your observations of family dynamics in a family-owned business?" That's a valid question, and one for which I have answer. You see, I began to notice that mom-and-pop operations, which is what your startup is likely to be, invariably begin to treat their employees as their pseudo-children. Most people opening their first business don't know much about management unless they've already had professional training. What's worse is that most people who have had professional training but never ran a business before go into survival mode on their first assignment and revert to the tactics of mothers or fathers. This is being a mother or father as they either currently practice it in their own home or as they saw it practiced in the home of their origins.

Think about what I've just said. At work they take on the role of Momma or Daddy to all the employees, their vendors, and even their customers. I'm going to ignore vendors and customers and stay specifically on how they treat employees. Mommas and daddies have different relationships with each of their children, and if Momma and Daddy aren't real careful not to show favoritism, there will be problems with their kids. If you take your momma or daddy role to the workplace, you're going to have problems, and it won't just be one child claiming, "You like Larry better than me." YOU ARE NOT your employees' momma or daddy. You can't play favorites unless you want a lawsuit. You can't be wiping tears and blowing noses for hurt feelings all day. You can't spend all your time trying to save a troubled child.

The analogies are nearly endless, but the outcomes are fairly limited. If you try to operate your business and claim "We're all just one big happy family here at Roscoe's Floor Coverings," you're going to be dealing with pseudo-children all day long instead of employees. Pseudo-children do not behave as employees because the rules that govern familial relationships are entirely different than the rules that govern employee-employer relationships in a business. Think of how hard it is to be Momma or Daddy to your own children and how even when you try your best to be impartial, firm but loving, and considerate of your children's futures, they still get angry at you and accuse you of liking Larry better. Is that how you want it to be at your business?

The other problem I've seen that I need to mention is sibling rivalry. Let's say you promote from within and you make a pseudo-child/employee office manager and another pseudo-child/employee shop foreman. What I've seen in these instances is this older-sibling dynamic take hold where the people managing derive all their power from being Momma and/or Daddy's favorite child; not always because they're the best and the brightest. The other pseudo-children/employees resent this, and in discussion with them you'll hear them complain that "I'm just as smart as she is. Why is she now my boss?" The really troubling aspect here is that when I'm asked to conduct aptitude testing, it's not uncommon to find that the pseudo-children/employees who've been chosen to lead are actually unqualified intellectually to do so, and others who've been passed over are significantly more intelligent and/or qualified.

If you are thinking about starting your own business, you need to stop and get a solid grip on the new reality you're about to immerse yourself in. I was a father for the first time at age nineteen, and up until that first little girl came along, I was an absolute expert on child-rearing. In less than a month, all the boasts I'd ever made about how I'd handle my newborn child went out the window and I was suddenly faced with an enormous and painful learning curve. In that instance, my wife and I had the patterns our parents had established to fall back on, and that spared us a total disaster. But with my first management slot and my first ownership experience, I was initially lost once again and had this enormous learning curve to master. I fell into the father role and had to unlearn it over time.

Unless you were raised in a business and were able to learn real management techniques from your parents or the professional managers who ran their enterprises on their behalf, then you're at a huge disadvantage going in. I work routinely with companies that are facing human resources issues, financial issues, or growth issues. The ones who handled their human resources problems like they were dealing with their children suddenly found themselves before some sort of hearing officer or a judge. The ones who handled their finances like they handled the family budget are surprised to look up and be talking with angry bankers, collections agents, or a plaintiff's lawyers. Those who handle their growing business like they handle buying the next family van find opportunity slipping away.

A lot of folks mistakenly think running a business is something anybody can do. When people first heard I was going to study business after industrial technology and natural sciences degrees, they were puzzled. By that time I'd already owned businesses and managed other people's companies. It was that experience that taught me there was a whole lot more to business and management than I'd ever suspected. I'm going to suggest that you begin to think about your business ownership a little more seriously. Some of you reading this already own businesses, and you know (but don't share with anyone else) that you're in over your head.

When this realization first hit me, I figured it was just going to be an on-the-job learning experience, and I tried that for a while. That approach didn't work well, and in time I sought out books, tapes, and eventually live lectures on business and management. I learned a lot there and, truth be told, you could probably learn enough under those formats to run a fairly substantial business of your own; not everybody needs a PhD in Organization and Management. For those of you who want to helm some great enterprise where you have managers or even C-level executives answering to you, it will take more than books, tapes, and weekend seminars. How much more will it take? I can answer that easily but opaquely: it will be different for each of you who choose to tread down that path.

What I need to leave you with is the idea that you can't be Momma or Daddy to employees unless you want to have family headaches of one sort or another from morning until night. You're the owner and the boss, and the quicker you start acting like one, the better your business will be. If you insist on taking the Momma or Daddy management route, you can expect your employees to behave like poorly disciplined children. They'll whine, they'll complain, they'll tell you "it's not fair," they'll throw tantrums, they'll make demands—and if they don't get what they need from you, they'll run away to another company in the hope that they'll find the Momma or Daddy they want over there.

When that last scenario plays out, if you're a real manager and not just some poor shmuck casting about for survival as a business owner, you'll watch them go and you'll move on as the seasoned owner of your enterprise. If you're a Momma or Daddy, you'll chase that employee like a runaway child and beg them to come back. You'll promise to be a better Momma or Daddy. You'll offer better working conditions and a raise (the equivalent of new paint for their bedroom and a bigger allowance). You'll even force other pseudo-children/employees (brothers and sisters) to accept the unhappy child back and act like they're thrilled that tantrums and running away from home got the pseudo-child what they wanted. You've brought your wayward child home, and in doing so, you've set yourself up for years of childish demands, sibling rivalries, tantrums, and headaches.

## They're My Employees, I'll Treat Them However I Want To

The title above exemplifies far too many owners and managers that I've met in the course of my career. Elsewhere in this book I talk at length about how I refused to work for abusive owners or managers. I'm going to soften that comment a little bit with my own recognition that I've had a gifted mind and skilled hands since I was young and had the enviable position of being able to pick and choose where I worked. I'm going to further admit that I know a lot of people have never had that luxury and have been forced by circumstances to work for owners or managers who were abusive on multiple levels. They felt they had no choice but to put up with the hand fate had dealt them.

Over the past forty years I've seen this change dramatically, and the changes came about because the owners who ranted, "They're my employees, I'll treat them however I want to" found themselves hauled into Fair Employment and Housing hearings, administrative labor law hearings, or civil court by employees who'd had enough and found a lawyer who'd take on their case on contingency. During my early years as an employee and in later years consulting with businesses, I've seen and confronted egregious abuses committed and unlawful liberties taken by owners and those they hired to manage. Threats, assault, harassment, demotions, and demanding sexual favors were and are just standard operating procedures in some workplaces. Fortunately today we see far more "days of judgment" on abusive owners and evil managers than we once did.

One of the jobs I perform for client companies is to investigate employee complaints. When they're found to be substantiated, I work with the company to figure out how to fix the problem and make things right. Sometimes that's as simple as apologies and retraining, sometimes that's reassignment and demotion for the perpetrator, sometimes that's a straight-up firing of the perpetrator with a recommendation the lawyers be brought in to work out a financial settlement with the aggrieved employee. With sole proprietors or a mom-and-pop, it's always tougher because they want to tell me right off that they make the rules, they sign the checks, and employees will do what they're told and they'll like it. Do yourself a favor as a business owner and adopt the mindset that you don't own anybody and you want to treat everybody as you'd want to be treated.

I've alluded to this elsewhere in this book, but it doesn't hurt to mention here that the average settlement today for an employee action against an employer where lawyers get involved is about $41,000. That number is only good if it doesn't go to trial. If it goes to trial, it will exceed six times that much. I can't change you into a good, moral person if you're not already headed down that road. What I can do is warn you that whether you wish to treat people altruistically or not will have an impact on your business ownership. A small business hit with $41,000 in settlement costs and attorney fees usually means you go broke and perhaps sell your house to cover it. Owners, whose history includes the details of having caused a lawsuit of this sort, whether legitimate or not, will find it hard to gain employees; don't kid yourself about the settlement details never getting out.

## Why Internet Sales Are Booming

I wanted to purchase an attachment for one of my welding machines. I went to the manufacturer's site and retrieved the names of the three local vendors. The manufacturer showed that all three had this item in stock. First thing the next morning, I called all three local vendors (I like to buy local when I can), and each of them parroted almost the identical line: "I don't stock that item, but I can order it in from the regional warehouse and have it here by next Monday."

Ignoring for a moment the manufacturer was either lying to me or has a supply system that is so inept they don't know where they have their stock, I knew I could buy the aftermarket part for half the cost. Now I like to use genuine parts, but I'm not married to the idea and I do like to save money. By ordering the part online from an aftermarket manufacturer, I cut my cost in half. They shipped for free, and they also had it here by that following Monday.

I believe most of us want to support local merchants and see jobs stay in our communities, but I also think most of us want service for the 25% to 50% premium we often end up paying to a local vendor. My point is that if you're a local merchant, the one thing you can do to build customer loyalty is to offer superior service over and above the level of service customers can get on the Internet. They have you on price already, and once they have you on service, your business is doomed.

## Don't Bother To Say Thank You When You Ring Up The Sale

I miss the days when employees in stores still said "excuse me" if they cut you off or needed to step in front of you to get to an item. Apparently, rudeness of this sort is a new marketing tool designed to get me to return to their store again and again. The problem here is this only works with people who are closet masochists. The vast majority will find some place to shop where they are not seen as a bother or an obstruction, and the rude business place will die one customer at a time.

I routinely try to shop at smaller merchants when I can, to help keep them in business. I already know the big-box stores are going to be an every-man-for-himself experience, but at least I usually get cheap prices to help ease the pain. Recently I went into a local small business establishment, was subjected to rude behavior of the sort described above by employees twice within five minutes, and paid three times the price for an item I could have bought at a big-box store ten minutes away.

Small business owner, you don't have a whole lot of things going your way these days. The economy is tough, regulations are tough, taxes are tough, and it's harder all the time to continue to have a profitable bottom line. Take five minutes this week and talk to your employees about old-fashioned concepts like manners, saying thank you at the sale, and "coming to life" when they begin to speak to your customers. No one has to do business with you; where people spend their money is still mostly a matter of personal choice.

## Ruined By Too Much Success

I received an email from a web hosting company I used to do a lot of business with until about two years ago. I know from following their fortunes in the financial pages that they've gone from having over 10,000 clients to less than 6,000 clients, and the number continues to fall. The purpose of the email was to ask former clients if they'd tell them why they left. It seemed the newest CEO was trying to figure out why the wheels were falling off their money machine.

My academic research side kicked in and I took the time to craft a thoughtful and lengthy reply and to wish them the best.

The bottom line for me was they went from being a friendly company where I knew many of their support staff by name, to being a company that tripled in size in just a few years and lost its willingness to let me ever talk to a human being. This left me with the impression that I was a bother whenever I called them.

Apparently there were a lot of customers (4,000+ to be exact) who felt the same way and took their business elsewhere. In my case, I had also referred my own consulting business clients to them when they were looking for domain registry, web hosting, and website construction. Once customer service went downhill, the referrals stopped immediately. Let this be a cautionary tale: if you begin to find your customers an annoyance, soon there'll be someone who steals them away.

There is an addendum to this tale. I received a nice reply sometime afterward and an admission that in growing so rapidly, they'd lost some customers and were trying to regain some of their customer support model from their "old days." They thanked me for my candor and promised to do better if I ever came back. I give them points for continuing to try to improve their model and still wish them the best, but I'm happy with the new vendor.

## Dear John

Over the last five business days, you and I have left more than a half-dozen voice mails, this despite me having tried repeatedly to speak to you directly. Earlier this morning, I redialed your number off and on for thirty minutes to see if I could ever get through; I always got your voice mail. Now, perhaps you folks really are that busy, or perhaps you just set your system up to screen calls so you can answer at your leisure. When I pushed zero (which you suggested I do if I needed immediate attention), of course, it routed back to the operator, who promptly put me back into your voice mail. What imbecile there at your West Coast headquarters came up with that brilliant stratagem?

John, I'm neither as young nor as patient as I once was. Moreover, even though I filled out your online sales form to make an initial purchasing inquiry, once I got your emailed reply, I thought eventually I'd actually get to speak to you. You did give me your direct line and you did say to call. I see now I was wrong in this assumption and it's clear to me even though you're in sales, you must be very well paid, or you just don't need to make the initial $1,800 sale my query mentioned. This is unfortunate for your firm because I was actually looking to make an initial order of eight of these devices for prototype testing. The actual production runs, beginning next year, will involve orders of eight units at a time.

John, please don't worry about me over this. When I was finally completely steamed, I called your chief competitor. The operator there put me through to an actual human being who talked with me for twenty minutes, asked and answered questions, and after first offering to take my order over the phone, walked me through how to use their online ordering system so I could customize each unit for the same price. Now I acknowledge I'm going to have to pay your competition about 9% more than what your company wants for the same products. However, I figured if I can't speak to a human being when I'm spending money with you, I'm very unlikely to get a human being on the line if I have a problem or a complaint on down the road.

John, in the manufacturing industry, times have been tough these past few years, and every sale counts for us. I genuinely hope you and your coworkers remain so busy that you cannot answer your phones. It must be nice to be so busy that you don't to have to worry about your company losing sales. Nevertheless, if you do find sales falling off, layoffs pending, and the phones not lighting up so they could go unanswered as they used to, you might want to apply for a job with your chief competitor. They took my business (and I suspect some others) away from you today with old-fashioned better customer service, and they definitely weren't the lowest bidder.

## Excuse Me, I'd Like To Do Business With You

Is there anything more mystifying about business than when you walk into a place of business, intent on doing business with them, and the staff behaves as if you are interfering with their conversation? Frequently (as I've gotten older), I actually ask for help from the staff in electronics stores, hardware stores, and other similar places. Invariably, if I come upon two staff members talking and stop next to them to ask a question, I find I'm ignored by them until I actually begin to speak. Do they think I walked up and planted myself next to them to eavesdrop? As much as I like a bargain, I find myself going to businesses where they actually behave as if they are happy to see me, even if it costs me more money.

## The Greatest Gift We Can Give Our Children

The call came late in the day on a Friday, and I was just getting ready to head home from the office. The year was winding to a close, and Christmas was less than a week away. My business in those days tended to be highly seasonal, but more in line with agricultural and industrial cycles rather than holiday cycles, so I wasn't actually expecting any calls for business at that time of the year. I considered just allowing the phone to go to voicemail and then reminded myself I had a duty to customers to be available when I said I'd be available. I was already standing to depart my office when I picked up the phone. The voice on the other end began to speak rapidly in heavily Chinese-accented but very proper English. I immediately suspected Hong Kong.

It was the voice of a young man, at least younger than me, and he was asking if I could talk with him about a line of business I was involved in. I politely explained that I wouldn't do that since I wasn't in the practice of giving away business ideas or trade secrets over the telephone. I'm sure he heard the irritation in my voice. He hurriedly explained that he had a business idea he wanted to talk over with me, was currently in Boston but had a condo in Los Angeles, was flying home tomorrow, and would love to drive up to Bakersfield the following week if I would give him a half hour of my time. He also promised to buy me lunch while he told me of his plan. The few facts he'd given intrigued me, and against my better judgment, I agreed to meet him the following week in a truck stop near Buttonwillow, California on Interstate 5, for a Christmas Eve lunch.

When Christmas Eve rolled around, I already regretted that I'd agreed to the lunch. God knows in this work you get tons of tire kickers, people looking for free advice, and outright mental cases. But I'd given the man my word, and I would be at the appointed greasy spoon of a truck stop at noon on Christmas Eve. I also told myself that if he was even fifteen minutes late, I'd pay for my iced tea and head on out the door for home; after all, it was Christmas Eve. At about two minutes until noon, a diminutive Asian man came through the door and I stood up. After all, how many diminutive Asian truck drivers do you see wearing a tailored three-piece business suit? He walked over and extended his hand; we introduced ourselves and sat down.

What ensued was to become one of the most amazing and pleasant relationships I ever made in business. My new acquaintance had a totally American first name for his totally American associates; we'll call him Patrick, though it's not his real name. I won't disclose his real name for reasons that will later become perhaps even vaguer. Patrick turned out to be charming, extremely well-educated, and as it turned out later, from one of the wealthiest manufacturing families in Asia. Somehow he held dual citizenship for both the United States and Hong Kong, and in addition to the Los Angeles condo, he kept a tiny apartment in Hong Kong. The family manufacturing business was all on the Chinese mainland. He wanted to be allowed back into the family's business.

The story that unfolded over the next hour and a half was both educational and eye-opening for me. Patrick's family had a practice that he swore was not uncommon among Asian oligarchs. He said that from childhood, all the children worked in the family business in various departments over the years. When a son finished his primary and secondary education, he spent a few years in the family business, found a suitable wife, and was sent to college, either in the United States or Great Britain. In Patrick's case, he'd been sent to Boston to attend a banking school and had graduated about three months prior. As I recall, he was thirty-two and had a wife and two children by the time of our first encounter. But in order for him to be accepted back into the family business, he had to first create his own profitable business to prove his professional worth to the family.

I'd never heard anything like that before in my life, and I was stunned. By his manner, speech, and clothing, he was clearly from a wealthy background. So I inquired about the name of his family's main line of business. When he told me, I immediately asked how many employees they had now; when he said about three thousand, I wasn't surprised. The company name is a common one in China but would mean nothing here. But the name of the family's primary line of manufactured goods is known the world over; there's not a home in America where one or a dozen of their devices are not on hand. I struggled to process all the things this likeable young man across the table was saying as he and I both worked our way through some greasy stir-fry.

At that point I told him that if he was comfortable, he could share his business idea with me. Up until then, I had no idea how I fit into the picture. He pulled a sheaf of papers from his jacket and laid them on the table. He was for certain a banker because he clearly wasn't an engineer. The papers were filled with pencil sketches and calculations for a building material idea that would be revolutionary. I realized within the next five minutes that Patrick was the real deal and not just some nutcase wasting my time. The idea involved combining two current types of building materials to produce a hybrid that was so clever and so obvious I wondered why someone hadn't already hit upon it. For that matter, why hadn't I already hit upon it?

Patrick and I soon parted, agreeing to meet again after the New Year for a half-day working session to sign some paperwork and iron out technical details on his new product. We met twice more to iron out chemistry and production details. Patrick already had strong connections to manufacturers in China, other than his family. By the time he'd been out of banking school one year, his product was in full production and for sale in major markets in Europe and Asia. He eventually sold the rights to a European building materials company for millions. After all, he'd jumped the entry hurdle his family had placed before him and was being welcomed back into the family business at a junior executive level.

I used to get regular calls from Patrick about management and building materials. They usually came after 11 p.m. due to the time difference between Bakersfield and Hong Kong. At first they were once a month, then once every two or three months, and finally once a year. In 2000, I lost touch with him completely while navigating my way through a divorce, and didn't give it a whole lot of thought for another six years. It was then that I ran across a business article about Patrick's family's company. I was unsure what to expect as I began to read since the title was somewhat ambiguous. It went something along this line: "New Leadership At Manufacturing Giant Leaves The Future In Doubt." Apparently Patrick's father had let go the reins of power.

Apparently the whole idea of putting your children out of the family business at a young age to force them to learn to stand on their own two feet has mixed results. I've been told in the years since I met Patrick that some of these young men Patrick had alluded to, and to a lesser degree these days young women, don't make it, and they're forced to make whatever life they can going forward. Their families don't allow them to starve; they just aren't allowed to bring their failure back to managing the family business. This brings me back to Patrick. It seems that his father and the board of directors, all family members, decided they'd place the future of their company in the hands of Patrick. By my estimate, he was around forty years old when that occurred. At the time, they continued to manufacture the one original family product on contract for a Japanese company.

They now manufacture several lines for distribution in seventy countries; specialty building materials are there biggest sellers. They weren't even in that market at the time Patrick and I met. When he took over the family business, they were grossing about $323,000,000 a year; nothing to sneeze at. When I checked to see where they were at in 2016, I discovered they were grossing about $724,000,000 a year and have opened plants around the world, including one in Georgia. As with everything else, automation has reduced the number of employees. At the same time, the value of their brand has soared. From where I stand, it appears Patrick has made a success for himself and his family. I'm also told his son attends a university here in the United States.

We are in serious danger here in the United States of destroying our offspring by insisting on propping them up in everything they do. None of us want our children destroyed, but trying to protect them from ever possible unpleasantness in life seems to have acted as a bad form of social Darwinism, leaving us with children struggling to navigate the real world. I want to leave you with a thought that's alien to most American parents at this time. It's a thought I hammered on with my own children, grandchildren, and the friends they brought around. I expanded on it in my second book, *In Your Times: A Twentieth Century Grandfather Writes To His Twenty-first Century Grandchildren.* Sometimes it's what we refuse to hand to our children that turns out to be the greatest gift we give our children.

# CHAPTER 3

CONSIDERING CORPORATE CULTURE

## First Impressions Can Still Make Or Break Your Business

Recently I've attended a spate of funerals for businesspeople that I've known, and as the custom dictates in my area, I showed up in a suit and tie. In this instance there were hundreds of people present, and among those hundreds were several people I've known and done business with over the years. One of the more outspoken ones among them thrust out his hand and said, "I've known you thirty years, and this is the first time I've ever seen you in anything more than a Carharrt® shirt, boots, and khakis." We both laughed, and I assured him I owned a couple of suits and did get out in public a little more dressy than he'd seen me on construction sites or out on his farm. As I was driving home later, it occurred to me that he and I were long past first impressions, but if we weren't, how would my "dressed up" appearance have affected him and our initial relationship if I'd showed up that way years ago?

In my generation, just about every man or woman I knew had heard the same mantra I'd received from my momma: "You only get one chance to make a first impression." What those new to business ownership or new to business management need to know is that the impression you leave isn't just about the kind of clothes you're wearing. It goes far beyond those basics and includes your haircut, clothing style, your perfume or cologne, the setting, how you walk, how you talk (speech and diction), your conversational skill level, and your ability to convey a persona that gives your potential client, customer, or patient a sense that everything is going to be okay. If you fail to pull that off, you're off to a very rocky start. While one meeting may not be the final judgment on you and your offerings, a couple like that, and even the most understanding person may be looking for someone else to do business with.

What business are you in or seeking to be in? You need to answer that question for yourself before you ever go out on that first client interview, sales call, presentation, or business social hour. I used to hear this saying a lot more than I do these days, but it still bears mentioning: "To get the part, you've got to look the part." I don't think that's a line meant just for actors and actresses. As the Bard said, "All the world's a stage, and all the men and women merely players. They have their exits and their entrances, and one man in his time plays many parts ..." We have many roles in our life, and being people in business is just one of them. For each of our roles, if we're to be successful, we develop a character, or persona made of unique schemata we've developed that works best for us in that role. If it isn't working, we modify it until it does or we lose the role. Arriving in the wrong persona can derail a career, wreck a marriage, and crush your business dreams.

Many of you know from my previous books that for about twenty years of my early working life I was a skilled craftsman and later a construction contractor. I was and am licensed in California in four different trade categories. In the early days, the three I most often worked in were industrial mechanic, plumber/pipe fitter, and electrician. You learn very quickly that there are certain expectations that go along with each of those crafts. You heard back then, and you will even hear people now who claim that appearances don't matter so long as you're skilled. I'm going to disagree with this premise. In my sixty-fourth year, I'm at the place in my career where I could show up for just about anything I'm skilled at, dressed in just about anything decent, driving anything I chose too, and no one would say much because I have a reputation that precedes me. All this gray hair also offers some measure of comfort to those who hope I've been at it for a while. A young person attempting the same shtick would probably be sent packing.

So, is that reverse-ageism? Is it sexism, racism, or some other -ism? No, it's just human nature that we expect our plumbers to look like plumbers, our ministers to look like ministers, and our servers to look like servers. This is our expectation because if we showed up playing our role as someone in need of a plumber, someone in need of a minister, or someone in need of a server, we're generally not in the mood to try and decipher the role they're playing; we want immediate and identifiable cues that they're in fact the answer to our prayers. In your new business or your new management job, you have to begin to get this right from day one. Restaurants are especially aware of this and will conduct free soft openings to allow their staff and management to sort this out so that the paying public and the local food critic don't show up and destroy them before they can hit their stride.

The setting of your business makes an impression and will immediately speak to the clientele who come there and come back with others in tow. Know who your customer is, know what your customer expects, and know what it takes to satisfy that customer to the degree that they'd return again and again. In business school, I ran across a term that I think all business people should keep in the back of their minds with regard to customer retention. The term is "satisficing," and *Investopedia* says it means:

"To accept an available option as satisfactory." Bad salespeople starve for lack of understanding this term and its implications, as do a whole lot of other lines of business. We've all went to buy cars or other items where we had a certain set of expectations in mind. We shared them with salesperson #1 and he said, "Sorry, I don't have all those options." We shared them with salesperson #2 and she said, "Let me show you what I have." The second salesperson knew we could be "satisficed" without every single option we desire.

It's not uncommon for a business not to be in a position to offer exactly what you want, but they may well offer an option that would be completely acceptable to you. You need to begin to change your thinking to see business this way. Let's say you own a beauty salon and it's located in an area of modest to average means. Or, let's say you've started a mini-mart and it's in an area of modest to average means. Or, you've opened a professional practice and it's located in an area of modest to average means. I'm repetitive here to make a point. This is a specific kind of neighborhood with a specific economic stratum of potential clientele. You don't have to tell them this; they already know their financial situation. The salon doesn't have to offer $200 haircuts; the mini-mart doesn't have to offer exotic cheese and $30 bottles of Bordeaux; and the professional practice needs to look professional, but it's not expected to look like the ones charging $500 an hour on Market Street in San Francisco.

Conversely, if your new business is aimed at a higher economic stratum of clientele, you must plan and execute accordingly. If you can't do this, don't launch until you can. It may be absolutely necessary for professional attire to be everyone's job uniform. Your office may need to be long on vaulted ceilings and cabinet-quality finished carpentry throughout. Your mini-mart may need to be elevated to fine delicatessen status, featuring an international variety of wines, cheeses, and cured meats. Your beauty salon may have to be upgraded to spa status, featuring $200 haircuts, masseuses, manicurists, estheticians, Botox injections, a Reiki therapist, and a consulting plastic surgeon. The level of what it takes to be able to offer a satisficing option to your clientele can run the spectrum. It's your job as an owner or manager to understand who your customer is, and then to create a business that can satisfy. If you're not offering them exactly what they want, offer them options that are satisfactory.

Some of you who read this will be younger entrepreneurs and will have seen the Hollywood image of the avant-garde young cyber businessperson who has poor personal hygiene, dresses outlandishly, speaks like a street urchin, locates in an abandoned warehouse, and has made millions or hundreds of millions by the time they're twenty-five. That does happen; but are you that kind of cyber genius? Most of us aren't. We have a certain level of skill, intelligence, and drive. We have finite amounts of money to invest, and we need to do everything we can to stack the deck in our favor. The first impression you make, your location makes, and your product makes cannot be underestimated. Look like the role you've chosen to play, at least until you're a roaring success.

I joked with someone recently that these days I could show up for a public speaking engagement in Carhartt® attire and Red Wing® work boots, and people who follow me would listen. But if I went into an entirely new business line tomorrow with new clientele, I'd dress, speak, locate, and act for that specific role. If I didn't, I'd fail to connect with the new clientele on a most basic level.

## Put Some Lipstick On Your Pig
I was looking at a license plate yesterday on the car in front of me at a stoplight. I read it a couple of times before what was

actually going on was clear to me. I had to recall this local business's advertising campaign. The plate was from an automobile dealership. On the top of the plate it said the name of the company (which shall remain nameless), and across the bottom of the plate were the words, "Fresh Start Program."

We're told in their advertising that this ownership program is designed for people with no credit, bad credit, bankruptcies, and repossessions. They use it as a big draw in their promotions on both radio and television. I understand people need a fresh start sometimes and I also understand they often pay an enormous risk premium within the finance rate; sometimes many percentage points higher than a good credit risk would pay.

The thing I like most about the clever wording here is that it's so much more appealing and acceptable to call it a Fresh Start Program than it would be to have people driving around with a license plate that says "Super High Credit Risk Program" or "The Bankruptcy Is Behind Me Now." Rethink how you talk about your business and the words you use to describe it. These folks have done that, and their effort seems to be working well.

Here's a case where a business decided to take what would otherwise be perceived as a severely negative situation and, by semantic manipulation, gave it a whole different and positive presentation. The facts all remain the same, the consumer's credit is still the same, but the consumer and other potential consumers now see the matter of having bad credit framed in an entirely different manner. The business also reaps a healthy return for its willingness to extend credit in these situations.

Take note here. You may not be dealing with bad credit risks. But as a business owner or manager, you'll encounter bad press and bad reviews. You'll experience a lack of expected product or deliver bad product. You'll have days when employees deliver poor service or no service at all. You'll encounter people making distortions of the facts of your business and other people telling outright lies in an attempt to hurt you. How will you deal with them? The people who survive in business learn to absorb all sorts of negative events, rethink them, and reframe them in the best light they can for their public.

You have to take your pig and give it a bath, comb its hair if it has any, and then put on some bright and happy lipstick. If you've got a charming ribbon that goes well with your pig's skin color, tie that around its neck too. Now, people will still know you've simply cleaned up your pig. They won't be fooled by the bath, the hair combing, the lipstick, or the ribbon. But what this whole ridiculous scenario will allow them to do is to see the issue in an entirely new light, a light you decided on, and a light that you directed toward the points you wished them to see.

## Playing The Appearances Game Can Kill Your Business

Far too many new businesses fail because they want to appear to be old, well-established businesses. By that I mean they load up with too much overhead in the form of staff and other things you'd expect in a business that has been open for many years. I've worked with businesses struggling to survive that appeared to be fabulously successful.

Hiring too many employees too early in the life of your new business leads to negative cash flow and the pain of layoffs unless you can easily afford to fund the excess out of your own pocket. Furnishing an office for $100,000 when you really just needed some cubicles and a cheap phone system may impress your friends and your mother, but it may also sink your dream.

The choice to own your own business is one that's driven to a greater or lesser degree by our egos. I know those of us in business often like to pretend that's not true, but at least consider that possibility. In its early days, your business likely can't afford to carry the lease on that Mercedes, your membership at the country club, expensive original artwork, and crown moldings in your luxuriously appointed office.

If you have self-image issues, trying to deal with them through your business is going to be much more expensive than getting into therapy. Certainly each of us wants to take a degree of pride in our business. Yes, some will demonstrate that pride by a lavish office and all the trappings. Others will celebrate it more quietly when they look at their bank and stock accounts and see lots of assets.

### Three Critical Management Truths

There are many reasons why the use of temporary workers has skyrocketed here in the USA over the last forty years. Admittedly, most of those reasons are purely economic. However, a growing number seem to relate to many of this generation's desire not to have to manage people. Managing people seems to have been difficult as far back as we can find recorded business history. Nevertheless, owners and managers took this in stride as part of what was involved in being in business and shouldered this responsibility. The great owners/managers learn how to treat their people, and their people in turn make them successful.

As past generations of owners/managers have faded from the scene and younger generations with different and decidedly more negative views of management have taken their place, a new and more confrontational era has arisen. These newer creators/inventors/innovators don't want to be bothered with confrontational people, so they're not. They contract out their labor needs to organizations that will willingly (for a price) be bothered with people and the inevitable problems that come with them. The ideas of past generations regarding owner-employee relations are fading, and a new paradigm is clearly upon us. This wanting to avoid the messy bother of managing people has had unintended negative consequences.

I interviewed a fifty-four-year-old man recently for a client. That man told me he'd worked for the same temporary agency for eighteen years. During almost all of those years, he'd been assigned to this same manufacturing company I was consulting for. He received all his wages and benefits from the temporary agency and spoke well of both the agency's management and the manufacturing company he was assigned to. What seemed lost in all of this was any sense of his wanting to better the manufacturing company where he labored daily. Why should he? His view was that it was not going to improve his lot in life since his paycheck came from the temporary agency. Think about the ramifications of this for a moment.

Many of America's greatest companies became great because their workers felt invested in those companies to such a degree they strove to come up with better ideas and better methods to improve both products and production. In general, a rising tide raised all ships and the workers benefitted directly from improvements in efficiency or inventions they brought forth. More and more I see this element being lost as any sense of investment has been replaced by the mentality of people as merely human machines. There's a loss for each worker who's no longer valued for anything more than the sum of his parts, and there's a loss to the owners in having workers who no longer feel partnered in their enterprise; their loyalty now lies elsewhere.

In business school, we're all forced to spend a great deal of time studying the management and production systems of other countries. The sense I gained from both the countries I've visited and the countries whose systems I merely read about is how each country, and even individual companies, see themselves in competition with every other country and company with similar industries. After sixty years, the United States of America is finally starting to grasp that we're not the only team on the playing field and the other teams are getting stronger. To solidify this sense of competition with the world, many of those countries and companies work extra hard to instill a sense of personal connection to the company, the team, and the nation.

American schools of business, seizing upon this team concept, figured if we just start branding everything a team then we'd suddenly have true teams. To this end, teams became the rage, and suddenly it was team this and team that. We handed out team shirts, we conducted team building, and we had team retreats. But what I saw with the Japanese is that their teams not only occupy the same work space during the day, they hang together after work, and they still feel the sense of investment many American workers once did, but no longer do. The Japanese teams know if the company does well, they'll do well, and their nation will do well. If the company goes under, they'll go under, and their nation will go under.

All the team building exercises in the world cannot replace people's internalized sense that they matter and they are important to their coworkers, their company, and even their nation. The place this starts is with a strong connection to the company through a great owner and/or manager. We've known for decades employee satisfaction and retention is very strongly correlated to how well employees like and get along with their immediate manager. If your business is to capitalize on this, it seems to me we need to begin to figure out what's gone wrong in management that is causing so many people to shun it like a plague. You can build a great team that's loyal to your business around great management; temporary agencies will only be able to provide you with human machines.

My first management experience was at age eighteen after I dropped out of college. As I shared at the outset of this book I managed a small drive-in restaurant that was open seven days a week, sixteen hours a day, and employed six people. I learned very quickly I was dead without my crews to staff each shift. I learned this by having to cover double shifts for crew members who were unhappy, troubled, addicted, or just wallowing in life as they tried to get launched and figure out what they really wanted to be. I also learned: 1) people want to be listened too, 2) people want to be respected, and 3) people want to be treated fairly. There's no rocket science in these revelations, but understanding these very human wants are at the core of the success of every great manager and every great business owner.

## The Leader Who Didn't Know It All

One of the most liberating things I ever witnessed in business was when the CEO of a company I worked for was hearing a presentation and he stopped the speaker and asked him to explain a concept he'd never heard of before. This shocked me because it was a current concept in this line of business; truthfully it had been around a couple of years at that point. The liberating part for me came from the fact that even though I knew what the speaker was talking about, here was the head of this multi-million-dollar company, in a room with forty of his top-level executives from all over the world, admitting he didn't know something.

As I looked around the room, I noticed several faces that looked relieved. It was then that I sensed that many in the room had no idea what the speaker was talking about, but they didn't want to look incompetent by asking him to explain. The speaker graciously took about five minutes and laid out the technical aspects of the concept, and then he picked up his presentation and took off from where he'd paused. It was in that moment when I saw that the great leaders (and this man, now deceased, was a great leader) were not afraid to admit they didn't know something. Contrast this with the leaders you've followed who would never admit that their own knowledge is any less than omniscient.

When I was a young man, I took great pride in my knowledge. I loved to learn and loved sharing it. I also loved the adulation that knowledge created. But as the years have passed, I slowly recognized that even though I knew more than some others, the areas of my knowledge where I know little or nothing are cosmically vast. Pride in all of us, not just our leaders, will make it hard for us to admit that there's something that others around us may know that we don't. It's a strange combination of pride and arrogance that borders on hubris in many of today's "great leaders." This holds true in all fields: religion, politics, medicine, science, art, and all of the others are not immune to this malady.

As an aging man working daily to be a wiser man, I find that upon someone's questioning, I'm admitting more and more often that I just don't know the answer. Yes, there are some fields where I am a Knowledge Area Expert. But there are literally thousands where I'm not. The great leaders allow the expertise of others to be recognized and acknowledged. The worst leaders pretend to know it all, to be able to do it all, and to be insulted if anyone so much as hints that maybe they don't know something. Institutions in America and around the world need more leaders who will admit they have gaps in their genius and are big enough to ask for others to lead in these areas.

## They've Fired Ron Johnson

I shopped at JCPenney® for most of my life. Then in 2011, the board of JCPenney hired a man named Ron Johnson to be their chief executive officer. Johnson, fresh off a successful stint over at Apple®, set out to remake JCPenney into a newer hipper kind of department store. Gone were the sales and the coupons; in were the fair pricing scheme and portable checkout systems. The end result, sales fell nearly 25%, and the profits followed. His effort to create "stores within a store" seems to have fallen flat, and droves of former customers stayed away. I haven't been back to JCPenney since I got my first look at the changes Johnson made. He completely did away with a brand of underwear my generation had worn for forty-five years. In my opinion, the board brought Johnson in for a face-lift and a tune-up, but Johnson did facial reconstruction and a heart transplant.

Apparently, the JCPenney board decided that the experiment was over, and in 2013, they gave Johnson his walking papers and a large severance package. It will take an enormous effort (read: tons of cash invested) to pull buyers back from Target® and Internet vendors after the drubbing they took from Johnson and his *New World Order* vision of this American institution. Here's what you need to take away from this if you own a business and you have a downturn that requires some fresh countercyclical thinking. If the basic mechanics of your operation are good, figure out which areas are problematic and deal with them. For God's sake, don't decide that because a screen door is damaged the whole house should be torn down. Furthermore, you might want to ask your present customers what it is they like about your company before you decide to scrap your moneymakers.

I've seen this sort of re-imaging happen far too much in recent years, and as often as not, the effort was disastrous. If you ever bought clothes at JCPenney, you may already know that some of their most successful old lines were dropped entirely while others were modified so much that customers didn't recognize them anymore. At the end of the day, many JCPenney customers did what I did and went elsewhere. If you're going to try and look like Walmart®, then I'd just as soon go over to Walmart and get the better pricing. Here's the worst of it. I'm glad to hear that they came to their senses and fired Johnson. However, that doesn't mean I'm heading back to JCPenney as soon as I finish today's writing. I've developed new preferences and loyalties while I've been away, and like most consumers, I usually take my time leaving, and I'm slow to return once I've been burned.

## When The Shoe Is On The Other Foot

Business owners would be well advised to remember that if your employees are helping carry your business in tough economic times, you should remember this devotion when times get better. Organizations often ask their employees to work harder, take pay cuts, endure furlough days, or even get paid late when times are tough and cash flow is slow. Be just as willing to help them when times are good again, or they'll leave you and never look back!

## The Family-Owned Business

Recently I heard about a local business where a large percentage of the staff just walked out the door. No doubt they took their talents and their business relationships with them. The word on the street said the exodus came about because one of the members of the family-owned business had just become too erratic to work with any longer. This can happen due to a multitude of sources (e.g., drugs, alcohol, mental illness, etc.).

Family-owned businesses are tough on the family, but often they're much tougher on the employees who lack any kind of power to protect themselves from a looney family member. Sometimes working in a family-owned business is like working for one of the multiple-headed gods of mythology. Just because one head is happy or easy to get along with doesn't mean the other heads are.

## Don't Worry, Nothing's Going To Change

So you decided you needed a new manager for your business to take your company in an entirely new direction. Great! Then help me understand why, upon introducing the new manager to your existing employees, you assured them "Nothing is going to change around here"? Worse still, as the new manager tried valiantly to effect the change you hired her for, you were the one who fought the change the hardest, and your new manager walked out.

## Figure Out What Hat You Wear

Are you primarily a business owner/manager, or are you primarily a minister, psychologist, or a social worker? You have to decide this at some point or your business will suffer. Too many owner/managers I meet feel like it's their job to fix their troubled employees, and they feel the troubled employee's coworkers should also help.

Here's a thought: maybe this isn't your forte. Maybe you should stick to making widgets and tell Roscoe in shipping to get some professional help. By the same token, your other employees shouldn't be expected to join in your personal efforts to save every troubled soul who lands a job with your company.

## Covering Problems In Gold

Kahlil Gibran has a piece where he talks about a rotting tooth and going to two different dentists in hopes of dealing with the toothache. In both cases he requests the bad tooth be pulled. One dentist refuses to pull it, then drills and fills the tooth with gold, which looks good and feels better temporarily, but then the pain from the deep decay again takes hold that night.

The second dentist says that the tooth is a total loss and that the drilling and gold has been wasted. So he pulls the rotted tooth and the problem is solved. Gibran then goes on to liken these dentists to his own country's politicians (Lebanon was under Ottoman rule at the time). He claims that some try to deal cosmetically with a problem that requires a much more serious approach, one that goes beyond merely covering over rot with gold.

At some point in time, all governments take both of these approaches. The first approach is taken because the citizens initially want to retain the tooth and refuse to believe that the rot has gone so deep it can't be saved. The second approach is finally taken because the pain has gone on so long that the citizens finally accept that the tooth is a loss, it is now potentially lethal, and they need to get on with their lives.

Many countries, and many businesses have been to the first dentist, and the tooth remains rotten and still aches despite all the gold fillings. At some point citizens or owners begin mulling over their options and soon realize more cosmetics may not be the answer; they begin to search for a second dentist. Yes, there will always be those who regard that second dentist as a hack and a butcher.

Pulling a rotted tooth is traumatic and leaves a gap, but it stops the patient from eventually dying from systemic infection. If your business or your nation develops such a toothache, you need to recall Gibran's story. Cosmetically dealing with deeply entrenched business or governmental failings will only work for so long. To be sure, pulling a tooth is traumatic and sometimes painful; it can change the shape of your face, your business, or your country. But all other possible outcomes are far worse.

## This Isn't The Old Country
As I sat in the waiting area while visiting a professional office a couple years back, I could hear the son of the owner having a

loud argument with one of the employees. The loud part came from the son, and the employee responses were barely audible. This didn't surprise me too much since I'd been in their offices several times over the years and had heard the father doing the exact same thing previously. On that previous occasion I cautioned the father that this yelling was a problem, bad for employee morale, and could lead to legal backlash. He laughed and smiled and said, "All these people know that I'm loud and wave my hands just like my father and his father did back in the old country. They know I don't mean anything by it." It was now apparent that the son had picked up this family trait and was in full force with it here in the twenty-first century.

Recently I encountered one of the other professional employees from that office and inquired how business was going. Her response: "Oh, I don't work there anymore. One of the clerical staff filed a lawsuit against the owner and his son claiming harassment and a hostile work environment. All the rest of us got sucked into that drama by subpoenas from her lawyer and ended up being recused; none of us were willing to perjure ourselves, and after that, those of us who could have found other work. The rest are looking." Now none of this surprised me. What did surprise me was that it had gone on for years in this office without previous legal repercussions, and even after I'd warned him this could happen, the owner and his son had apparently continued in the same vein. Consider that he's lost key personnel, is fighting a serious lawsuit he's likely to lose, and word of this behavior has rippled through his profession and his clients.

Hypothetically, the United States of America is more of a melting pot than other places, and we have dozens of ethnicities and cultural backgrounds present here in ownership, management, and workforce. You can't treat employees however you want and legally support the claim that "In my culture, it's okay to talk to people this way." Your business place is not your home, it's not a family reunion each workday, and it's not a place where you can abuse your staff based on your interpretations of interpersonal relationships. There's now a massive body of legal statutes and case law out there that will be used by opposing counsel to cudgel you into understanding the error of your ways. Much of what I write in this book deals with problems with employees, but owners and managers can be just as guilty of being "Out Of Brains" as anyone.

## Foiled Again

> "The greatest enemy of a good plan
> is the dream of a perfect plan."
> CARL VON CLAUSEWITZ

## The Dead Sea Effect

The first time I heard the *Dead Sea Effect* introduced was in a sermon I listened to when I was in my mid-twenties. Over the decades, it's taken on new meanings to me at different seasons in my life. Unfortunately, the actual lesson I needed to learn from each of those seasons was a sort of personal Black Swan Event (a concept you'll fully understand later in this book) in my life and usually didn't come to me until after the moment had passed and the damage was done. I hope that by sharing how I learned the relevance of this concept in my business life, it will help you avoid the same pitfalls that brought me to my knees.

The *Dead Sea Effect* is a common problem and one I suspect is deeply rooted in psychological issues some of us have based on a combination of childhood poverty, above-average intelligence, the desire to succeed, and a strong belief that we can be our own brain surgeons. By this I mean that children who are poor often have great ambition to accumulate wealth when they're grown because they know from firsthand experience that poverty is nobody's friend. Now couple that desire to succeed with strong intelligence, drive, and survival coping methods, and you have a recipe for problems in business and business management. The person may be smart enough to arrive at a plan, but the plan is hindered by the biases of that inner child.

Many of us come away from that early period in our lives able to perform technical tasks and handle intellectual problems that our more financially stable counterparts didn't have to even consider. We learned to be our own physician, mechanic, nurse, plumber, seamstress, electrician, secretary, and accountant. In short, we developed an "I don't need anyone else but me" mindset born out of not being able to trust that other people were going to be able or willing to help us. This usually serves us well and makes us the go-to people in a lot of business situations. If this is you, the employers you've worked for loved the fact that you could do three jobs and they only had to pay you for one.

The problems arise when you decide to become entrepreneurial. If you're just trying to start a business or you're a first-time manager of a business, it's not such an obvious problem. And if your business remains a one-, two-, or three-person operation, you're likely to be just fine. It's at the point where your business takes off and you need to expand that business that you get into trouble. Previously, you wore three hats; suddenly, there are twelve hats to wear and you decide you can handle a dozen easily. As you shift from juggling your normal three roles to twelve roles, it's like a juggling act where they keep throwing balls to the juggler until the inevitable occurs and all the balls are falling to the ground and rolling helter-skelter. You will eventually drop all the balls.

Money is certainly an issue that adds to this problem, or more precisely the lack of money, or the perceived lack of money.

Here's how this unfolds. You need an outside specialist to help you with some task (e.g., accounting, plumbing, engineering, sous-chef, etc.), but you don't want to pay that professional or hire that extra set of hands because if you just juggle a little bit faster, you can figure the task out, take care of it yourself, and avoid the expense. You reason that it will either save you money you don't have and don't want to borrow, or it will allow you to put a few more dollars in your IRA, or it will allow you buy that condo at the beach sooner. Eventually you will still drop all the balls.

So you're saying to yourself, "I can handle this and I'm a better juggler than people actually think I am. I don't need anyone else but me." I expect that response from most people reading this, and it's the excuse I offered to myself and my advisors for the first twenty years of my business life. It came to a head for me when I had mastered yet another task (i.e., the creation of computer networks, their hardware, and their programming). It was just another ball to juggle, and I'd done it. I was extremely proud of myself. Then one day I decided to go back to college and earn a doctorate. I was faced with the realization that I could be a jack-of-all-trades for the rest of my life or I could focus and be the man with a doctorate, but I couldn't be both.

In my own businesses and even as a manager of other people's businesses, the *Dead Sea Effect* has been a problem and one I still fight with; old age has made it less so as the physical limitations born of the years began to take their toll. Now I've written hundreds of words already and have yet to tell you what the *Dead Sea Effect* is with regard to you, me, and our corporate cultures. Here's the concept in a couple of paragraphs. In Israel, the Jordan River flows into the Sea of Galilee and out again. It then flows downstream to the Dead Sea. The Sea of Galilee is full of life, with commercial fishing having taken place there since ancient times. The Dead Sea, downstream of the Sea of Galilee and having no discharge, is filled with everything picked up by the river and deposited there.

There are such inland seas all over the world, and they're all either saline, brackish, or briny—terms which denote their increasing degrees of salinity. These salt seas are great for mineral mining interests, but save for a few species of brine shrimp and other similar salt-tolerant creatures; they don't teem with commercial fisheries. They tend to smell and don't attract people like a fresh-water sea would. There's one at Trona, California, which is about ninety miles from my home, which has produced minerals for more than fifty years. What the Dead Sea does by hanging on to every form of mineral riches that pours into it is to effectively diminish its ability to sustain life; smelly briny minerals yes, but not much life. It's a great source of salt and other salt-borne minerals, but there's not much fishing there.

Here's the correlation I want to make for you from the *Dead Sea Effect* and the propensity you may have to want to take on every job in front of you in your business. If you get to the place where every dollar you take in becomes so psychologically precious to you that you won't release any of those dollars to allow your business to grow, to pay your people a fair wage, or to buy that new piece of equipment instead of a used one you think you can rebuild, your business will eventually salt up and die or never achieve its full potential. If you won't hire needed employees, if you won't buy needed new equipment, and if you won't contract necessary outside professional help, your business will die. You have to release some of what comes into your coffers to remain fresh and vital.

This is one place your parsimony will be your downfall. Of course, once your business is dead, someone will eventually come along and mine the salts of your endeavor just as they do these salty seas I spoke of. They'll sell off the parts and pieces at ten cents on the dollar, and others will profit off your failure. You need to open your hand, open your heart, and open your mind to the idea that if you can keep your financial Jordan flowing and not dammed up, you'll do far better in the long run than if you go total Scrooge in the early days and the years beyond. Free yourself up to be the owner/manager and not the janitor, clerk, machinist, welder, or sous-chef. Allow other people's giftedness to make you happier, healthier, and wealthier. Let your financial Jordan flow.

## If It Ain't Broke, Don't Fix It

On occasion, I used to drive about twenty miles round-trip from my office for a special lunch, which consists of a gourmet burger, fries, and a soft drink; the food is legendary. There are at least fifteen other burger joints I could stop at on the way and get a respectable burger, fries, and soft drink for about half the price. The one I like costs about $10 with tax. Instead, I took extra time, extra wear and tear on my automobile, and extra money to eat this specific meal.

About two years ago, it came under new ownership. I was concerned at first that they would tamper with the burger. But for the first year, they left the product alone, and it continued just as it had for the previous thirty-six years I'd been going there. Then last year, I noticed some tinkering going on with the grade of meat, the amount of meat, the quality of the buns, and the condiments they used. I know a thing or two about this; you may recall the first business I ever had a stake in was a burger joint.

It seemed odd to me that the woman who'd been the long-time manager was sent on down the road about this same time. One had to wonder if she was an obstacle after all her years to the new way of doing things. The surviving cooks, though amiable and doing the best they could with what they had, no longer went through the tedious steps they previously did to get the great flavor and just the right char on that meat; a flavor and char that people had been willing to pay handsomely for.

I happened to stumble into a small burger joint a while back and low and behold, the old manager was cooking and managing there. This place is only about eight miles from my office. I ordered their burger basket, and she recognized me. We began to talk about the hamburger business, and she told me the new owners had wanted to increase their bottom line by reducing costs. This cost reduction effort had affected the quality of the buns, the meat, the condiments, the cooking time, and even the temperature of their cooking technique.

I recently went back to the old burger joint I'd visited regularly for thirty-six years. I was sincerely hoping the quality had improved since the last visit. The burger was even worse than the last time I'd come in. The meat shape had been changed (now somewhat oval) to hide the obvious reduction in the size of the patty, and I no longer saw the formerly posted guarantee of "eight ounces of hamburger meat before cooking." Further cost-cutting was obviously underway. They'd even changed their burger basket to a smaller size to fool the uneducated eye.

The reality is that what these people have done is to cut their own throat. The business will dwindle over time as people like me will no longer drive that extra distance to pay those inflated prices for a mediocre burger. Their formerly enthusiastic customers will also tell their friends and family about the experience. In a metropolitan area today, there are many options for a great burger at a moderate cost. So to own a unique "mom and pop" that people went out of their way to patronize, and then to callously eviscerate what made it great for even better profits, happens more than some of you would imagine.

If you buy a business, any kind of business, and it's been successful for generations, unless the market changes dramatically, you need to be very careful about tinkering with a working profitable formula. People were already driving miles out of their way and paying 100% more to get their hands on that product; when the bottom line started to shrink or they needed a better margin to fund their retirement, maybe they should've just raised the price instead of killing the goose that laid the golden eggs. Keep this in the front of your mind, it doesn't matter if it is burgers, widgets, or cappuccino, if it ain't broke, don't fix it unless you want to risk ruining a profit stream.

## Capture That Idea

Very creative people from many different walks of life come across my path each year. The truth is, I know a lot of people who are ascribed the title of genius. The most interesting thing for me in knowing these geniuses is that the ones who are able to make anything more of their genius than cocktail party banter, are constantly jotting down their new ideas.

Some of them have desks and workbenches covered with scribbled scraps of paper, backs of old envelopes with drawings, and legal pads filled with their sudden epiphanies. If you didn't know any better, you'd think upon meeting them that they were just terribly disorganized. But ask them where in that pile an idea of a certain type hides and they can grab it almost instantly.

Yes, just like you and me, they have a lot of what would be generously called stupid ideas. Yet because they capture so many of these ideas for later studied consideration, every once in a while they hit a home run that's worth lots of money. Write down your ideas when you get them; if you wait half an hour, it may be too late to pull them back to your conscious mind.

Inventor Thomas A. Edison is credited with saying, "Genius is 1% inspiration and 99% perspiration." However, even if that's true, that 1% inspiration is priceless, and the perspiration would be worthless without it.

## Kill Them While They're Young

Reflecting on companies I've worked with who conduct their hiring by teams of other employees, one of the pitfalls I've seen is that if a candidate is "too strong," she may be killed off in the hiring process by potential coworkers fearing for their own future. True leadership requires rising above self-interest, and not every employee or manager will be up to the task. As a business owner, you have to keep your eyes open for this problem, not only at hiring time, but also in the day-to-day of your workplace.

My friend, Leonel Martinez, was once a newspaper editor and he shared with me what I think is a powerful insight and something everyone trying to build a great organization needs to imitate: "When I was at the newspaper, I was asked to hire a secretary. We had half a dozen or so candidates, and it was obvious the sharpest one was a woman with a very strong personality whom I'd clashed with in the past. I chose her because I was certain she would excel at the job. We became good friends, and I never regretted it." This is solid reminder that good manager/leaders are hiring for the good of the company and not just to have sycophants around them.

True leaders like Leonel, will hire people who are stronger than themselves, smarter than themselves, and more driven. In doing so, they build great organizations. Weak leaders hire people who are weaker, less intelligent, and less motivated than themselves so they pose no threat. As the owner of a business you have to demand your managers rise to the level of leadership required to bring in the best brains to your company or risk losing it all. A business owner who tolerates weak leaders making poor hires, sows the seed of the destruction of their companies. To be a successful business owner you have to be able to spot brains, recruit brains, hire brains, and hang on to brains, even if it discomforts other employees.

## Do They Bring More To The Table Than They Take Away?

When you are finally able to hire employees, keep in mind that each person you add to the mix of your workforce has a direct impact on everyone they interact with, not just customers. Be sure that your new hire brings more to the table than they take away. Will they add to your business's harmony and productivity, or take away from it? A great deal of my graduate and post-graduate work dealt with the psychological aspects of the people-mix in a workplace. Ignoring this aspect of each new hire is inviting a lighted match to an open can of gasoline.

## Your Attitude On Safety Either Costs Or Pays

In each business there are unique risks for which we buy insurance. In recent years, worker's compensation insurance (WCI) has become one of, if not the most, expensive forms of insurance businesses buy. I started handling safety programs for the company I worked for back in 1981; we had fifty-two employees, and WCI rates of about $17 per $100. Today throughout that industry, they'd be more than twice that high; prices have exploded.

Your safety program can help you contain these explosive costs. Any company that implements and enforces a good safety program is at a direct cost advantage over its competitors. Any company that doesn't implement a good safety program, implements a hit-or-miss safety program, or fails to enforce their own safety policies eventually sees its experience modification (X-Mod) factor skyrocket along with operating costs.

Let's say you have an excellent employee safety record and your X-Mod is 1.00. You pay $20 per $100 for WCI for each of your widget makers. If your competitor has an X-Mod of 1.30 from a series of accidents due to poor safety practices, they're paying $23 per $100 for WCI for their widget makers. You have a competitive advantage because that money, which goes to your bottom line, ends up going to insurers over at your competitors.

If you produce the same goods or services as your competitor, you can bid lower or manufacture cheaper than your competitor for the exact same items. Lower operating costs improve your chances of survival and success. I've seen many companies fail due solely to escalating X-Mods; they failed to keep an eye on their WCI costs, and the costs broke them. When you consider that some jobs have routine WCI rates of $35 to $90 per hundred dollars earned (that's right, some businesses pay almost as much as their employees earns for WCI), the added costs can be devastating.

If you don't have a safety program at your new business and you have a business requiring WCI for your employees, implement one as soon as possible; today wouldn't be too early. If you have a bad safety program, evidenced by your X-Mod being above 1.00, you should scrap it and find a good one if you haven't already. If you have an existing safety program and you've been lackadaisical about it, revitalize it quickly. In tough times, the lean operating companies survive; in good times, the same lean operators get rich.

## The Training Never Stops

Early in my career, I had two industrial accidents that left me with lifetime scars and injuries. I began to realize that the companies I was working for at the time placed no particular interest in safety, and so I began to do so as an act of self-defense. When I came to a new employer in 1980 and safety had suddenly become a big issue with insurers, one of my bosses who'd noticed how safety-conscious I was about myself and my crew suggested me to the owner as the guy to head up the company's fledgling safety program. In the ensuing thirty-six years, safety and safety programs have never been far from my mind and have usually been part of my portfolio of assignments. Below are some insights into a common failure to train properly for safety; pay close attention because your life and/or your business may be in the balance.

I happened to be on a jobsite visit some time ago, where a young man who had been employed by that firm for about two years had been placed in charge of orienting a new hire. I could tell the young man was excited to have his first opportunity to be in charge. There was only one problem there: in the two hours I was in a position to see them working, I noted several serious safety violations from the would-be mentor, which he expressly passed along to the new hire. I like to refer to this as "sharing your ignorance." Any of us can only pass along that which we've learned and inculcated. If we learned it wrong and made it part of our existence, it's still wrong. I spoke with the owner later that day and was quick to point out how enthused this young fellow was and that I felt he was an asset to the company, so long as he and the new hire were completely trained and/or retrained in the safe practices related to their areas of responsibility; the owner agreed and thanked me for my candor.

I cannot overemphasize to you how critical it is that somebody who actually knows the drill be placed in charge of any new hire training. Most companies that I work with initially take the attitude that any of their older employees are capable of teaching the newer employees. Wrong! Unless you know for a fact how long-time employee Charlie actually behaves and operates on the work site, you have no idea if he's capable of doing anything more with his charge than teaching him or her a series of bad work habits developed over thirty or more years. Bad corporate cultures related to work habits and safety didn't just suddenly get that way. Too many times we take the attitude that if no one has gotten killed or lost a limb lately then everything must be going okay. Too many times we fail to recognize the little precursors to horrific events. In one instance I recall, a chemical plant experienced a severe accident due to an ongoing misformulation of a product, which had gone on undetected for years.

Many in that plant's chain of responsibility had noticed the quality assurance people were flunking more and more batches in recent months. Yet it never occurred to anyone that this indicated the operators were off in their batching, or the load cells were off in their weighing, or the temperature was being allowed to rise too high in the cooking, or the mixing process wasn't mixing homogeneous batches, or that the component chemicals were still dangerously reacting hours later in the sales stockpile. There is a saying that it's the little foxes that spoil the vines. Frankly, I've never been sure exactly what that means, but in real life I can tell you that sometimes it's the smallest of details that pave the road to calamity. So what can we do? I find that the most wonderful thing to run across is an energetic and motivated employee who sincerely wants to do the job correctly. I hear the same sentiments from other business owners and managers. This being so, it stands to reason that no organization would want to waste all of that employee's energy and motivation by failing to provide good initial training and great ongoing training in processes and safety.

For your sake, your employees' sake, your customers' sake, and the sake of your business, you must initiate training at the beginning of your business. Then you have to stay ahead of new developments in your industry and retrain your employees as needed. Accidents, injuries, or product failures are highly correlated with poor training. My wife and I own a small business where new products come into the market all the time. This means that new awareness and training has to take place with employees routinely. It also means that if an employee is seen performing a task or using a product incorrectly, retraining must take place. It will be no different in your business if you're baking breads or building graphite composite spaceships. The training never stops, or problems will ensue.

## Already Broke

There was a local business I knew well that started out profitably but slowly went broke over the next couple of years because they kept trying to follow the television business model. "What's the television business model," you ask? It's the model we all see on television where a business has all new equipment, the best of furnishings, above-market wages, ridiculous perquisites, and their office is a social hub. By the time they looked around for management advice in order to sort out their decline, they were already broke and didn't realize it.

Television, the movies, and novels paint an imaginary picture of how a business runs and what that looks like. In the real world there's old furniture, old computers, cranky printers, erratic copiers, and oftentimes the boss doesn't get paid but a handful of times a year. Unlike the television office, the real-world workplace isn't full of men and women who could step onto the pages of a fashion magazine. Unlike television, real-world workplaces aren't filled with talk of sordid affairs and plans for galas at the country club. To hire those people and provide that imaginary workplace would be a short-lived fantasy.

# CHAPTER 4

## MUTUAL CONSIDERATIONS FOR BOTH OWNERS AND MANAGERS

### Overheard In The Workplace

"I didn't say it was your fault, I said I was blaming you." Think about this phrase the next time one of your employee's blames another employee for something that's gone wrong; sometimes, the most charming, likeable, or downright sycophantic employees become quite adept at blaming their own mistakes on subordinates or co-workers.

### Management Isn't A Passive Undertaking

One of the surprises associated with a new business for many budding entrepreneurs is their discovery that their workforce may not share their internal motivation for the job at hand. What that new business owner had hoped for was that the employees they hired would be just as excited about their new business as they were. To their dismay, many business owners soon learn that for the vast majority of employees, "…it's just a job." There's nothing inherently evil about that because all of us have had jobs where we felt the same way. The problems flare up when a new business owner thinks those hires will manage themselves, stay internally motivated, and want to be the world's best at whatever the task at hand might be.

As an owner or manager, you cannot afford to be passive in managing your people assets. In addition to hiring them, you're going to have to train them, constantly motivate them, and then keep them on task. These are not small undertakings, and many people who see themselves as creators more than as managers soon find themselves overwhelmed by the role of manager. Some of the overwhelmed eventually begin to embrace their role as manager, some hire other people with management skills to run the business, some are miserable for years trying to fill a role they hate, and others finally throw in the towel and say they can't take the stress of managing people anymore. I heard that last mindset expressed by a successful business owner at lunch this past week.

Like just about every other skill set out there, the role of manager can be learned if the person being trained possesses the proper aptitude. I've trained managers at every level, and some take to the role naturally while others take to the role only reluctantly. Without management, and good management at that, your new venture is doomed to fail unless you're a one-person shop. Every employee you hire will have their own self-interests, their own ideas, and their own internal motivations. If you can't figure those out, tap into them, and turn them to the benefit of your enterprise, then your life is going to be miserable. As I said, management skills can be trained, and there are resources out there capable of training you. You must reach deep inside yourself and determine to become competent in this area or hire someone who can.

There are management books, seminars, community college classes, and university-level management training if you're up to it or if you wish to send your staff. I'd love to think that people will read this and plan ahead for that training. However, the truth is that most people don't realize they're drowning until they're already out in the deep water and sinking. Most of us realize we're in management trouble only after we have our first few bad encounters with employees in our role as "Boss." By then we're already working eighty hours a week and don't have five extra minutes to ourselves, much less the time to attend management classes or weekend seminars. If you are to survive, you'll have to find that extra time and energy somewhere. The business highway is littered with the bones of those who didn't.

## Oh No! You Did Exactly What I Told You To Do

Yesterday I was talking with a business owner who's owned successful businesses for nearly fifty years. We were talking about how easy it is to miscommunicate with employees and how devastating the outcomes can be. Here are some tips that will improve your chances of getting the message you intended across.

1) Think before you speak or write to your employees. Who is the audience? What's their age? What's their educational level? Is your first language their first language?

2) Make sure you're being as precise as you can be in what you say. Just because you and your generation would be familiar with some terms doesn't mean employees twenty, thirty, or even forty years younger would be.

3) Impromptu meetings and casual off-the-cuff speech, emails, or texts can get you in trouble. These spontaneous efforts at what professionals refer to as "relationship maintenance" often backfire.

4) Ask someone you trust to listen and/or read your communication first; preferably someone from the age group and of a similar background as the person or persons the message targets.

5) Once communicated, ask the employee(s) targeted to tell you in their own words what you just attempted to

communicate. I find these efforts almost always surprise and dishearten the communicator.

6) Draw pictures or diagrams and use multiple examples to go along with your words or speech; the goal here is to communicate, not to be brief. Time management is another topic altogether.

Now some of you reading this will say, "Hey, I'm the boss here, and I write the paychecks. It's up to these yahoos to listen up and get it right." I agree that you're the boss. I further agree that you write the paychecks. But so far as who the burden of communicating directions falls upon, we disagree.

There's a humorous story that goes along the lines of two men meeting after they were killed in an accident in which both men were involved. As they talked about it, neither would shoulder the blame and both claimed they were "right" in the course of action they'd taken. Eventually it occurred to them they were "dead right."

Even with these additional efforts on your part, there will still be miscommunications. If you have a workforce that's intended to be long-term or the task at hand is of a critical nature, consider bringing in someone to teach a communications class to the whole group...including you. You don't want to be dead right.

## You Must Manage The Problem Employee

Someone reminded me recently that unhappy/problem coworkers are also frequently angry coworkers. If you've ever had an angry coworker, you know they can completely dominate the atmosphere of a workplace and force everybody else to tiptoe around them to avoid conflict. If you're a business owner/manager, you owe it to your other employees to deal with an angry employee unless you can afford to have your productivity, profitability, and workplace harmony ruined by this kind of dark cloud in the workplace.

This business of employee relations is one of the hats a small business owner or manager has to wear whether they like it or not; no one enjoys conflict with employees or coworkers. If as an owner or manager you refuse to manage chronically unhappy or outright angry employees, your other routinely happy and cheerful employee assets will be sending out resumes and going on job interviews at lunch time as they try to find another happier and more peaceful workplace. You and your customers will be left with Mr. Unhappy, or Ms. Angry, or both.

## Roller Coasters Or Steady State Management Models

While management styles and objectives differ, each of us has to operate our businesses in a manner that will allow us to survive both the fat and the lean times, which inevitably will come. I counsel all clients to operate their businesses as if a downturn is always coming; there's much to be said for stability. One of the management styles I see, I'll term the "roller coaster." I call it this because it seems to have economic rises and falls, which alternately scares and then thrills both owners and employees like a ride on a roller coaster. The other style I see is one I've termed the "steady state." In the steady state, the owners and employees are working diligently to keep business and the finances stable and moving along at a constant sustainable clip. This style doesn't thrill the owner or employees with fat times and lean times as the roller coaster does, but it also doesn't scare them to death that the doors might close and their paychecks might bounce.

Roller coaster's finances are fat one month and then lean for the next three months, and then things get fat again; the financial boom-and-bust cycle goes on continuously. This frays the nerves of employees, clients, and creditors. In the case of employees, especially good employees who crave financial security, they'll take their brains and go elsewhere. Soon roller coaster finds itself out of brains. Clients may or may not be aware of the happenings, but if they do become aware, they too will become concerned about whether or not roller coaster will keep the doors open and complete their orders. Creditors crave stability and predictability, and they'll look deeply at your financial history to see if those qualities exist in your business. If a graph of your finances looks like the track of a roller coaster, they'll of course look for a trendline, but if it isn't to their liking, they'll pass on extending credit to roller coaster.

Steady state owner is financially boring since she's the same all the time. There's no financial boom-and-bust cycle at steady state. The employees don't have an extravagant beer-bust on the last Friday of every month, and they don't suddenly see unexpected tickets for a Hawaiian vacation, but they also know they're going to see a check every payday that won't bounce. Brains who crave financial stability often flock to gain employment over at steady state. This occurs because they worked for roller coaster and jumped off. Clients never hear much about steady state, and it's boring dropping by for a visit as they go about their tasks efficiently. Creditors seeing the instability of loaning money to companies like roller coaster actually seek out boring businesses instead, which operate at a steady state. The graph of their finances tends to be boring, but the trendline is slowly and steadily moving upward.

Which way do you manage your business? Which way do you want to manage your business? There are certainly gradations of the two extremes I've offered here. You need to brutally assess where your business is at on this continuum. I've worked with clients and for companies that operated at these extremes and several points between. There are examples I could provide (if confidentiality didn't prevent it) of both of these extremes being very successful. Conversely, I could also offer examples of companies that failed miserably, leaving anywhere from dozens to hundreds of employees out of a job and out of their last month's pay.

Let me close out with an oddity. Frequently I've seen brains migrate from one extreme to the other due to having experienced either too many scares or too much boredom. As with all continuums, perhaps somewhere in the middle is the safest ground.

## Improving Your Management By Understanding Your People Better

Making good business decisions has been on my mind as I think back over my career to what the bad business decisions I've either made or seen made have cost me or other business people I know. Then there's that secondary wave of repercussions for our customers/clients, employees and their families, and our own families. As I've aged, I've slowed down dramatically in the speed with which I make a business decision. In response to this slowing down, some people who know me have been straightforward enough to ask me if my mental processes are slowing down. An honest answer on both counts would be "Yes, my mental processes have slowed down as I'm in my sixty-fourth year" and "No, the speed with which I arrive at decisions these days has very little to do with that natural mental slow down." I'm reminded of an old adage my momma often spoke, "I'm older, but I'm wiser."

When you're young, you have a very limited palette of decision-making colors to paint with. When you have forty years or more of decision-making colors added to that palette, you certainly have the opportunity to paint a more nuanced picture of the issues than you could four decades earlier. Anyone looking back over a life in business who can't identify the outright mistakes, questionable decisions, and arguably terrible decisions they've made is either self-deluded, senile, or a narcissist. Many of you who'll read this book are either early in your careers in life or early in your careers in business ownership or business management. In the years ahead you'll be called upon to make thousands of decisions, and some of the most critical ones you won't even recognize as important at the time you make them. In true Black Swan Event (still later in this book) fashion, you'll look back later and assure yourself that it was otherwise.

The biggest factors I see in looking back as to why I made so many decisions that I'm now second-guessing have to do with the actual or imagined lack of time, lack of information, or lack of knowledge. But before we go there, I'd like to talk about a small evaluation tool in working with training people and helping them understand themselves. It's not certain who created this tool, but it's brilliant in its brevity and the degree of insight it provides. After the assessment is completed, people are grouped in one of four categories. They're classified as a jaguar, an owl, a dolphin, or a butterfly. (I've seen other animal terms used, but the gist is the same.) Each of these types brings a different perspective and a different set of tools to the way they view problems and how they arrive at solutions. Each of these types has strengths and weaknesses in their interactions with others and their decision-making ability.

**Jaguars** tend to be natural born leaders, and they like to consider the big picture; jaguars get things done. Terms used to describe them include focused, decisive, driven, and bottom-line thinkers. They dislike too much information, feeling it often confuses the core issue around which a decision must be made. Jaguars tend to be goal oriented, don't listen enough once they feel they've got the picture, and can easily be too bossy. Jaguars may fall into workaholism and lose patience with other people who don't want their jobs to be their life.

**Owls** are attentive to detail and are often accused of wanting too much detail, becoming paralyzed in decision-making; owls bring stability. They prefer to work and play alone. Owls will rarely share their true feelings about a matter. They don't like change, even when change can be a matter of life and death. If changes have to be made, owls don't generally handle them well. This tendency to resist change can unintentionally create business obstruction. The owl's strength is holding back too rapid a decision-making process.

**Dolphins** are great listeners, strong givers, and the most loyal of friends; dolphins create strong interpersonal relationships. Dolphins love teams and don't thrive if they're forced to work alone. Dolphins like to serve other people, and this penchant toward freely serving can inhibit their realization that profit is critical to business success/survival. Dolphins also excel as peacemakers in businesses. They are notoriously slow decision-makers, sometimes infuriating their coworkers or partners, but they can be counted on to stick with a decision once it's been made.

**Butterflies** are highly social by nature; they love people, parties, new ideas, new places, and they like to create a happy workplace. Butterflies are born for fun. They like to be the center of attention, and they actually enjoy chaos as a means to producing novelty and adventure. Butterflies can get easily bored with dull people and mundane ideas and have earned the identifier "butterfly" from their habit of flitting from one newly interesting flower, idea, person, or place to another.

Now that you have those briefest of primers, let's get back to decision-making and how it's affected by our personality types. I'll confess first off that I'm a jaguar, and I have all of the faults and some of the strengths of a jaguar. That being said, I am and always have been highly productive whether in my own business or in those I've operated for others. But I must also confess that I can see where I made decisions too hurriedly because I was on the way to my next "kill." I have detailed daily lists of what tasks I've worked on and whether or not they were completed going back decades. But I also have the jaguar's fault of cutting off debate and new input at some point if I feel we've drilled down into too much minutiae. Early on I acted without really thinking about outcomes. When the outcomes came back later and beat me down, I was forced to rethink some of my approaches and to more highly value my owl counterparts

I want to skip now to owls because owls are the jaguar's greatest enemy in the business of making decisions; they can also be the jaguar's greatest asset if they learn how to work together and respect what each brings to the process. The owls I've worked with tended to be the perpetual foot dragger because they look for a near 100% certainty before they willingly make a decision. They're strong researchers but can get buried in the minutiae of the research. They're wonderful at bringing details to the decision-making process, but they can also show up with so many details that the process can become muddied by their desire to balance the information they offer with a million pros and cons. Owls tend to be deep thinkers and think alone, which can also lead to conveying the sense that they mistrust others who work to make decisions with them. Owls and jaguars need one another.

Dolphins struggle with the decision-making process because they are so much about the needs, wants, feelings, and desires of others. Dolphins I've worked with are the people in the workplace who are always trying to pour oil on troubled waters because they dislike unhappiness among those they care so much about. As I mentioned earlier, they struggle with the profit-making motive and do far better in my opinion in a not-for-profit environment because they can easily get behind a noble cause and feel the need to have money available for good works justifies having to find a way to gain it. I acknowledge the dolphins I've worked with over the years softened my sharp edges in business decision-making and many times caused me to not be so abrupt, harsh, or cold when hard decisions had to be made. Dolphins will also help all the other types mentioned here "buy in" to whatever business decision is finally made and convince them it's for the greater good.

I've saved the butterflies for last because they have an important and often unappreciated role in business and business decision-making. More often than not it's a butterfly that brings in the new client, the new idea, the new direction, and the new money to a business. Admittedly they can't be counted on to stay with any of them long because of boredom, but if you can spot the value in what they've found and turn it from a passing fancy into a reality, they'll make you rich. Think of butterflies as the host or hostess you know who's so excited about the adventure of getting ready for the party that when the party finally starts, they're exhausted, excuse themselves, and either slip into the background or go home and go to sleep. Without butterflies, I see where there would've been a whole lot fewer opportunities for me to make fortuitous decisions.

I've learned to slow down and think about the decisions I would make and the ramifications of those decisions going out days, weeks, months and even years into the future. That did not come to me naturally because my tendency is to kick in the door and take on whatever is on the other side. The butterflies brought me opportunity and the sense that work should be fun. Owls brought me reams and reams of data and questions and naggings, all of which better informed my decision-making and kept me from looking even more dim-witted. Dolphins showed me that decisions are not made in a vacuum, that they have repercussions close at hand and far away. Butterflies I've worked with brought opportunity to make decisions that would have otherwise never existed. In short, you're better off to have broad input with ideas other than your own before you make a decision.

I need to wrap this passage up but do so by echoing the ancient proverb in its admonition from Proverbs 11:14 that "… in the multitude of counselors there is safety." Focus in your business ownership or management life in making "higher quality decisions" than you would make if the only voice you listened to would be your own. Don't be such a closet-narcissist that you think the only brilliant mind in the room is yours. I've found arrogance to be perhaps the most expensive fault we can purchase in our lifetimes. My suspicion is that the earlier you embark on a slower, more counselled and deliberate course of action, the sooner you'll make better decisions and decisions you'll regret less in your later years.

## Who Speaks For Your Business?

It is necessary to have an emergency plan for your business in the event of some sort of accident, crisis, disaster, terrorist act, etc. A key part of such a plan involves your media policy. Will you speak to the media? If not, who will be authorized to speak to the media on behalf of your business? Will they just blabber along incoherently and make you and your company look like fools, or will you give some time and training for potential scenarios and appropriate comments in advance so the responses are regarded as objective, well-reasoned, and caring?

Having worked for four years as a regional manager for a publicly traded company, I can tell you this is an ongoing issue in businesses both great and small, and one on which a lot of time, money, and training is invested. Offering the wrong information or offering it in the wrong manner can not only cause your stock price to tank, it can leave you open to needless litigation, and leave the public with a bad taste in their mouths about your organization forever. Many businesses never fully recover from such an event because they handled it so poorly.

Your small business needs to give this area some careful consideration. It's not just publicly traded multi-nationals that experience emergencies, tragedies, and crises. Your little mom-and-pop business can suddenly become big news if you have some sort of an unfortunate event take place associated with your business and you handle the event or aftermath badly. Today, any business can become the scene of a shooting, a fire, an accident, a death, a hostage situation, or a dozen other events that can immediately put you in public view. What's your plan? Who speaks for your business?

## Both People And Systems Break Down

Once I was once called in on a weekend to a worksite by a client at a time when the employees weren't around to try and figure out a cash flow problem in the accounting department. Their revenues were off by a half million dollars over a three-month period. I found three things hidden in the responsible A/R clerk's desk that were telling. It contained almost $500,000 in unbilled sales from the previous three months, an empty bottle of prescription anti-depressants, and several empty airline-sized vodka bottles.

Part of being an owner/manager is actually watching people, what they do, and how they do it. Some will disagree with this, but in my opinion, snooping is part of your job description if you own a business. This particular clerk had been there for quite a while and had previously been a reliable and valued employee. Consequently, the managing had ceased, and an auto-pilot mode had been engaged with regard to her activities. We'd later learn her marriage had imploded; she'd slipped into severe depression, and had resumed an alcohol habit she'd abandoned years earlier.

The old craftsman in me will tell you that no matter how good a piece of equipment may be or how much you once paid for it, it will wear out over time and break down. Fortunately, those kinds of machines can be repaired, but only if the damage is caught in time. With people assets, it's no different. They age, they experience life's ups and downs, sometimes they break down, and sometimes they cannot be salvaged. This is why as an owner you need to keep a thumb on the pulse of your employees. A good employee assistance program is also critical.

This clerk hadn't stolen anything, which was the client's main concern. However, the clerk had been there day after day for over three months melting down, and no one was noticing it. Where was her immediate supervisor? Where were her coworkers? In many industries predictive and preventive maintenance are honed to a science because potential mechanical failures can be catastrophic. It certainly wouldn't hurt if every business put slightly more emphasis of a similar sort on their people assets to avoid potential meltdowns.

## Decision-Making; Beware Euphoria And Depression

On the day I began to consider writing on this specific topic, a local businessman I'd known for over twenty years took his own life. I was shocked to the core and saddened for his wife and family, having experienced the suicide of my own son nearly twenty years earlier. Over the next two days, I heard of two other businesspeople from the area who had also taken their lives. What it reminded me of almost immediately was how many people who own businesses have all the other pressures in life that anyone else does, and they have the added pressure of constantly being at the point of the spear. Some folks actually thrive on that kind of pressure and it energizes them and their decision-making processes. I suspect they're the exceptions and not the rule. My own experience is that being under constant pressure from multiple directions and sources doesn't always leave me, or a lot of other folks, in the best frame of mind to make well-balanced decisions.

About this same time, I was dealing with another local businessman and personal friend I know who was considering a major change to the way he operated his business, a business that had existed for over thirty years and was highly successful. We both knew the businessman who had taken his own life, and of course we both were shocked and saddened at his passing. At that point I took the opportunity to share with him my own sense that we (people in business) often make critical decisions about our lives or our businesses at inappropriate times. I'd consider an inappropriate time to be one where you're experiencing either an extreme high or euphoria over things going well or an extreme low or depression over things going badly. I cautioned him to give protracted thought to a decision this critical and not to ever make such a decision when passing emotions could play such a key role.

Business owners, people wanting to start businesses, and new managers must constantly work against their own emotions or they can destroy their future before it ever arrives. People will receive a financial windfall of some sort and hastily decide to sink it all in a business dream they've had for a lifetime. Business owners can be having a great quarter and erroneously attribute it to a turn in the tide of their business fortunes when it could in fact just be an anomalous quarter. By the same token, they can be having a terrible quarter and erroneously attribute it to their business going under when it's just a single bad quarter. New managers often haven't yet had the time in their career to understand the ebb and flow of the particular line of business they're in. Consequently, they may make emotional decisions based on fear of failure and the loss of their new position.

In addition to being business people, we each have our personal lives, made up of our spouse, our children, extended family, friends, business associates, and community relationships at our churches, synagogues, or clubs. Every one of those relationships carries with it the potential to impact our emotions and either directly or indirectly impact our thinking and decision-making processes. If your marriage or some similar relationship starts to have problems, don't fool yourself into thinking that you're being as clear-headed as you might be otherwise. If you just learned a loved one has a serious or terminal illness, you'll reason you can handle that and still make decisions. Personal experience and a multitude of interactions with business owners have taught me this is a form of self-delusion we embrace to help us cope at such times. Conversely, a beautiful day, waking up feeling unusually happy, or "feeling lucky" may not be the very best time to jump into a new business venture.

I want to add a final area of warning here based on personal experience, and that's the danger of too many voices. I warned my grandchildren's generation in my second book about the problem of hearing too many other people's voices and not your own. Let me add here quickly that I like the biblical advice, "There is safety in a multitude of counselors." The problem arrives when your "counselors" are in fact just offering opinions or theories they heard in school and not offering counsel based on a solid wealth of experience. God only knows how many businesses have been launched or sunken over family dinners, casual drinks at a bar, or people sitting around the shop on a rainy day. Every one of those people is subject to their own emotions. You have no idea what may be going on, good or bad, in their lives. Be willing to accept counsel, but first consider the source.

I use the metaphor of marriage constantly throughout this book with regard to the relationships we have with businesses we own and/or manage. Marriages have good days and bad days, they have fat times and lean times, they experience sunshine and rain, and a lot of times the decision to enter a marriage or end a marriage is made hastily on the basis of a euphoric feeling brought on by good times or a period of depression brought on by bad times. Business life will be much the same, and what I look for in marriage and in business is a sort of "running average" of how things are going. If the marriage is running a fairly steady average or even improving, I feel like my marriage is going well. If my business life is running a fairly steady average or even improving, I feel much the same. However, if the marriage or the business life is tailing off or nose-diving, that calls for some serious work to save it.

Marriages rarely fail in a single day. The same can usually be said for businesses. Just be cautious that you don't make such an emotional decision on a single day, based on a single wave of emotion, that you destroy your marriage or your business.

## Out Of Brains

One of the most poignant stories I know, which is relative to the importance of having competent employees, involves a couple of wealthy and successful businessmen who decided to expand one of their existing businesses. In writing here, I don't want to be too industry specific because this could happen in any organization regardless of whether they're repairing widgets, manufacturing rocket engines, or baking pastries.

It seems they were doing very well with this new startup they'd launched, and in just a matter of a few months, they had enormous demand for their new service. This led them to realize they could go regional and perhaps even national with this idea. They had ample personal capital, and so they almost immediately began to open branch offices in other key markets in the western states.

At first, things seemed to be going quite well as they personally went to each new locale and set up the office, hired the team, and started the marketing campaign rolling. In their business, a lot of the marketing is personal contact, and they went out with their team and made those initial contacts. Business began to roll in, and the owners returned to their California office expecting new profits to pile up rapidly.

It was a while before there began to be trouble in this newfound business paradise. At first things went smoothly, and then there began to be problems with the sales, service, customer satisfaction, billings, cash flow, and personnel. The businessmen returned to the new branches and tried to work through the problems as they cropped up; each time they worked with their teams to smooth out the bumps in the business.

Over the course of the next year, they continued to open new offices. But soon this pace slowed and stopped because they were routinely called back to the existing locations they'd launched to put out operational fires. Customer issues, accounting issues, and personnel issues consumed more and more of their time. Eventually they were so busy fighting fires that their California businesses suffered.

At this point, the two businessmen sat down and began to reconsider this business venture and what was going wrong. Not all of the locations had problems, but most of them did. After a lot of soul-searching, they made the decision to shut down the problem locations entirely. Eventually they closed down all out-of-state locations they couldn't personally access rapidly in case of problems.

A year or so later, with the full benefit of hindsight, they were asked by another businessman they knew what had happened. They offered him a number of insights into the individual problems that had cropped up at various branches. But when he pressed them further for how this could have happened at so many locales, they gave him what I consider a classic answer: "We ran out of brains."

What had happened here is far more common than people starting businesses, managing businesses, or attempting to expand businesses realize. Just because you understand your business and all of its nuances, doesn't mean you can move about the country and easily find other people who'll have the same mental, educational, and motivational talents you do to carry out your master plan.

For years in business schools, we've taught that there is a "Talent War" being fought in businesses all over the world. In fact, there's a popular book out entitled *The Talent Wars* that you might want to read. The idea that there's an unlimited supply of people out there who are as intelligent, educated, and motivated as you are is a false concept. The truth is, talented people are in shorter supply than your optimism might otherwise assume.

I write about employee recruitment, pre-employment testing, and other aspects of employee selection throughout this book, but right now I want to pound that little mantra into your burgeoning business brain: "We've run out of brains." This won't just be an issue in hiring managers; it will be an issue from the bottom of your organization to the top. It will deeply impact your corporate culture. The sooner you understand its importance, the better.

Every day, in every country in the world, new businesses die, growing businesses falter, and old businesses go into a prolonged decline with eventual death from running out of brains. There are hundreds of reasons this happens, but whatever the reason, the result is the same: businesses decline and/or die. To launch your business, build your business, or sustain your business, it will take adequate brains. Without them, your dreams of business greatness will never be achieved.

Now when I speak of brains here, I'm using an expanded definition where brains involve intelligence, education, training, and drive. If you don't have this yourself, or you can't find it, hire it, or steal it, your dream will be like a mirage; always in the distance. Your new business will suffer stunted growth, or your successful business will eventually decline and die. During more than forty years in business, I've found no adequate substitute for brains.

I want to add an emerging insight on my part. I believe the reason there is such a rush at present toward Artificial Intelligence is not just that it offers superior abilities for decision making and action. I am coming to believe that it is also driven in part by the recognition that brains are in short supply and there is enormous demand. People with brains, people with a highly valued skillset, can often name their wage and benefits. Even with that level of inducement it is difficult to find all the brains needed.

## Learn To Say No

As a business owner or a business manager, one of the hardest things you'll ever have to do is to learn to say NO. Closely allied with learning to say no is learning to walk away. Let me expand briefly on both of those without stretching this out to 1,000 words. In this instance, we're talking about learning to say NO to many of the voices that pull at you to say YES. As far as walking away goes, we're talking about the 1,000 great ideas, products, or business deals people will try to pitch to you once you're in business. I'm not suggesting you never say yes and I'm not suggesting you walk away from every deal; I'm suggesting you need to use your time and money resources wisely and limit your battles to fights you can win.

In the years ahead, if your business ownership stays intact, you'll only have so much time, so much money, and so much mental energy to expend. If you lose focus on what is essential to you and your success, you'll look around one day, realize you "yessed" yourself to excess and sadly see where you hurt yourself, your family, and your business. Once it's known you own a business, you will be overrun with people who have their own dreams, ideas, and sales quotas to meet, and they'll want you to help them meet them. You'll encounter them at work, school, church, markets, little league games, soccer matches, and your fraternal club. To survive you must learn to sort out the wheat from the chaff and say NO.

Now the response I get to this line of reasoning when I share it with students or newly minted business owners is that I'm a cold person and this approach is cruel, heartless, and something they could never do. Truth be told, many of them never do learn these lessons, and so far as I can tell, they're very glad being back in their role as someone else's employee. They're much more comfortable remaining a wage earner for somebody who's already learned these lessons and has put them into practice regularly. You only have so many hours in your life, so many dollars in the bank account, and so many psychic energy withdrawals you can make in one lifetime. Don't think of what I've said here as being selfish; think of it as acting out of your need for self-preservation.

## Are You Empowering Brainless Behavior?

It's a noble idea that we'd want to be kind and forgiving in our businesses when the people who work for us make mistakes. However, it becomes a weakness instead of a noble strength when mistakes are made or rules are violated routinely because managers or employees know there will be no consequences for their actions, whether deliberate or accidental. The problems arise when these mistakes or behaviors begin costing you dollars on your bottom line.

Let's say Owner has a donut shop and Employee drops a tray of donuts one day. Owner comes along and sees what happened and doesn't blow her top, instead she assures Employee that it's okay and that these kinds of accidents happen from time to time. Owner suffers the loss of the value of that tray of donuts but gains some rapport with Employee and other employees who saw the accident forgiven. In those first instances, Owner almost never investigates what the cause of the accident was.

As days or weeks go by, perhaps more of the employees drop a tray of donuts, a stack of pies, or a champagne cake. Owner's lost revenues add up, but since everyone is forgiven for these events, there's no incentive to try to get to the root of the problem. I'm not saying accidents don't happen; I'm saying that people who know that there will never be repercussions for their actions do behave in a different manner than people who understand that being routinely negligent will cost them their job.

Inattention to work these days is a bigger problem than ever with people having so many electronic media distractions in the workplace. I've had to deal with this with young people coming into the workforce who were having "accidents" because they were busy reacting to the phone going off in their pocket every three minutes. Others were distracted because they had to be carrying on social conversations with everyone within earshot. Then we have the age-old problem of employees who lose major efficiency because they're either smoking or trying to figure out how to get outside for a smoke break.

With people we hire as managers and supervisors, there are those who just aren't intellectually equipped for the job and are always making "mistakes." These are mistakes like failing to schedule employees for work properly, failing to schedule supply pick-ups or deliveries in a timely manner to meet orders, forgetting to have a production run for a product out of stock, and failing to deliver customer orders on time. Owner is covering for all these mistakes through erosion of her profits and is likely angering customers or vendors at the same time.

Another issue I often see with managers and supervisors is that when they lack adequate brains and technical skills, they can become lackadaisical with regard to bringing in outside "experts" (i.e., Owner will cover this) to handle problems that are actually part of their job description. Sometimes this is handled by some other employee being forced to step up and cover for the manager; this is still an inefficiency Owner is paying for. At other times, the outside expert shows up and leaves Owner an invoice for hundreds or thousands of dollars.

As an Owner you should have fixed expectations of your employees and other supervising personnel within your organization. Employees at all levels need to be hired or promoted into their jobs based on their aptitude; meritocracies work. Then they need to be adequately trained for the work and held accountable for their outcomes. Mistakes will happen, but if you allow them to become routine, they will become a routine part of your corporate culture. Owner, you're efforts to be a kind and forgiving boss have to be balanced against holding people accountable for their jobs. If you don't, you'll soon be Former Owner.

Businesses that find themselves out of brains may have actually cultivated a brainless corporate culture that encourages brainless actions; they degenerate from a brainy operation to a brainless one. If the brainlessness is at the top, it will flow down. Such behaviors have been cultivated by Owner through unintentionally encouraging routine failure to perform. Employees failing to fully apply their mental abilities and focus to the job at hand have become the acceptable status quo. In those instances, tough business competitors will eventually consume that company.

You're going to need policies and procedures in place at your business that address all the issues I've written about above. How will you recruit? How will you evaluate for new hire? How will you train? How will you evaluate current employee performance?

How will you promote? How will you discipline? There are at least a dozen other considerations I won't mention here, but these few should get you started thinking about your present policies and whether or not they're promoting brainlessness in your workplace. Recognizing this problem and turning it around is a laborious and painful process. If this is you, your business life is at stake.

## Own Your Successes And Your Failures

When you suffer a real failure in life, it helps you to define the boundaries of what doesn't work. Wallowing in near failure is not the same as outright failure because we don't learn the hard lessons from near failure, and may go back there again. So accept failure and learn from it when it does come, just as you should own your success when it finally arrives.

## Don't Expect The Impossible Of Your Employees

Some employers I've worked for quite literally demanded the impossible of employees and then were puzzled and/or angry when employees would become unproductive or simply quit. I believe most employees want to be successful at their work. A sure recipe for employee failure, employee dissatisfaction, and subsequent high turnover rates is the employer who creates a corporate culture which refuses to provide the necessary resources to employees, but still demands the tasks be done on time and correctly. Unless you're able to recruit and hire sorcerers who can conjure up everything they need in the way of resources, workers will need you to spend money on the necessities.

Much of my work in life has been technical or even highly technical. I've encountered many non-technical employers and managers who have no idea how the technical things over which

123

they are the boss actually work. Yet they'll demand an employee make a piece of equipment that is burned out or broken work like new again without the required parts or services. Cost is usually the driver here, but they become angry at their employee when the improperly repaired equipment doesn't function correctly. They then conveniently forget it was their unwillingness to provide proper resources that brought about the subsequent failure. When this mindset becomes part of the corporate culture it's a slow-growing Cancer.

If you act this way as an owner, you're doomed to a second-rate or third-rate operation, presuming it even survives. You're doomed to high employee turnover as the stress of being unable to ever get a win at their job drives good and caring employees (brains) away. You're doomed to be plagued with higher than normal absenteeism as workers seek mental respite from your constant unwarranted harangues. You're doomed with higher than normal worker's compensation claims as people seek any and all means to survive economically and not have to come to your workplace. I hope you're starting to get a picture here because the data goes on for miles, and it's all bad. Have realistic expectations about what can and can't be done and your true costs to do business.

## Ignore Your Employees To Your Own Loss

In 1949, a young engineer fresh out of USC, after a stint in the United States Navy during WWII, went to both the manager and the owner of the company he worked for with an idea he had. The bosses were busy and each quickly shot the idea down. He was foresighted enough to get their rejection in writing. The young engineer never forgot his idea, and nearly thirty years later, he borrowed $25,000 and set about implementing it. When I worked for him in 1980, he was already worth about $2,000,000. He's gone now, but the company he left to his family today is said to be worth in excess of $200,000,000. Take time to listen to the ideas of your employees, young or old. You're paying them, and under most circumstances, the ideas they generate using your time and resources belong to you.

Let's say the idea is far-fetched or is in an area in which you have zero expertise. You should still listen to the employee's idea, later do some research, and if the idea seems to have even an iota of possibility, you might want to run it past someone who is an expert in that field. Now, even if it's not a business you want to be in, ideas have value in the marketplace, and you could do some development and pitch it to another company. If you are successful, you'd pick up a spot of cash, some back-end participation, and you'd reward the employee who came up with the idea. My point here is to think of your employees' thoughts and ideas as potentially valuable to you.

A final point here to remember, that boss of mine was incredibly kind and generous to his employees because he knew they'd helped him achieve his dreams. He took us to the 1984 Olympics, we shared his box at Dodger stadium, and we got to sail on his beautiful sixty-two-foot yacht. Twice I was with him when we encountered some of those old bosses from 1949. They were elderly men by that time, and he was always gracious to them. He later told me: "The biggest favor anyone ever did for me was rejecting that idea." He knew they had a legal right to it; he'd made sure they were aware of the idea and that each rejected it in writing. This left him free to pursue it on his own. They both retired; one with a modest pension and the other with a small buyout of his company. My old boss retired worth over fifty million.

## What Does Your Success Look Like?

I suggest to clients who talk about wanting to achieve success in their business or their personal life to first take some time and figure out what success would look like to them if they actually encountered it. I do find many people know what the other person's success looks like, but simultaneously are unsure what their own success would look like if they ever came upon it.

## Destroyer-Culture Or Creator-Culture, It's Your Choice

A friend posted a piece on social media the other day and it reminded me of something I believe and have been passing along to mentees for years now: "It's not necessary for other people to fail in order for you to succeed." Sadly, some folks never understand this and spend their business life trying to get ahead by destroying others.

There are two schools of thought here in creating a successful corporate culture; 1) The pie is limited and you have to fight everybody and everything to get the biggest piece you can, or 2) The pie can be expanded limitlessly and you can have all you create. This leaves some organizations as destroyers and some as creators.

It's your choice what kind of corporate culture you'll foster, will you be among the creator cultures or among the destroyers?

## Figure Out What Really Matters In Your Life

If you leave work Friday, die this weekend, and never come back, someone will take your place Monday and the business you formerly helmed will somehow manage to move on without you. On the other hand, if you die today and never come home again, your family will miss you forever. Part of being a successful business owner is figuring out what really matters and then pursuing what really matters. If you get your priorities right, your entire life will come together, and not just your business life.

## Never Be Afraid To Be Proven Wrong

A man I respect as an extraordinarily successful entrepreneur/ investor (nine-figures kind of extraordinarily successful) told me once that, "You should never be afraid to be proven wrong. It doesn't do you or anyone else any good to hang on to an erroneous idea."

## Don't Throw Them To The Wolves

We've all known instances where business owners promoted their best worker into a management slot and were seriously disappointed with the results. Some people are natural born managers, others can be trained to be competent managers, but most people are not managers, and no amount of training will fix that.

I believe that each of the categories I mentioned above can gain some benefit from management training. With that in mind, before you throw one of your best workers to the wolves by promoting her into management, how about giving her some management tools first and seeing how she handles it? If you don't, you're likely to lose a good worker or a potentially good manager.

In my line of work you see people who attended management training come back to their jobs and at the very least they have a better feel for the bigger picture of how the business runs. However, it's not unusual to have some folks come back from those same trainings and say, "I'm not interested in being a manager. The training showed me it wasn't a job I want."

## Communicate The Truth With Your Employees

I've worked with many clients who found they couldn't make payroll on time. I always advise that rather than springing this on your employees at the very last minute, call them in as soon as you know what's happening. Tell them the truth and tell them when you think cash flow will get you back to being able to meet payroll. This also allows them to avoid all those bounced check charges for the bills they might otherwise send off in the mail while expecting the check to come on payday as you promised.

I've found most employees will hang in there because they are invested in the job, their coworkers, and the life they have in the local area. They know it would be more onerous in most cases to find a new job and get the new paycheck rolling in. They'll also respect the fact you didn't try to con them. Now I want to offer a word of caution about this whole missing payroll issue. Employees will generally be patient with you once or twice, but if money isn't coming on time week after week, they'll find another job or just go home.

## Trim The Dead Wood

A client I once had told me one of his key staff members was going to be out for a month for a stress-related disability. When I asked why, he said it was because she'd cracked under the work-load. Apparently she was the only one he could get to do any work, so he just kept piling it on her. I asked him if he ever considered firing some of the dead wood and getting her some help instead. He looked at me like I was the one who'd lost his sense of reason.

I then asked him to figure out what this absence was going to cost him and get back to me. I really wanted him to think about the business costs of his actions. Most owners and managers are never forced to do this. It's a great way to learn how not to manage in the future. The path of least resistance is a common choice for owners and managers. Ineffective employees are often shuffled around, sidelined, or transferred when they should in fact be terminated.

## Phone And Internet Backup

In late February 2012, an Internet cable that fed much of East Africa was cut by a ship's anchor. It knocked out Internet service to six countries, and they worked for many weeks to get it fully restored. It created business chaos. Our society has become so wired that I have to wonder how people and businesses would survive if they lost Internet service entirely for days or weeks at a time.

Most of the businesses I know would be crippled if they lost phones or Internet for fifteen minutes. To be without service entirely for a day or days would be devastating. What's your backup plan if fire, flood, hurricane, tornado, or earthquake knocks out your home or office phone or Internet? There are workarounds, but they need to be thought out and made available beforehand.

Our dependence on phones and Internet is the reason I'm stressing this to you. When you lose those services, employees are frustrated and stymied in their efforts, and your customers will be disadvantaged and likely furious at being unable to communicate with you. Create a strong corporate culture that prides itself on being prepared, come what may.

## Food For Thought From Peter Drucker

"Most of what we call management consists of making it difficult for people to get their work done."

Peter Drucker

## Where Are Your Employees?

We routinely track valuable pieces of equipment by satellite these days to be sure it's where it's supposed to be; not stolen, not on someone else's job site, and not sitting in front of a bar, casino, or motel when it should be working. In the old days we'd drive from known hangout to known hangout looking for wayward employees because we lacked a better means to track them. The latest technologies use an employee's photo identity cards to allow for the same thing. This doesn't eliminate the problem; it does offer new tools to deal with it.

Having owned multiple businesses and worked at every level of management from foreman to CEO. I can tell you that I've gone out and pulled on-the-clock employees who were drinking in bars, gambling in casinos, banging their coworkers' wives in seedy motel rooms, and running a full-time manufacturing business on the side with the money and equipment of the company that employed them. If you own or manage a business, this may not be an unusual aspect. In some businesses (Bible bookstores), I hope it's unheard of.

When I locked the gates at the office parking lot one recent night, it was overcast and spitting rain, and I began to laugh at a memory. The reason I was laughing was the memory of an afternoon twenty-five years back when the weather was similar, and I spent two hours driving around in a cold drizzle, tracking down one of my unaccounted for salesmen. I knew of three bars that he really liked, and I eventually found him in one thirty miles from the office. Today I'd find him from a warm office with a smart phone.

In all those instances I mentioned earlier, they were driving or operating company vehicles or equipment, and we had the vehicle set up with a satellite tracker. The trackers in those days were about the size of a loaf of bread and under the dash. The technology today has advanced considerably and now exists in a much more compact form. Yes, employees can be compelled to consent to wear such a device as a condition of employment, and they have no say in the tracking of other company assets.

Some of you reading this are appalled and disgusted with this surveillance approach by businesses in America (around the world for that matter). If you're in that mindset, I suggest you not go into business. You should absolutely never try to manage a company. Yes, you'll have stellar employees who'll become your life-long friends. But just as surely, you'll have employees from Hell who regard you from day one as "The Man" (regardless of your gender). They'll conduct an insane and relentless campaign to punish you for every authority figure they've ever known. When it all goes to a lawsuit, you'll finally see the pattern when their five most recent employers are deposed for the same issues.

How you approach the use of technology with regard to labor tracking is up to you. I know that some of you reading here have feelings ranging from unease to disgust; I understand. I'll throw in for free some insight from old law school lectures regarding the concepts of servants, masters, agency, and your near-total liability for employees or other people who may act on your behalf. In thirty seconds, one errant employee operating company equipment (e.g., car, truck, tractor-trailer, airplane, dozer, grader, etc.) can potentially cost you everything you or your employer has built in a lifetime.

## Don't Ignore Your Gut

A colleague and I were discussing gut checks today and their role in managing people. We agreed if your gut (intuition) tells you something is not right, you should listen to it even when you can't quite put your finger on the problem. Case in point, I tested a controller for a company many years back; she was extremely bright and very personable. Yet after the sessions I had a nagging suspicion something was wrong. I met with her three times during the testing and some follow-up.

I told the owner of the company who'd requested the testing that I was troubled about her but couldn't quite determine why I felt that way. I suggested some other testing relative to my uneasy sense that she was being evasive in some of her answers. He told me she was already his right hand and reminded me I'm notoriously suspicious of people until I get to fully know them. We left it at that. She would later serve two years in prison for the roughly $400,000 she embezzled from him to use in support of her online gambling habit.

Sometimes those nagging feelings you're getting may well be that you're picking up information at a subconscious level. Our senses are taking in far more information than any of us can handle. The brain sheds most of the unneeded information so we don't have to deal with a constant state of garbage-information overload. Our own ancient sense of danger and the body's desire for survival seems to pick up on danger signals civilized people often miss. If something feels off with a person, place, or situation, then respect your gut.

## When Asking Employees To Do More With Less

A large body of research in recent years indicates what we all knew; employers are trying to get the same amount of work done with a third fewer employees than they had a decade ago. For most employers, it's not that they're deliberately being harsh, it's a matter of economic survival. Unfortunately, some of the side effects are a tired, stressed out, depressed, and often angry workforce. Incidents of spousal abuse, road rage, and employee-on-employee violence are on the rise with no end in sight. You'll need to get ahead of it.

As an employer, it's more important than ever that you find ways to "tap off" these negative impacts from your workplace. With money short, being able to spend or give raises is not always an option. It's an old axiom, but money isn't everything. Even simply thanking employees for hanging in there has been shown to result in positive benefits to enhance employee satisfaction. So instead of holing up in your office, why not make a point to get out and practice some of that "management by wandering around" stuff academics like me talk about?

## Hard Work Still Pays Off

Despite all the new management gurus, ideas, books, and advanced training programs, old-fashioned hard work continues to pays off again and again! You'll be surprised how much you can accomplish by simply working harder than your competition. I'm not saying that your volume of work alone can overcome all odds; I am saying that if you're an already productive person who is persistent, you can often outperform the purported business geniuses.

# CHAPTER 5

## HUMAN RESOURCES; WELCOME TO THE CONUNDRUM

**The People Component Is The Hardest Part To Get Right**

When I've been asked by business clients or business students, "What's the hardest part of business to get right," I always offer the same response: "Assuming you have a business that is already operating and perhaps even profitable, it's the employee part that is hardest to get right and keep right." The mechanics of almost every major line of business are old and well known. Some have been written about extensively for centuries and in all cultures where a written language exists.

There are myriad business schools around the world dedicated to the mechanics of business. The mechanics can be reduced to a science; the employee issues cross over dozens of disciplines and land nowhere solidly. If you're a person who feels like you have to have a rational/logical handle on every aspect of your work life, you'll be lost in areas of human resources. Why? While employees will include some very rational/logical people, the truth is that most members of the human race are not given to being rational and/or logical all the time. Our emotional component acts as a wild card.

What is well known yet poorly understood is that employees bring all sorts of variability and geometric complexity to your business equation. If you're a checkers player and not a chess player, business will be hard for you. If you're an employer/manager, then consider the huge amount of mental and emotional variability you and your employees each bring to the workplace and how it can change from day to day and even hour to hour. Can you shift gears and move the pieces fast enough to not be checkmated out of your business?

If you're currently an employer/manager, think about how much of your time is consumed dealing with employee problems and the myriad non-business issues employees can and do create on the job. I'd wager it's your least favorite part of ownership or management. The hardest news for my professional clients to hear is that this isn't going to change no matter how many degrees follow their names; people are complex. Employees will continue to be variable in their skills, production, affability, and mental stability for the foreseeable future. Get used to it.

Employees will continue to have personal problems (e.g., relationship issues, addictions, financial difficulties, physical illness, mental illness, etc.) that come to work with them whether you expected this upon hiring them or not. The upside to this is that those same people also bring their personal gifts to your workplace (e.g., intelligence, perseverance, good humor, loyalty, compassion, vision, genius, etc.), and you get to profit from them if you can manage those people effectively.

In more than forty years at this life of managing businesses and people, I've come to accept and reluctantly embrace the fact that you get some bad people and some bad experiences. If you're a delicate individual who doesn't understand that business is a full-contact sport, you best leave now. However, I can assure you that if you can handle the rough and tumble of the business world and all it entails, all the good people and the good experiences can far outweigh the bad.

## Your Employees' Talents Matter

I watched a local business owner let his best millwrights and machinists slip away over the years. He lost some over wages and some over his refusal to adopt new technology, but most simply left him because he took them and the talent they brought to his company for granted. His competitors stole talented and discontent employees away from him one by one. But the talentless and the yes-men were never in danger of being taken away; in the last years, he was totally surrounded by poorly-performing sycophants.

When I heard he'd finally closed his shop at the end of June, I was saddened but not surprised. It was the end of an era in which he'd once been a major player. I had quit bringing him work years ago; others did the same. Some of us tried to tell him employees and their talents matter. When they took their talents elsewhere, we took our work to their new employers. I sincerely wish him good luck in his retirement and I'm genuinely sorry he couldn't have passed the machine shop along to his son the way his father had passed it on to him.

## Management Truths That Never Go Out Of Style

Managers learn more than a dozen major management theories in grad and post-grad studies. Many are fads that come and go. Basic management concepts have been around for hundreds of years. Yet the concept that we should treat those we manage as we ourselves would like to be treated has been well known for thousands of years. Respect, fair wages, decent working conditions, an open ear, proper training, and providing the necessary tools to do the job never go out of style.

## Great Fiction Writing

Of all the great fiction I've ever read, some of the greatest has been job descriptions I've been asked to review for clients. Why do companies routinely put together job descriptions which only remotely resemble the jobs they're offering, the environment people will work in, or the support and/or expectations the organization will actually offer/have? In some cases it's idealism, in some cases it's poor management skills, and in some cases it's outright deception.

It costs you as a business owner or manager a lot of money to recruit, hire, and retain an employee, even the ones you hire at minimum wage. New business owners and managers usually haven't learned this yet. Why not try to put an accurate depiction of what it is you want from this employee in the job description? Do you really think if you do manage to hire someone that you can fool them forever about what the job actually involves? Do yourself and your employees a favor, figure out what you and your company need before you start recruiting. Then write an accurate job description.

## The Dumbing Down Of America

There are those who routinely muse that the average American is not quite as well educated or at least not as knowledgeable about the country and the world as those in prior generations. My mother was born in 1918, and her formal education ended with the eighth grade in 1932. Other than algebra, I'd guess that my mother was at least as well educated as the high school class

I graduated from in 1972. This begs the question as to whether there's been a decline going on for a long time. I still encounter the occasional young man or woman who is in love with learning and has benefited from all that entails. But more often than not, I encounter young people who seem to be completely unaware of their personal history (i.e., who were your ancestors and where did they come from?), much less knowing anything about their state or nation.

I saw a YouTube® video the other day where someone was claiming that the government has put fluoride into much of the drinking water in an effort to dumb down the populace to make us easier to control. I have a hard time swallowing that one (no pun intended), since it implies the ability to create an enormous conspiracy and carry it off over multiple generations without anybody ever finding the smoking gun it would take to blow the lid off such an undertaking. I have my doubts because we can't even seem to run the postal service efficiently or use the IRS to attack our political enemies without falling on our face and having the whole world find out about it. So, if we're dumbing down, it may be as simple as weakened curriculum, poorer study habits, larger classroom numbers, or Mom and Dad not caring enough to get involved in assuring the kids get a proper education.

For you as a business owner this means that the pool of applications that floods across your inbox may have spent more years in school than ever before and yet be less educated than past generations. A high school diploma means almost nothing to me today when I see a new entrant in the job market list this and his or her alma mater. A bachelor's degree means a bit more, but I also know that the applicant's actual skill levels may be more commensurate with those of a high school graduate from thirty years earlier. Faced with a 1980 high school graduate and a 2010 college graduate, I will give the high school graduate nearly equal consideration if all other aspects of the job are equal. In past generations educational attainment helped prospective employers quickly cull the herd of applicants. Today it's not nearly so clear cut.

## Maybe You Are Hiring The Exemplar

Based on over forty-five years of work experience including twelve years of higher education in the field of business management, three years of law school, and having managed people for forty of those forty-five years, I'm convinced that despite a job having the same name at another business, no two identically named jobs are ever exactly the same. It's an old axiom that whenever one is hired, he or she is completely unqualified to perform the job they're hired for. This is true because of the unique features I alluded to above. Conversely, after years on the job and being ready to move on, an employee becomes completely qualified to perform the job he or she was hired for years ago. Ironically, it's now time to change jobs to build a career. This goes on in businesses, ad infinitum, ad nauseam.

If I'm looking to recruit a person in the field of sales, I don't necessarily have to look for someone who sold an identical product or service to the one I'm recruiting for. Some of the worst job fits I've ever seen were when people had previously filled the same titular position with another business. As I said before, they were uniquely qualified by their experiences there, for the old job. The problem is that I may have to retrain them entirely or break bad habits they learned there, and they may not be willing to make the required change. In fact, there are times when it might be easier to start with a lesser candidate having the basic skill set.

Every job in the world is unique. The combination of unique circumstances and a unique person trying to "own" that job results in the performance variability we find throughout businesses around the world. There's nothing wrong with this; we're just seven billion individuals with individual facets. At the same time, if you're a business owner or manager and you're tasked with selecting a single employee or many employees, in most cases you're going to be tempted to hold up the person who previously filled that roll as the exemplar. What you can't know is that the true and ultimate exemplar may actually be one of the folks you're interviewing later this week.

### Do You Have A Facebook® Account?

We've all heard stories of people who posted items that should have remained private on their Facebook accounts, only to be haunted by them later in a job interview or during a performance review.

Now there's word some job interviewers are concerned if people DO NOT have a Facebook account since they're so common around the planet. The questions at the back of that are: "What's wrong with you?" and/or "What are you hiding?"

As an employer or manager, you are responsible for weeding out bad job applicants. I think that calls for more effort at balance than ever before, as well as the ability to winnow out the wheat from the chaff. Be understanding of people, but be cautious.

### So They Didn't Perform A Basic Background Check?

Over the last fifteen years, I've worked for several companies who called for advice on terminating a problem employee. Sometimes they wanted to release them because the employee's production was low or their attitude was bad. Sometimes they wanted to release them due to economic downturns. But the worst cases have been when they discover an employee has a serious drug, alcohol, or mental health issue that puts the lives of other employees at risk.

Admittedly, an existing employee can develop a drug, alcohol, or mental health problem after they're employed. We're working with humans, not robots, and these things happen. When they happen, there are laws in most states that dictate how the situation can legally be handled. In other instances, there are union contracts or company policies that can intervene on behalf of the employee. You must obey the law, any labor contract, your company policies, or expect to pay the consequences.

One instance twenty-five years back an employee who had drug and alcohol issues was terminated and showed up for the exit interview with a handgun. He'd made the threat in advance about his intent to shoot me if he were terminated; I took his threat seriously. Fortunately he wilted when I pulled a bigger gun and told him to either put the gun down or I'd shoot him in the doorway. He wisely chose to lay the gun down. He was discharged and law enforcement was called.

This incident should've never happened, and I don't recommend the approach I took to anyone. He'd originally been hired by a previously discharged and discredited manager who was a buddy of his. The previous manager had vouched for his fitness for the fairly important job he held. The company had a strict background check policy, which was completely ignored by the buddy on the inside. Workplaces should be safe and peaceful for all workers, and one of the ways we assure this is to weed out the problems in advance through good screening practices, including thorough background checks.

Violence in the workplace is a real problem and one you need to consider as you contemplate going into business for yourself or entering a career in business management. I can't think of a single owner or manager I know who's been in business for more than a few years who hasn't been threatened or assaulted at some point. Drugs, alcohol, and mental illness all played a role in those encounters. Unfortunately today, these social problems are pervasive at all levels of our society. You have a duty to your other employees to safeguard their well-being and make sure you've done all you can to weed out bad actors who may represent a workplace threat.

## Bad Background Checks And The Need To Correct Them

Recently published information indicates that as much as 40% of the information supplied to employers by the companies that offer employee background checks may be erroneous. This does a disservice to both you as the employer who paid for it and the potential employee who agreed to undergo a background check in an effort to gain employment. One bad hire can ruin a company. One erroneous background check can ruin a career. Owners, become more aggressive in getting reliable background checks.

There are two pathways for correcting this problem long-term: Congress and state legislatures can shore up the laws to bite these background check companies for their shoddy work, or a couple of well-placed lawsuits (perhaps even a class action lawsuit) will bring this to a sudden halt. Contact your lawmakers; they don't seem to be too busy these days. If you've been victimized as either an employer or a potential employee, call a lawyer.

## Why Not Just Toss A Coin?

Frequently replicated management research over the years indicates that hiring a person when your only screening method is a job interview improves your chances of making a good hire by

2%. A coin toss (heads or tails) would give you only slightly worse odds (50% versus 52%).

## Don't Look At Me, You Hired Them

Whenever you're called upon in your role as owner/manager to make a hiring decision, consider what's best for your organization and not so much whether or not the new hire will make a good drinking buddy, first-rate golf companion, or red-hot lover. I've seen owners/managers go down all those roads, and pretty soon they find they've surrounded themselves with problems of their own choosing; both they and their organization suffer. Eventually, any enterprise run in this manner either winds down to near nothingness or dies off completely. So what's it going to be, a successful organization, or a group of affable but failing sycophants?

There'll always be the temptation to surround yourself with people you like. Whenever the goals of your enterprise and this hiring-people-you-like approach are compatible, more's the better. But if you make business decisions based on who's your friend, who's your lover, or who's your best bet for a sympathetic ear, you've headed down a path that's only going to get more treacherous as you go along. Your first duty, whether the shareholders are you and your family or you and 30,000,000 public stockholders, is to maximize shareholder value. That means your duty to maintain a successful business has to be placed above your friendships and your romances.

## Help Employees Understand That Safety Is Also For Their Family

I was a manager tangentially involved in a lawsuit twenty-four years ago where a contractor's employee died after deliberately ignoring the job-specific safety training everyone involved with the project had to undergo. The company I worked for was in and out of court weekly for two years, and near the end of the trial, the lawyer asked if we would still settle for the original offer made to the wife five years earlier and long before this lawyer got involved (less his fee and inflation of course). We did agree to settle.

I happened to run across the case file recently while cleaning out a storage room, and it brought that time back vividly. The pity here is the dead man waited until all the other employees and supervisors had left the site and told his helper, "They don't know what the hell they're talking about. I've made this same kind of repair a dozen times before without any problem and without all that stuff they're asking me to do to be safe." These were his last words; less than twenty minutes later, he was dead.

Over the years while working in heavy industry, I've seen four men die in industrial accidents on projects I was involved with. In this instance I didn't witness this death, but this was the most senseless one of all of them. There was no hurry to get finished; it could've been finished safely the next day. There was no incentive to finish early; there was plenty to stay busy with. He left a wife and two small children. Safety procedures can be tedious, but they're there for the worker's protection.

We try more in conducting safety training these days to appeal to a worker's sense of what their family will endure once they're dead than we did thirty years ago. Frequently there's a false bravado amongst workers that is difficult to crack; I've seen it in both men and women who "don't want to go against the team." However, the specter of their spouse and children being destitute for five years while lawyers haggle over a pittance for their life seems to dramatically sober their perspective.

As an owner and/or manager it's on you to do your best in your safety programs to make them effective in communicating the inherent dangers in your line of business. Failing to do so can not only result in needless injury or death to you or an employee, it can also bring about law suits and workmen's compensation issues that can cripple or kill your business. Make it your highest priority that each employee goes home healthy each day, do it for their family, do it for your family.

## Employee Training Adds Value

Back in 2009, *Forbes* magazine published an article on the monetary value of employee training. Their data indicated each dollar spent on employee training yields a $4 return in improved productivity and reduced accidents. In some of my own academic research, I've found it also improves morale when workers see you care enough to put some money and/or time into them in the form of training.

I know times are tough and dollars are tight; this is always going to be the case in a competitive business environment. But failure to properly train and retrain your employees leads to lost productivity, higher maintenance costs, lower morale, and more accidents. Do yourself and your workers a favor, re-examine, and recommit to your training program today!

## Pareto Principle Of Problem Employees

A common variant on the Pareto principle states, "20% of your employees will create 80% of your employee problems." Stop making the 80% of your staff who are productive carry the 20% who aren't. You'll be happier, more productive, more profitable, and your remaining employees will bless you for your actions.

## Managing In The Age Of Narcissism

There's some interesting writing in management circles at this time about what it's like to try and manage a generation of young people who are essentially narcissists. Others have gone so far as to deem it an epidemic of narcissism. In its simplest terms, narcissism means a person is totally self-absorbed, which is evidenced by an almost complete preoccupation with personal preferences, aspirations, needs, success, and how he or she is perceived by others.

Twenge and Campbell wrote about this problem extensively in their 2009 work, *The Narcissism Epidemic: Living in the Age of Entitlement.* I'm seeing it more and more in those under the age of twenty-five who struggle to fit into workplace paradigms that don't orbit around them. They struggle to take direction and fit in because after all, why would THEY need direction, and even if they did, who would be qualified to direct THEM? Additionally, why should they fit in? Shouldn't the rest of the world revolve around them?

If mistakes are made, equipment is damaged, or losses are incurred, it will never be the narcissist's fault. Then, due to their ability to charm, they will in fact often convince the gullible that the mistake, damage, or loss was the fault of a less gregarious coworker. In this capacity, they remind me of a pseudo-alpha animal's ability to elevate itself in a pack hierarchy by deceptive means. They also seem to have the ability to spot a weaker animal in the business pack and redirect the pack's aggression toward that weaker pack mate.

We used to think that narcissism cropped up as a defense mechanism created by some type of serious earlier emotional trauma in childhood and from which the patient had never truly recovered. But these days I'm forced to rethink that approach in light of what appears to be huge numbers of young people, perhaps even massive segments of entire generations, who are now similarly afflicted. There's also the possibility that our entire culture has simply elevated narcissism to worshipful status and made it a behavior to be desired, admired, and widely emulated. My advice to you as employers and managers is to seriously consider this personality type when you conduct job interviews. Narcissists are experts at manipulating people around them and can be absolutely charming so long as they need you. They seem to share this trait in common with sociopaths. Thus, your most engaging interviewee may in fact be your worst potential choice for an employee. Can you really afford to have an employee who believes and acts as if your business, and the world, should revolve around them?

Failing to weed out the narcissist in the hiring process, you are in for some kind of honeymoon period that may take anywhere from a month to a year before the narcissist is fully revealed. We can only hope that in the interim you haven't lost or fired other good employees due to the narcissist. We can also only hope that you have documented grounds for termination. The narcissist will be formidable in a hearing setting as they play so well to judges and jurors.

I can get a better work product out of a team of average workers who work together than I can from a team of superstars. Make no mistake about it, a true narcissist believes in their own mind that they are the superstar among a galaxy of superstars and that you and the rest of the staff are just there as bit players in their ongoing life drama. Be careful as they can be angry when finally cornered and confronted regarding their behavior. At the end expect to be insulted and talked down to like you are a worm; when their self-image is in danger, they can become dangerous.

## But I'm A Nice Person

If you're a business owner and have employees, you know all too well the cost of workers' compensation insurance has skyrocketed. Many of us have seen costs quadruple over the past ten years. In line with this, a client of ours recently conducted a refresher course of "confined entry training" for their employees. The very next day he caught an employee who had attended the training violating the policy by entering an excavation without proper safety measures.

My professional advice to the business owner was to terminate the employee immediately, since his policy allowed for a termination in this kind of situation and the employee was insolent when confronted while still in the hole. Why be so cold to one of your employees? This employer has other employees who want and need to work and are willing to follow the rules to stay safe and keep costs down. By flagrantly risking injury or death, this employee jeopardizes everybody's employment.

How does ONE employee jeopardize everybody's employment? If Employee is severely injured or killed, Employer's workers' compensation insurance will climb for ALL employees. Since business is a competitive undertaking, Employer is now at a cost disadvantage with other's who compete in the same marketplace.

This harsh reality needs to be brought home forcefully to ALL employees on a regular basis so they can help keep one another working safely; here's a place where group psychology can work in everyone's favor. Construction, chemical, and mineral extraction companies know these truths all too well; many have gone broke over their workers' comp insurance costs. When that happens, every employee goes home, and not just the offenders.

Employers, if you allow ONE employee to ignore the safety training of your company, rest assured when it comes time for a trial to help compensate the employee for an injury or the survivors for the death of their loved one, no one will remember you were trying to be a "nice person." The only thing that will matter is Employee was injured or dead and you are at fault because you failed to enforce your own policies. Telling the court, "But I'm a nice person" is not a defense.

## Good Boss, Bad Boss

One would hope that you treat your employees well all the time. But on the offhand chance you don't, consider that when the economy improves, employees who feel as if they've been unappreciated by their current employer will often start to test the waters of an improving job market and seek out a new employer. They won't hit you with the news until they give you their notice.

You put a lot of hidden expense into your employees. You had to recruit them, you had to train them, and then you had to carry their inexperience and low productivity for some period of time before you ever began to see a return on your investment. If they did turn out to be good or even great employees, you'd be a fool to allow them to be stolen away.

A company avoids the loss of its best people by being proactive in this area. If you're not looking at yourself and your competition and comparing what you have to offer your employees versus what the competition does, you're going to be in for some sad times as you lose your best workers again and again. Being a good boss is cost effective; being a bad boss creates "people capital" loss.

## Employees Have Rights That Applicants Don't

I was talking with a long-time local business owner and his sons yesterday afternoon, and they told me about their most recent efforts to hire a new office employee. They had contacted the local government program charged with identifying and sending out applicants, which dutifully sent out four potential hires. One especially memorable applicant arrived with fingernails so long; they had a full curl on all the nails.

When the business owner asked during the interview how she would use a keyboard or adding machine, she told him she used the eraser ends of two pencils held in her palms. The questions about whether or not this affected her keyboarding speed or accuracy went silently unanswered. She was not selected for the position. I frequently see personal choices (e.g., nails, hair, piercings, scarifying, tattoos, clothes, etc.) impact people's ability to find a job.

Individuals have every right to personal choices, and I fully support it so long as it doesn't infringe on others' rights. In this case it would infringe upon the rights of that employer to a fully functioning employee. As an employer, you have an applicant pool made up of the current society. Despite what you're being told, there are good applicants out there who are qualified and want to work. Don't become lazy or panicky and hire a bad employee just to be done with it. If you do, it becomes an "act in haste, repent at leisure" experience.

You need to remind yourself the job you're offering is not a constitutional right, and as an employer, you don't have to hire people whose personal choices might negatively impact your business. Consider how an applicant's personal choices in matters of clothing, body ornamentation, speech, or grooming will impact your workplace BEFORE you hire them. Consider also what it reveals. After the hire, a different set of rules is in place based on the law, your policies or lack thereof, and any labor contract you entered into. The new employee now has rights the applicant didn't.

## Cell Phone And Internet Policies

I'm reviewing cell phone and Internet policies right now for a client so they can be updated to stay in touch with the times. For you who might wonder, if an employee is involved in an "on the job accident," either as the victim of the accident or as a potential contributor, one of the first places the accident investigation is going to go today is whether or not they were talking, texting, or surfing the Internet while they should've been focused on their immediate task. Lawyers are always looking for legal means to shift the liability.

As an employer, questions of whether or not you had adequate policies in place, how sufficiently your staff was trained to your policies, and how stringently you enforced your policies will play a major role in how any tort liabilities or administrative fines shake out. I'm seeing more and more instances where equipment operators (both light and heavy) are on their cell phones when they should've been focused on the task at hand. Sometimes they only injure themselves, but just as often, they injure or kill others.

## Thou Shalt Not Muzzle The Ox

"Thou shalt not muzzle the ox when he treadeth out the corn" is Old Testament Scripture from Deuteronomy 25:4, and also sound advice for business owners. Employees who are allowed to share in the profits of a company, even in a small way, are generally much happier to show up and on time, work harder while there, and work with a better attitude than employees who feel muzzled.

Both oxen and employees tend to get grouchy if they're forced to walk around all day within sight of the fruits of their labors, but are never allowed to stop and enjoy even a single bite of what they produce. When considering your compensation plans as you go into business and in the years thereafter, give this verse and your compensation policies some serious thought.

## The Unsung Hero

During my time in the workforce, I've noticed an often over-looked aspect of work life that is critical to the success of any organization. I think of them as the unsung heroes, and though they are a staple in small organizations, the mega-organizations have them as well.

They are the ones who make sure the supplies get ordered, the shop gets picked up, the software gets upgraded, birthdays are remembered, and the client gets the promised return call before close of business. They are often the least flashy individuals on the team and may go all but unnoticed.

In short, they are the organizational grease that keeps all the other slightly out-of-sync gears from grinding themselves to pieces. They are rarely employee of the month, seldom receive the big raises or bonuses, and may only be noticed for their absence once they are gone and the gears start to grind.

If you are an owner/manager, be on the lookout for these characters. Once you identify them, you need to make certain to give them the tools they need to keep doing the things they do out of their own sense of responsibility. Usually it's all they require to keep them humming along happily for years.

I have found that with this type of employee that if you rec-ognize their work, call them into your office and praise them for that work, and make sure to remember them when raises are given or bonuses are handed out, they are your employee for life. Conversely, where I'm seen them taken for granted, they just as unobtrusively move on.

## How You Gonna Handle Those Old Folks?

With an aging workforce and more people planning to work lon-ger before retirement due to the unpredictable economy and poor retirement planning, you need to be thinking and planning now about how you'll accommodate older workers so they can remain a productive part of your workforce. I value older workers for their knowledge, their skill sets, their loyalty, and their work ethic. Such qualities seem to be in shorter and shorter supply as I survey today's workplaces. Unless you have older workers retiring at fifty-five, sixty-two, or sixty-seven, you might consider what it will be like to have a workforce with septuagenarians in it. Teenagers and robots can't replace everyone just yet. Making the investment to keep older workers productive as they age will be money well-spent.

## Employee Compensation: Who's Guarding The Henhouse?

I explained to the board of directors of a local enterprise recently why you don't allow your CFO to conduct the salary survey for himself, the CEO, and the COO. I have no problem with a CFO doing a salary survey for those below the C-level, but my mother used to talk to my siblings and me about the inherent problems of having "...the fox guard the henhouse."

While I'm nearly certain there's never any larceny in the hearts of C-level executives, I did find it strange that the CFO in question chose to make comparisons with executives from San Francisco, San Diego, and San Jose. Local companies of similar size and in similar industries in our Central California county don't tend to offer comparable salaries to those cities. Don't let your fox guard your henhouse.

## Watching YouTube® Wasn't In The Job Description

My first stop one recent Monday morning was to go by a contractor's showroom and pay him for some work he did on my wife's shop on the previous Friday. When I came in the door the buzzer sounded, but after five minutes, I became concerned when no one came out into the showroom.

Other customers had arrived by that time, and I told them I'd step in the back to see if anyone was around and if everything was okay. Earlier this summer, the contractor had introduced me to his recent high school graduate grandson as, "…someone I'm trying to teach the ropes."

I found the grandson ensconced in the back office with headphones on, watching something on YouTube®. It startled him when I tapped him on the shoulder and said, "There are three of us out here who'd like to do some business with your grandpa." He was embarrassed, which is exactly what I had intended.

Much of my livelihood comes from being on the computer and the Internet. The same is true for many others reading this. In the case of the grandson, he was supposed to be watching the front, stocking the shelves, and greeting and serving customers. I doubt his job description includes watching YouTube.

## We Don't Know What We'll Do Without You

There does come a time when the only way to deal with an employee who just can't or won't rise to their assigned tasks is to assure them that you don't know what you'll do without them, but you're going to begin finding out tomorrow morning.

## Fire Him

Early in my business career I was certain that every new hire could become a great employee if I just took the time to figure them out and then put sufficient effort into them; years in business proved me wrong. I learned we can put an inordinate amount of time into trying to turn around a bad employee. In grad school, I asked one of my management profs who'd been a chief operating officer for an international company how to deal with a manager I'd inherited that I kept trying to fix and never could.

She asked the details and I laid them out for a couple of minutes. Her response surprised me, "Fire him, Mr. Neeley. You can't fix everybody, and the scenario you're describing is just wasting your time and your company's resources trying to turn a bad hire into a good manager." In a small business or a startup, good employees and managers are critical. You're an entrepreneur, not a psychologist, social worker, or marriage counselor. With some employees, there is no salvage and a firing is in order.

## You Might Want To Check Those Employee Files First

In consulting with a client about their plan to terminate a problem employee, we discovered the employee had no job description, had been written up by supervisors who were not his supervisor, was in two instances written up by a peer, and had been given five verbal warnings by his direct supervisor for the same policy violations. The company policy called for a verbal warning, a written warning, and for the third violation of the same policy, immediate termination. It's not a good idea for management to violate its own policies and then note it in the employee's personnel file. As surprising as it may seem, I run across that very thing routinely when reviewing employee files.

The details I uncovered in that instance showed the employee actually had good grounds to claim he didn't know what his job was. There was no evidence of a written job description, much less one he'd acknowledged having read and verified by his signature. He also claimed he hadn't been properly trained; coincidentally, there were no training records in his personnel file. Privately I asked the client how he'd explain all this to a judge; he struggled to form an answer, and then admitted he couldn't.

I suggested a layoff with the ability to draw unemployment. It might not be as emotionally satisfying as an outright firing, but it also wasn't as certain to prompt a lawsuit the client would most likely lose.

The better course of action here would have been for the client to have had good files, with good records showing how his management team had followed the companies policies and procedures. Further, they would have shown the employee was familiar with those policies and procedures and had acknowledged this by his signature. There would have also been detailed training records that began at hire and then showed every new task that the employee had been trained to in his nearly two years on this job. I know how tedious you must be thinking all of this will be for you as an owner or manager. But I assure you it will not be even half so tedious or nerve wracking as a labor hearing, or being deposed by opposing counsel for a wrongful termination.

## You Could Have Been Anything You Wanted To Be

Over the past eighteen years, I've conducted aptitude and intelligence testing on more than one thousand people. I want to share a story here about the man I tested who scored the highest on those tests of anyone I ever examined. I have no way of knowing if he's still in the workforce; he was in his early fifties at the time and had already completed one career and was retired from that with a secure pension. I have no desire to embarrass this man in any way because there has never been any doubt in my mind that he was the victim of a callous high school teacher/counselor who for whatever reason didn't like him and had crossed all sorts of ethical and professional lines in his treatment of this man when he was a teenager.

I met him in my role as a health care administrator, and one of the things I routinely did there was conduct some pre-employment testing of job applicants and later with new hires to assess their intellect, personality type, and their fit for the job they were taking on. This man had been hired as a physician's assistant (PA), and his story was interesting to me because he hadn't come to that role late in life by the usual route of the many other PAs who'd worked for me before. He'd completed a lower level healthcare career with a state agency, and as he neared the end of that career, he realized he'd accumulated enough vacation and sick leave to allow him to enter a prestigious PA program at a university.

I was to learn as we chatted after the testing that his dream as a boy had been to become a physician. He'd gone to high school and done his best, but there were some problems, and apparently he hadn't been the most studious kid in his classes. This had somehow raised the ire of the teacher/counselor assigned to him; they clashed. Word that he was a problem student began to get around, and some of the other teachers began to treat him differently too. By the end of his high school days, he was graduating, but he wasn't headed anywhere in particular, and the teacher/counselor had already assured him he wasn't smart enough or studious enough to ever take on a professional career, so he might as well forget it. And he did.

I recall he had gone into the military, and when he came out, he went to work for a state agency. I don't want to name the agency or the job he had for fear again of bringing unwarranted embarrassment on this man. But in the course of his career, he got into the medical field and served well and with distinction there. Hence the budding sense in him that he might have enough brains to go take the PA course, and if he was "really lucky," he might get through. Not only did he have the brains for the course, he excelled in the classes and graduated at the top of his cohort. I'm not certain if anyone was more surprised than he was when he passed the state exam on his first attempt.

By this time, his vacation and sick leave had run out and it was time to retire. He took retirement and began working for various small health clinics on a temporary or *locum tenens* basis. When he'd seen my ad in the newspaper for a full-time PA and that the job was within fifteen miles of his home, he'd promptly applied. He was a genuinely kind and likable man, and employees and patients in the clinic took to him quickly. Hence he came to be sitting in front of me after the testing, and we began to go over his scores. I shared with him that he had scored the highest on his tests of any man or woman I'd ever tested in my career. Not only had he outscored all of them, he'd outscored them by a 20% margin. I looked at him and said, "You could have been anything you wanted to be."

His reaction couldn't have stunned me more if he'd reached out and slapped me; he began to weep. I was caught off guard by this but gave him a moment. I didn't know what I'd said that had elicited this reaction, and I wanted to give him time to regain his composure. After a moment I immediately began to apologize, and he raised his hand to silence me. "When I was a boy," he started tearfully, "my counselor didn't like me, and we didn't get along. When it came time for career guidance, he told me that I was a problem and not very bright...I'd never amount to anything. Those words were branded in my mind and I couldn't shake them. I gave up any dream of a professional life and eventually ended up in the military. After working in healthcare for thirty years and being around physicians daily all that time, I began to wonder if I could have a little piece of my dream of being a physician."

This wonder caused him to learn about the PA program and what was involved. He figured out a plan for payment, his pending retirement date, a workable timeline, and got himself accepted to the PA program at Stanford University. His tears had stopped by now, and he assured me I had nothing to apologize for again. "Dr. Neeley, I want to thank you for what you've said here. For a lifetime I've been marked by what another professional said to me about my ability and my intellect. What you've told me and showed me in the scores helps me see that I was smart enough and studious enough to have had my dream."

As I write this, it's been eleven years since I last saw that man, and at that time he was happily serving as a PA in a Federally Qualified Health Center. He stands out in my mind as the prime example of how some of the best brains around us are missed and misbranded. When this happens, the person with the brains is harmed, the person who missed the opportunity to encourage them and help them achieve their dreams is diminished, and the world as a whole suffers an incalculable loss because superior brainpower of almost any magnitude is a precious resources we all need to see being maximized. Please remember this story when you're interviewing people to work for you. Over the years I've found more than one diamond in life's resume coal pile, and you might too.

# CHAPTER 6

## THE BUSINESS LANDSCAPE BEFORE YOU

### Survey The Business Environment You Plan To Enter

It never ceases to amaze me how many people will come to me to talk about starting a business and when I begin to ask them about what kind of research they've done, it's almost always minimal, to the point they seem embarrassed to share it with me. Let's say you want to open a coffee shop/kiosk. Now you would think in this instance that people would want to learn everything there is to know about owning and operating a coffee shop/kiosk before jumping in (like the friends I dedicated this book to did when they went into that business nearly twenty-five years ago). But what I frequently get instead as feedback from clients is that 1) they've spent a lot of time at Starbucks®, or 2) they love hanging out at Denney's®, and 3) they have some extra money burning a hole in their pocket, 4) it looks like an easy business to enter, and 5) they're excited about its future prospects. Wow!

If I'm brutal I just say, "So let me get this straight, you want to risk your nest egg on a venture you know little about other than that it makes you feel good and you're excited about its future prospects?" I caution that while those emotions are all well and good, it's certainly not how Starbucks, Dunkin Donuts®, or Denney's go into a new marketplace with one of their stores. They look at demographics that are often so detailed that the detail becomes laborious to wade through, even for a business wonk like me. How many homes or apartments are within five miles? What's the average income? What's the disposable income? What are the age demographics? What are the educational levels? How about ethnicity? How about religious beliefs? How about traffic? How about parking? Are you getting the picture?

Now there are companies that exist for no other purpose than to sell people like you information packages on how to start a business and what to look out for and consider. Usually if you find their web sites they'll be able to offer you a package (one of dozens); which usually amounts to a divided binder of information, disks of information, links to download information, their website, and a hundreds of useful' business and governmental links, all for a small fee. Having once availed myself of such a service, decades ago, I can tell you that most of it is useless boilerplate, but there may be useful general information in their content as well. What they'll lack is specificity about the business you want to jump into and the marketplace you plan to enter.

To solve this problem, there are companies that can provide you with exhaustive demographics…at a price. Now I'm not saying that a lot of this leg work couldn't be done by you, your family, or some other local professional company. What I am saying is that someone needs to do this research on the business environment FIRST, in order to see if it's conducive to receiving and nurturing the seeds of your dream. Dreaming is important to seeding great ideas and creating great businesses. But dreams that lack any grounding in reality are generally doomed to only be dreams. I know most people hate this numbers stuff, but numbers really do matter when it comes down to going into business and staying in business. Ignore the numbers at your peril.

Throughout this book I talk a lot about business plans and their importance. I won't even attempt to write a business plan for a client unless they have either done the research and can provide it for me, hired someone else to conduct the research and provide it for me, or hire me to take the time to do the research for them and use that as a basis for a business plan. Without that information "...it's all just doodles on cocktail napkins." The essays which follow are meant to make you consider potential pitfalls and triumphs ahead if you go into business. I'll offer one guarantee, if you don't take the time to fully understand the landscape you seek to enter, it will consume you like the Western American deserts once consumed old pioneers.

## Limit Your Risk

How vulnerable to change is your dream? When I was in my twenties, I was befriended by a much older man who'd been the head Linotype operator for a major newspaper on the East Coast. He'd moved to California and reinvented himself as a hardware store manager after his career suddenly ended. This happened because the Linotype machine was made anachronistic by the invention of computerized typesetting. That happened in the late seventies; it was the first time I realized a career and an industry could suddenly disappear. The message I want to convey here is that you can sink your life savings or your retirement money and all your dreams into a business thinking it will be there for you and your family for generations to come, only to see it vanish like morning mist on a warm day. No matter how much of a sure thing you think it is, there's risk to getting into any line of business.

## What's A Small Business?

The term small business gets tossed around so much by pundits and politicians these days that I'm fairly certain most people have no clue there is no single definition for the term. For many it conjures up a picture of some mom-and-pop operation in a small burg out on the Great Plains with three employees. Let your business knowledge begin to expand now. As I'm writing this book, the Small Business Administration (SBA) has a forty-eight-page document that sets the standard for hundreds of different types of small business.

Your company could be defined as a small business in some industries if you have gross revenue of $750,000 a year or less. While in other industries, your company could have gross revenue of $35,500,000 a year or less and still be a small business. In some industries, you're a small business if you have 500 employees or less regardless of income; while in others, you're a small business if you have 1,500 employees or less regardless of income.

Many business people (from both political parties) have lobbied hard over the past forty years to help us arrive at this point. Why? They did it so their lines of business could qualify for SBA loans and for bidding on government contracts limited to small businesses. Now you may be beginning to understand why it's so difficult to speak accurately about small business. Maybe you have a small business, maybe you don't. The truth is there are dozens of definitions dependent on the industry involved.

So the next time you hear any politician (Democrat, Republican, or Libertarian) speak about small business, know he or she speaks of a near mythical creature. Ask yourself if he or she is speaking about the potato farmer who has four employees and is limited to grossing $750,000 a year to maintain small business status, or the property and casualty insurance carrier with 1,500 employees and no limit on gross income. I suspect that after reading this essay you may in fact know more about what constitutes a small business than many of your elected representatives do.

## The Future Is Upon Us

I remember as a boy when industrial robotics was a concept that was going to happen in the distant future. Fifty years later, I have clients who routinely sell new industrial robots and buy back old ones to refurbish and sell again. It's best to remind yourself when you lie down to rest each night that every morning the future is upon you, and if you decide to rest in the past, the present will begin to move on by you that very day.

## Why Even Go Into Business?

Why do sane people go into business for themselves in a capitalist economic system (or any other economic system for that matter)? Ignoring the arguments for self-actualization, personal fulfillment, job security, and the joy of working for yourself, I want to look at the economic drivers for being your own employer. I must first posit that self-interest is natural to the survival of any species. Humans, as a species, are not an exception to that generalization.

If you work for someone else, that person has put their own money at risk in the expectation that they can get a dollar and more back for every dollar they put at risk. They do this by leveraging their expertise, connections, money, and someone's labor with the expectation that they can get a better return on investment (ROI) than if they just put their money in the bank at 0.5% interest.

You may recall that passbook accounts at your bank and treasury notes are low RISK and have a low yield. Being in business for yourself is high risk, but also carries with it the possibility of high yields. People who are risk-averse put their money into low risk investments and accept the lower yield because it's safe. People who are willing to place their money at high risk do so because they expect to get a high yield when they take a high risk. Of course, they can also lose everything!

With regard to launching a business, the situation I encounter most often is people who have a special skill/talent (or at least think they do) and are tired of the boss making all the money off their skill/talent. Hence they decide to go into business for themselves. This group includes people from all walks of life and all kinds of backgrounds. A few are successful in their efforts, the vast majority are not!

As an example, an electrician might see that s/he is being paid $28 an hour plus benefits, but that the boss is charging $65 an hour for that work. A bookkeeper might see that s/he is being paid $15 an hour and no benefits, but the boss is charging $35 an hour for that work. Seeing an opportunity to make more money and a better life for themselves and their families launches most small business efforts.

My goal isn't to debate wages and benefits or classes within society, but rather to provide an example of what drives people to launch their own businesses. The logic will go somewhat along these lines. "Why shouldn't I put my capital, my skill/talent, and my time into an effort to make the big money for me instead of for my boss?" All learn quickly it's a little more complex than that. All will pay for what they learn with ROIs varying from 0% to 5,000%.

In concluding this section, let me say that I've never had anyone approach me in the past thirty years and tell me they wanted to put their capital, their skill/talent, and their time into an effort to make the big money so they could give it away to their neighbors, their friends, their church, or their government. If they survive, they may well be generous to all those entities. Most folks are concerned first about the welfare of themselves and their own families; as they should be.

## How High Are The Hurdles To Your Business Success?

Two of the most important questions new business owners, old business owners, and business managers should be asking themselves regarding getting into business initially or entering a new line of business are: "What is the hurdle to entry?" and "How high is the hurdle to entry?"

I'd been a business owner and manager for decades when I first heard these questions in a master's business class. I'd never even thought about them previously, much less asked myself about them regarding any business I was associated with. Sometimes if we've never heard a concept stated succinctly, we're vaguely aware of the problem but have never been able to get it into manageable terms. Put simply, there are hurdles to many aspects of business that have to be overcome, or the effort will never succeed. There's the initial and very critical "hurdle to entry." After that, there are the secondary hurdle-height issues as we learn about employees, marketing, sales, cash flow, logistics, taxes, expansion, product lines, and so forth.

Have you ever sat down and thought about going into business, and while considering all the possible businesses you could try, you realized that for many of them, you didn't have the money necessary? If so, you've encountered the concept of hurdles to entry and just didn't realize it at the time. Money is the main hurdle to entry for most businesses, but certainly not the only hurdle to entry. For instance, if you want to own and operate a business in Hawaii, one of the hurdles you'd have to clear is relocating yourself to Hawaii. Gaining any necessary licenses and permits there would be another hurdle. As you think about this example and extrapolate it, you'll start to see some of your own hurdles to entry.

Staying with the concept of money as a hurdle, let's talk about the height of the hurdle. When most of us were children, we set up the little lemonade stand out on the corner or the sidewalk in front of our home and launched our first business. Here the money hurdle was extremely low because we used our parents' financial resources. We were able to use their lemons, their sugar, their water, their pitcher, their spoon to stir it with, their ice, their cups, and their table upon which to sell and serve. For advertising, we used their paper and their writing instrument or magic marker to tell our story of lemonade sales and what a cup would cost. The height of the financial hurdle to entry is never that short again.

I'm involved in the manufacture of fertilizer and soil amendments. From time to time, we consider entering new lines of product manufacturing. Sometimes we already own all the equipment and have all the permits and licenses we need in hand. So long as we have the required knowledge and the capital needed to make the startup, we're good to go. But if we lack the equipment, the permits and licenses, the knowledge, or the capital, we have one or more hurdles we can't immediately clear. Some years back, we had all of the pieces at hand except for a federal permit on the product itself. It turned out that even though the soil amendment had been around for two hundred years, and that both my farmer-grandfather's had mixed the two basic chemicals and boiled it up on their kitchen stoves; we'd need to conduct a $500,000 environmental study to gain the permit.

Bear in mind it didn't matter that twenty other manufacturers had already conducted the same study; we had to conduct our own study or pay one of them a royalty to use theirs. The royalty would've taken such a bite out of the net profit that it made the project infeasible. We abandoned the idea because we couldn't overcome the height of the permitting hurdle necessary to entry. It would be highly instructive here to say that at one time, this specific permitting hurdle didn't exist. What brought the permitting hurdle to life wasn't public safety. It was a lobbying effort by the manufacturers already producing the product who now claimed it "might" pose a health risk; they were of course already grandfathered in. Frequently your competition will throw up hurdles where none previously existed.

In another instance, which I'm painfully aware of, I worked with a family who wanted to create a small business using the husband's disability settlement from an industrial accident. The idea was they could take less than $50,000 and turn it into a business that would provide them an ongoing livelihood. After conducting the business analysis and creating a business plan for them, it became obvious they didn't have enough money for the business as they envisioned it. The lesser alternatives offered didn't appeal to them, and I encouraged them to shelve the plan until they found more capital. We had numerous conversations about "faith versus reality," which went nowhere. They proceeded with 65% of the plan and were broke within one year.

My point in all of this is that whether it's an existing successful business or a mom-and-pop startup, there are going to be hurdles to entry that have to be overcome. They can't be walked around and they can't be ignored. I was a hurdler in high school. If you went around a hurdle or ignored a hurdle, you were disqualified. In life, if you ignore a hurdle or walk around a hurdle, you'll be punished (i.e., fined or jailed for failing to acquire licenses/permits). If you ignore a hurdle and pretend it won't matter in the long run, you will fail (i.e., your business will die for lack of a critical piece of the puzzle). No matter how right you feel about ignoring the need for a license/permit, there'll be consequences. No matter how much faith you have in God,

God rarely allows the immutable laws of commerce to be ignored without consequence.

If you follow my writing or have read any of my books, you already know I think faith and hope are wonderful things. But I also think that a good survey of the line of business you want to go into and the resultant solid business plan go a long way to assure you'll clear all the hurdles. We've all heard that failing to plan is planning to fail. I didn't come to this place solely via academia. I've come to this place having made many of the same mistakes I now teach, write, and counsel against. If you're a student of the Bible, you know there is a repetitive phrase that crops up over and over again. It goes along these lines: "Him that hath an ear let him hear..." I've always taken it to mean that a reasonable person listens to sound counsel.

## Chaos In Your Business

A recent occurrence in the business of my daughter and son-in-law reminded me of something those of us who've been in business for decades can easily forget. A business can be a really chaotic and unpredictable thing. With degrees in business, it's easy to overlook that in the real world, day-to-day business doesn't unfold like it did in all those grad and post-grad business classes. Those textbooks, supplemental readings, and cases studies tend to be nice and neat and tidy up rather easily. The graphs and charts depicting business operations are built on the finest mathematical algorithms and three hundred years of business history. The problem here is that the real world hasn't seen the graphs or charts and isn't mathematically bent toward predictive algorithms.

The real world of business is more of a full-contact sport akin to football, where you're hit from the right, you're hit from the left, and before you can recover, you're hit from the front and the rear simultaneously. One day there are no customers, the next day there are too many customers. One day the phone doesn't ring at all and the next day the phone rings so much you want to take it off the hook. Sometimes you have too many people on your payroll and you wonder how you're going to make ends meet and who to lay off. At another time you can't find enough qualified workers and you fear going under due to your inability to meet customer needs. The idea that businesses move in any sort of a straight line is true in only the most limited number of cases.

In almost any business you own or manage, the element of chaos will be one of the toughest aspects to deal with. Some personalities thrive on chaos and are energized by it, while others implode from the constant shifting of the landscape ahead. For the vast majority of people whose abilities reside somewhere between the thriving and imploding poles, I'd suggest that in time you can find a livable medium if you don't have a nervous breakdown first. It truly helps if you have a spouse, partner, or strong right hand that has the ability to balance you out in these matters and keep you from jumping off the cliff in a bad moment. It also helps if you have a spouse, partner, or strong line of credit that can help financially with the inevitable aspects of financial instability this chaos produces.

Keep dancing is old advice I've heard given to children and adults who are part of performing dance ensembles. I take this to mean that even if you stumble or fall, as long as you keep dancing, the audience will barely notice it, or they won't care if they do notice it as long as the performance goes on. What your business audience will care about is if you stumble or fall, become exasperated, throw a hissy fit, lose all reason, and lie down on the floor of your business and go catatonic. People expect businesses to have operational hiccups from time to time. Learning how to handle those hiccups and to handle them gracefully in front of an invested audience will determine if you remain in business for years or if you implode at the first real trial.

The companies I've dealt with who handle all these matters best, whether mom-and-pops or publicly-traded giants, have given thought to what they might do in the event of a whole series of catastrophes or misadventures, and they've developed contingency plans for how they will respond. A company I worked for more than thirty years ago sent me to training for making public statements on behalf of the company in times of crisis; they did this with all managers. In addition, they'd devoted a lot of space in their management training documents and program as to how managers were to respond to certain situations that could arise unexpectedly at any time. Now even if you're not a big operator, you would do well to think about a whole host of what-ifs that might come your way. Jot down some ideas as to how you or your employees should handle them before you're actually fighting that fire.

Here are a few ideas to seed some thoughts for your own business.

1. What will I do if employees call in sick?
2. What will I do in the event of a power failure, phone failure, water failure, etc.?
3. How will we handle customer complaints?
4. What's our policy on employee appearance and dress?
5. Who speaks to the media in the event of some crisis or occurrence which impacts the business?
6. How would we handle an armed robbery?
7. What do we do if an employee appears impaired by drugs or alcohol?
8. What do we do in the event of a fire, tornado, earthquake, or other disaster?
9. How would we handle a bomb scare?

10. How do we handle an incident of workplace violence?
11. What if customer demand exceeds our abilities? How do we keep them happy?
12. How will information inquiries be handled and by whom?
13. Do we offer discounts to any person or group?
14. Do we donate to charities?
15. What's our policy on employee background checks?

I hope that these fifteen sentences get you thinking about your specific business. Whether you already own a business or if you're just trying to go through the mechanics of starting a business, it's never too early to begin to think about the legal and safest way to deal with the kinds of chaos your business is likely to encounter. Truthfully, each line of business has its own unique problems that are likely to come up again and again. The sooner you recognize them and create polices and contingencies for how you're going to get through them, the sooner your nerves will settle down, and the sooner you can focus your attention back on other aspects of the business that create revenue. Growing pains can be managed, as can every other bit of chaos you'll encounter, but it's easier if you expect them to occur and have a plan to deal with them.

## Predicting The Future

An ancient wise man is credited with saying, "There is nothing new under the sun." The older I get, the more accurate those words of wisdom seem to be.

Part of our task in business is predicting the future for ourselves, our customers, and our employees. You can't accomplish that by watching the six o'clock news or reading the latest tripe from a political pundit (pick your party) with an axe to grind, a career to hype, or a new book to sell.

It comes from research in boring areas like history, business, geography, economics, meteorology, new inventions, old inventions, and political science. With those as a basis for comparison, all you have to do then is lay those templates down over current events, and an outline soon emerges.

There's no magic to it, but it does take more than thirty minutes a day to stay current, so ignore the promises your local media claims such as, "If you'll give us thirty minutes a day, we'll bring you up to date." If you want to have an inkling of the future, take some time to look at similar periods and situations from the past.

## Data Mining

Data Mining has been going on in business for countless years, accelerating dramatically in the computer age. It's sped up in order for any of us to have a glimmer of hope of keeping up with the deluge of data we receive daily. Companies hire people whose only task is to work back through tons and tons of data to see if a "golden nugget" of valuable information got missed along the way. Think of it as modern-day gold miners working through old tailing piles.

The explosion of information sources has inundated all of us with more data than we can easily process, so the information ball gets dropped more often than ever before. This means it's more important than ever that we develop our critical abilities to spot valuable information quickly and discard all the garbage that comes across our path just as quickly as we can. How much of your day and mental power is stolen by inane blather in social media, broadcast news, or ethereal tweets from the celebrity de jour?

When information crosses your path (e.g., desk, PC, television, radio, smartphone, mail, etc.) you have to work to develop the ability to scan it quickly, triage it's degree of importance to you, then act upon that triage accordingly. Otherwise you'll have one hundred unread trade magazines, eight hundred dangling emails, snail mail awaiting replies, and a backlog of smartphone data that grows by the minute. Mental garbage is something you can no longer afford if you want to win at business.

We all have email that doesn't need to be opened, magazines that don't need to be read, phone calls we shouldn't answer, tweets we shouldn't look at, and snail mail that should be recycled unopened. If we develop the habit of taking these simple steps, we'll find we have more time in our day to devote to information that is relevant to our lives and our jobs. It seems to me it also leaves less clutter in my mind so that when I do finally see one of those gold nuggets in the data stream, I can actually recognize it.

## You Never Own The Same Business Two Days In A Row

In today's constantly connected world, you never own the same business or work at the same job two days in a row. Our world is in constant change, so even while we sleep, somebody in another part of the world is trying to build a better mousetrap or work more efficiently than they did yesterday. This constant change forces people and businesses everywhere to step up both their levels of creativity and productivity. The days when we took our businesses and the jobs they created for granted have passed. Accept the fact that you'll likely never know the kind of stability previous generations of business owners did.

When I left high school in 1972, many of my peers went to work in jobs where they remained until they began to retire in 2012. The industries (e.g., agriculture, trucking, mining, chemicals, oil and gas, manufacturing, etc.) they were in were stable and remained relatively stable for forty years. That world still exists, but to a much lesser degree; even those bedrock industries are now forced to rapidly innovate, downsize, and compete with the entire world. I still have dealings in all those business sectors. I can assure you they've learned that as they slept last night, the business environment they will function in this morning, changed from the one they fell asleep to last night.

## Mercantile Fatalities

The following appeared in my second book, *In Your Times: A Twentieth Century Grandfather Writes To His Twenty-first Century Grandchildren.* It was intended to offer some guidance for their lives, both now and after I'm gone. It offered advice in many areas, but because so much of my life has been spent owning or managing businesses, business was a major theme throughout the work. I decided to edit the work down from 240,000 words written specifically for my grandkids to a more succinct and less personal 80,000 words for general consumption. This was after I was given encouragement from friends who saw the manuscript and wanted copies for their own kids and grandkids. I hope you'll take a couple of minutes to read the following passage and contemplate what I've said there.

*Online shopping is here to stay and by the time you are grown I can only imagine how it will have innovated even more! That statement shouldn't surprise anyone among you since you haven't been marooned on a distant planet. Most Americans, just like me, have shopped online. I began my online shopping in earnest more than a decade back and then it was focused mainly on books for grad school. I could buy a volume online for $80 that was going to cost me a $120 at the school's bookstore. I wasn't a math major, but I figured the math on that one out pretty quickly. When you toss in the convenience, time savings, gasoline savings, and reduced wear and tear on your nerves from dealing with parking and other shoppers, you can quickly see why the popularity of online* *shopping is growing by leaps and bounds and will continue to do so for the foreseeable future.*

*Major retailers that don't want to simply become local showrooms where people go to window shop and then head home to buy online have had to retrench their businesses in order to survive. It's difficult if not impossible to name a major retailer (and a bunch of minor retailers) who doesn't have an online presence. From Sears to Walmart to Target, and even Sam's Club, they can all be accessed online 24 hours a day, 365 days a year. This is reshaping the way America shops as well as most other nations around the world. One of the features that I and apparently millions of others love is that I can shop many stores in a matter of minutes and can often find products and/or services for sale at deeply discounted rates. This ability to rapidly compare pricing and the resultant price competition will only accelerate in your times.*

*Now this raises the issue of "…online shopping is killing local businesses." I think that there is a high degree of truth in that statement. Just as there was/is a high degree of truth in the statement "big-box stores are killing local businesses." This begs the question for me as a businessman and a capitalist: Why exactly is it that people shouldn't be able to buy the goods and services they need from the cheapest provider? I've been a small businessperson for decades and experienced that phenomenon more than once. I didn't like it, but I value the way our system makes competing interests wrestle one another to be the more efficient, and therefore favoring the more cost-effective provider. The benefit is to your pocketbook as a consumer, yet you remain free to shop where you will and support who you will.*

*I encourage you to engage in online sales and online shopping as it benefits you. I also encourage you to support all those "moms and pops" out there that continue to provide value to you with the goods and services they offer. The tough economic times we're in right now force each of us to look for new ways to make economies in our own budgets, whether we are businesses, families, or individuals. Tough economic times have been a hurdle in each generation and will be in your times as well. There will be mercantile fatalities along the way as businesses that can no longer compete are overtaken by new business concepts. This has been the case throughout history and throughout the history of a concept called mercantilism. The Internet has simply provided its latest iteration. No doubt your future will hold other iterations just as tumultuous to the future marketplace.*

*Study them, embrace them where they benefit you, and make sure that if you go into business yourself, you learn to ride on the tiger, not inside the tiger.*

## Reality Check

In the study of business at a graduate and post-grad level, you spend a good deal of time learning about business practices in other countries. Despite the Foreign Corrupt Practices Act (FCPA), I can tell you that what Americans term bribery is just regarded as good business in most places in the world.

I saw a well-funded and solid business effort completely fail in China over a personal friend's unwillingness to pay a "courtesy fee" of less than $20 to a low-level local official. In another instance, a charity group I knew of had a cargo container full of shoes confiscated in East Africa over a similar amount. The chief of police is said to have then sold the shoes.

The very first time I left this country on business was in 1981. We were negotiating an oil-trading deal in a "second world" country. I learned on that trip that companies in other nations do whatever it takes to close a big deal, and competitors will do whatever it takes to derail a big deal. Threats, bribes, blackmail, and even death come into play. I'm not suggesting you break the law, but maybe you should just stay home.

Am I shocked by the recent allegations of bribery against Walmart® in Mexico? Not in the least. Will I now stop shopping at Walmart? No, I'm headed to Walmart as soon as I finish typing this passage. If you really care, you might want to look at Walmart's two biggest competitors in Mexico (Sanborn and Sears Mexico) and see how they figure in the bribery story.

If we really want to fix this problem, we need to demand that members of Congress have real-world business experience, and at least some of it needs to be in the blood-and-knuckles world of international business. Congressional junkets NEVER take these boys and girls to where the actual sausage is being made. Instead, they enjoy their taxpayer-funded vacation and come home to praise the business paradise they just left.

## Location, Location, Location

Some businesses really can be operated effectively from your home; some can't. If you're planning to start a business that can't be operated from home, you're going to hear the old axiom, "location, location, location," many times from people who either are already in business or already went broke because they didn't heed the axiom. The idea arises from the old question, "What are the three most important things to consider when starting a new business?" You may chuckle at that now, but after you're in business, or go out of business, you'll know how true those words are.

When I was young and had limited business experience, I reasoned that if I had a great idea and a good product, people would beat a path to my door, regardless of where the door was. Wrong! Unfortunately, many of you considering business for the first time are as ignorant of how things actually work as I was. People are creatures of habit and crave convenience. If you're trying to get them to make a habit of coming to buy your better mousetrap, you better make the location convenient. By convenient I mean an area that people pass by often, is highly visible, has good lighting, and has plenty of easily accessible parking.

I've yet to own a business selling products or personal services to the public (versus selling business services to the public) where location didn't start as a major factor or become a major factor over time. Location is more than just geography. It includes things like visibility from the passing traffic, how easy it is (or isn't) to find parking, and how safe is the location from criminals. All of these reasons and a dozen others factor into the location you must select for your business. Just as important is the fact that a location can get better or worse with the passing of time due to changes in the neighborhood. I urge you to carefully consider these issues and take them into account before you begin to sign that five-year lease and pay that first rent check.

People will not travel five miles out of their way to get to you unless you have a product so unique that it can't be bought anywhere else nearer their locale. People will not fight for twenty minutes to find parking unless you have a product so unique that it's exclusive to your business. People will not shop in a location where they feel that their personal safety is at risk. This holds true even if you have a product so unique that it can't be bought anywhere else. Finally, people will not seek you out just to help a young business. Business is a rough-and-tumble world, and the uninformed, financially weak, and marketing deficient will not survive. By reading this essay and picking a good location, your odds of survival just went up dramatically.

## In Life, Not Everyone's A Winner

I was contemplating a game we played in the grammar school classroom on a rainy day back in 1962. The substitute teacher, who was with us many days that year, was a kindly, elderly, retired teacher and she was one of the best teachers I ever encountered. So you're thinking, "There's not much to report there." Hold on, here's where the screw turns. This game involved her performing a task that required rhythmically tapping a stick on the floor while reciting, "...little is the man who can't do this." The students were each asked to do exactly what she had done, and the point of the game was to see how closely we were watching the teacher so we could mimic her behavior. Each time a student failed, she would repeat the instruction. Time after time, students failed and went back to their desks. Eventually, some of the students caught on. In the course of using up all the recesses for the day, everybody finally managed to figure it out. The trick was that each time she started the mantra, she pretended to clear her throat just before she began to speak. Kids focused on the words, the tapping, the posture, and just about every other nuance of the teacher while trying to get the point of the game. Eventually everybody figured out how critical the throat-clearing was to satisfying the game criteria.

In the course of the day, kids got upset, whined, became petulant, sulked, and manifested all the emotions that go along with "losing." You have to recall that in 1962, we still accepted the fact that in life there would be winners and losers, and this teacher was willing to take all day for that scenario to play out. Eventually, every classmate was a winner, but for some of the less observant classmates, it took all day. When some classmate burst into tears at their failure, the teacher never stopped and said, "Oh, never mind, I'll tell you what the answer is." She ignored their unhappiness at failure, and the game went on. I contrast this with some of what I've seen over the years with my own children, and now my grandchildren, where we seem to do everything we can to assure that a child never experiences a profound sense of failure. I recognize that a constant diet of failure is deadly. Yet I suspect that a constant diet of always being a winner may be just as deadly, it just takes longer. We do both the child and the society a disservice by creating a make-believe world where everybody is a winner every time. Loss can be one of the most powerful and important teachers in life.

Or, we could pretend that every response is a winning response and every performance is a stellar performance and eventually come to a point where we live in a narcissistic age of teens and young adults who've never been allowed to fail. They would be alternately crushed or furious when they begin to encounter it in a world where not everybody gets to be honored as "student of the week." Having never previously been allowed to fail, they would blame their parents, their schools, their curriculum, the employer, the church, the state, their fellows, and their god. Many would go on to feel angry because they were being denied their "right to win," which they heard of from their parents, their teachers, their ministers, their politicians, their fellows, and their god. When it's written down in stark contrast like that, it almost seems as if we've reached that place in many first world countries today. Meanwhile, those people and businesses in nations where there are still winners and losers learn to overcome failure and fight on. Is it any wonder that in adulthood they are consuming those little children who were always allowed to win, when they meet in business or on the playing fields of life?

## Black Swan I

There was a time in Europe when an exceedingly rare event was likened to the probability of seeing a black swan. You see, in those days in Europe, there were white swans and black sheep, but there were no black swans. It wasn't until British exploration found itself in Australia and New Zealand that suddenly reports of multitudes of black swans were being talked about incessantly. It was not that black swans did not exist, it was just that the concept was so far outside the thinking of everyday life that no one had stopped to consider that there could not only be black swans, there could be thousands of black swans. So, even today, an exceedingly rare or unexpected event may be referred to as a black swan. In recent years, there's been an effort to address the black swan because past failure to do so has been deadly.

A really smart fellow named Nassim Nicholas Taleb has written a book entitled *The Black Swan: The Impact of the Highly Improbable*. It's caused something of a stir in many circles, but especially in government, business, and finance. I want to spend some time sharing about this concept and why it is that we are often betrayed by linear thinking when the appearance of a black swan in a given field can turn the linear-thinking world upside down. We've all seen these black swans, we all know the effects of black swans, and we've all experienced the black swan's ability to destroy the world as we knew it yesterday. My reason for striking this vein is to help you be open to the coming of black swans and to be agile enough to live with them rather than be destroyed by them.

## Black Swan II

Nassim Nicholas Taleb's Black Swan Theory posits the following regarding a Black Swan Event: 1) it is a surprise to the observer(s); 2) the event has a major effect on the specific field it occurs within or it may affect the entire world; and 3) the event is said to be recognizable in hindsight. That is to say that with the benefit of hindsight, one feels they can rationalize what has just occurred. Taleb says he developed the theory to help him explain: "1) the disproportionate role of high-profile, hard-to-predict, and rare events that are beyond the realm of normal expectations in history, science, finance, and technology; 2) the non-computability of the probability of the consequential rare events using scientific methods (owing to the very nature of small probabilities); 3) the psychological biases that make people individually and collectively blind to uncertainty and unaware of the massive role of the rare event in historical affairs."

While studying macro finance, I came across this idea initially in Taleb's work, *Fooled by Randomness*. Over a period of several years he refined the idea, and his most recent book, *The Black Swan*, develops the metaphor more completely. What so captured my attention was his assertion that while Black Swan Events would be regarded as extreme outliers, they're nonetheless extremely influential in their impact on all of us. In fact, I'd say they are disproportionately influential in their impact on human history and all of its various facets. They would include things like major scientific discoveries, historical events, and unique artistic achievements. My own fascination with these powerful random events in history is how often they have entered an otherwise static world and literally turned it on its ear. Events like discoveries of the laws of physics, the precipitating events of World War I, and the ability of artists to create the appearance of three-dimensional drawings all register as Black Swan Events.

I'd like for you to think about your own life and times and consider how many Black Swan Events you've lived through. At first this will seem a very difficult task to undertake. But then when I mention things like the development of the atomic bomb, the birth of rock 'n roll, and the advent of the personal computer, you'll start to see what I mean. The fact is, your and my lives have been full of these events, and there are more such events ahead; many more. With this in mind, we have to decide if we plan to live and order our lives as though every day from here on out will be the same as every day that came before it, or if we realize that at any given moment, a new dynamic in the form of new ideas, new inventions, or new technologies can burst upon the scene and transform our world, for better or worse. Taleb's work initially caught the attention of people like me in business and finance. Suddenly, every other field is watching too.

## Black Swan III

Let me jump in here and point out the critical nature of this information. Throughout human history, we have fooled ourselves into thinking that we are able to predict future outcomes based on our current knowledge. This happens in business, finance, science, medicine, politics, stocks, bonds, and religion regularly. Beyond those fields, it happens in our everyday lives with far too much regularity. The technical terminology would use phrasing such as "low probability events," and most people's eyes would glaze over and they'd stop caring or reading right there. Yet the reason I find this area both fascinating and important is how often these low probability events actually happen, and when they do, the tremendous chaos they create.

Admittedly, not all chaos is a bad thing. Chaos introduces change to a system that may in fact be quite positive. But when the chaos introduced is unexpected and adverse to one's circumstances, the importance of Black Swan Events begins to come into focus. Let's use the stock market for example. You and I get bombarded with people wanting us to purchase stocks all the time. They paint a picture of a rosy path lined with profits and opportunity for even more profits along the way. Then, seemingly out of the blue, some happenstance will occur that derails the stock we've invested in and our position is diminished or wiped out entirely. Let's say you bought a stock based on a precious metal, and within months, a new and almost limitless supply of this metal becomes available to the world. This Black Swan Event has just had a major impact on your life.

Now remember, you went into the metal deal assured that your precious metal purchase was incredibly safe and stable and had been for the entire history of mankind. Then suddenly a new massive source crops up, seemingly from out of nowhere. This black swan may have just flown away with your life savings. The Black Swan Event is no longer a mere philosophical matter.

The event has now altered your world from that point forward. In my lifetime we've seen this happen to things as diverse as typewriters, Linotype machines, ironing boards, butter, giant steel mills, and farming. All of these were established products or fields that were blindsided by a low probability event that either diminished their importance or wiped them out entirely. I hope at this point you're beginning to see that this field of understanding isn't just academic. These Black Swan Events have impact on every one of our lives.

I'm concerned with Black Swan Events in our mundane everyday lives. But I'm much more interested in how they relate to matters that affect the entire world. If you're a student of history, you already know that seemingly improbable (low probability) events have changed the course of history repeatedly. Ask yourself how the assassination of an obscure duke in Europe somehow led to the outset of World War I? If you are a student of science, ask yourself how some mathematical conjecture by an obscure patent clerk led to the atomic bomb, the cold war, and the world we live in today. If you are a student of religion, ask yourself how the appearances of Buddha, Jesus, and Mohamed have changed and continue to change the course of history. Ponder these and consider what Black Swan Events could benefit or destroy your existence.

## Black Swan IV

If we can accept the fact that Black Swan Events do occur and that they seem to occur with an uncanny frequency, we must also accept some uncomfortable truths. The fact that Black Swan Events seem to almost creep up on us and then jump out from behind a moment in history to reveal themselves should bring us to the realization that we're not nearly as clever or as good at predicting critical events as we like to convince ourselves that we are. I remember how intelligent I felt when I realized that I had mastered quantitative analysis. I came away from those years of study with the sense that if I was just given the correct numbers, I could be almost prescient about how an organization was going to fair in the coming months and even years ahead. This is a dangerous form of arrogance that education in general and math education in particular tends to foster. Black Swan Events seem to exist to slap the arrogant smile from the faces of the *cognoscenti* who buy into such foolishness.

Taking this a step further along the road of uncomfortable truths, can we really take the word of bankers, realtors, economists, scientists, politicians, or lawyers as definitive in any matter, when so many times in the past, Black Swan Events have made them all look foolish? If bankers, realtors, and economists were so prescient and quantitative analysis so foolproof, explain the Great Depression, routinely unforeseen economic downturns, and the Great Recession to me. If scientists employing the magic of their knowledge were such sages and assured us they could see the future, explain their bewilderment at stoichiometry, black holes, Higgs boson, powered flight, the personal computer, stopping and restarting a human heart, superconductivity, and relativity, to name a few. If politicians and lawyers were as on top of our world as they pretend to be, explain to me the legal quagmire and the economic/monetary mess that every country on the planet now finds itself in.

The Black Swan Event, each time it is encountered, should first and foremost act as a wakeup call for mankind. It should remind us that events we cannot easily foresee or quantify are coming down the road of history and, at their given moment, will reveal themselves to our collective dismay. Yes, afterwards, with the benefit of hindsight, doublespeak, and obfuscation, the aforementioned cognoscenti will assure you that they now see the separate links that went into the Black Swan vent. In doing this, they hope that by convincing you they understand it, you will also begin to think that they foresaw it. In truth, they cannot admit that they were unable to capture lightening in a bottle, and when it crashed about, they were just as surprised as everyone else was. Most frightening for all of us should be the realization that they won't foresee the next one either.

## Black Swan V

I'd guess that by now you've heard as much about Black Swan Events as you'd ever want to. If you have read all five of these passages and still don't grasp Black Swan theory, I'll take the blame for that. Those of us in business, finance, philosophy, mathematics, or history are either aware of the theme and are concerned or have already become frustrated trying to get our heads around the concept. I find myself in the concerned category, simply because of the hubris of the leaders in their fields I've met who feel like they have all the facts at hand, and that they need to make the critical decisions for all the rest of us. We are not the Masters of the Universe, despite how much we work to convince ourselves that we are.

In some circles, this black swan theory has truly caused people to stop and begin to consider how often there might well be circumstances where the information available leaves too much to pure chance and beyond the reach of our ability to analyze. In other circles, it has prompted discussion about the fragility or robustness of existing business models and whether or not, at times, there are unacceptable levels of risk at play that we may not even be equipped to contemplate. And in political circles, where there really should be pause for contemplation and discussion, our elected brain trusts listen politely to expert testimony from Taleb and others similarly concerned, and then go back to the status quo.

My interest in this area of low probability events comes from studying history these past couple of years in an attempt to see if I could understand what kinds of events trigger economic decline and total financial collapse, or what kinds of trigger events signal the end of a nation. What's been most unsettling for me is how "unpredicted" the events that have brought nations to their knees have been; the sages seem to be batting zero. When I looked at our historic economic markets, we always seem to have seen the end coming, but no one has been able to recognize the trigger until well after it has been pulled. I had hoped to be able to see through all that haze and offer some insight. Instead, what I found time after time were black swans.

Black Swan Theory and future Black Swan Events should come as a wakeup call to all of humanity. When I was a boy, I always had this sense of well-being based on all the "really smart" people out there who were making the world go 'round. I was sure that the finest minds in science, finance, history, politics, and religion were in control of everything, or at least had such a superior understanding of everything that a child like me needn't worry. Then I grew to be a man and slowly understood that even the finest minds only understand a fraction of the knowledge within their own chosen fields. My conclusion: it might be time for the rest of us to take all the wise men around us less seriously and begin to ask some questions about the future for ourselves.

## It Doesn't Hurt To Listen To Failed Business Owners

The benefit of a bad business experience can be obtained either by living through that experience oneself or by being humble enough to actually listen to people who have had such an experience and then learning from their failures. These are rare opportunities, and not everyone is willing to admit, much less share, the fact that they've failed at a business effort.

The latter course of really listening is easier than the former course of being unwilling to receive what's being shared. For some reason, many of us seem to keep being held back a year in the school of hard knocks because we insist on taking the position of "I have to try it for myself." If you can vicariously learn from others' mistakes, it's dollars in your pocket and days added to your life.

## Cheap Business Locations

Here's another piece to consider on location, location, location.

Upon learning what I do, people at social gatherings often tell me they want to go into business and then they begin to ask my advice. I advise them not to go into business because business at any level is fraught with high levels of financial risk. But for those who ignore that first advice and insist they want to push ahead, if they're going into a business where foot traffic is at the core of success, they shouldn't next tell me they're going to rent a place because the rent is cheap, it's near their house, or their kids' schools are nearby.

In businesses dependent on foot traffic, as I said a few paragraphs earlier, it's location, location, location. Whether the economy is up or down or sideways, that old axiom rings true. Prime locations cost more because they're prime locations. This is a case where the cheapest location is cheap for a good reason; almost no one wants to be there, including your potential customers. If you don't have the financial resources to site at a location that's ideal for your business, why not wait until you can secure the needed monies?

## It's Always A Challenging Time To Become An Employer

Business owners routinely report that despite the fact they want to hire people, they're regularly met with applicants who they consider of questionable appearance. They note that these same potential employees almost immediately begin to ask about modifying the job description to fit the applicant's lifestyle, beliefs, or values. Imagine a workplace where no two employees live by the same rules or expectations. We know this would be a problem. But is there some flexibility in your employment scheme that would allow you and those potential employees to benefit one another?

The business environment, or more aptly as I call it often call it, the business landscape, is seeing a groundswell of change around these and associated issues. You have no choice but to begin to become informed of the mindset of the generation(s) you will employee, and then to figure out how to best utilize their talents in your workplace. Now I don't mean they're handicapped, are devoutly religious, or need some kind of reasonable accommodation. I mean if the hours are 8 a.m. to 5 p.m., they want to work 6 a.m. to 3 p.m. If the days are Tuesday through Saturday, they want to work Monday through Friday. And if the dress is business attire, they want extreme casual. They'll have different clothes, different hair, different modes of dress, multiple tattoos, and piercings. The challenge is to find, and work with, the diamonds among them.

We seem to have raised a generation or two where the parents stressed their child's right to self-expression and self-determination, but forgot to explain that when you become the employee of someone else, limits will be placed on both how you express yourself and what you can and can't do at work. This is touchy territory and one you'd best tread in lightly in the current litigious atmosphere. Know your rights as an employer, but know their rights as employees just as well. The fact that there are laws seems at times to be a real shock to Junior or Sally. Frequently, the only reason Junior or Sally doesn't get fired for violating rules or laws is because firing would be traumatic, and there's always the potential for lawsuits or hearings before the labor commissioner. Instead, the first time business gets slow, they're laid off and never called back! But what if Junior or Sally have real ability? You now face the delicate issue of how do I create a great employee out of one or more of these folks?

Of course, unless parents or grandparents planned to directly hire Junior or Sally, buy them their own business, or fund a startup, they could have done us all a huge favor and helped them avoid years of anger and confusion. How? They could explain to them the working appearances and lifestyles they see on reality television rarely exist in reality. They could teach them about the compromises we all make to work and survive in a complex society. I'm dreaming here, aren't I? As an employer, you are going to have to stop dreaming and figure out how Junior and Sally fit into your business, because they are part of the business landscape you are faced with today. You've got to have employees in most businesses. If you want to own a business where this is the case, how will you deal with the current crop of prospects? I've said elsewhere in this book that getting the people part of business correct is the most difficult task you'll face. Consider that point reiterated here.

Many of my clients are now in their 40s, 50s, 60s, and even their 70s. They come from generations with an entirely different set of workplace appearances and behaviors than the people who approach them for employment. I like to offer the insight that some hills are big enough to die for, and other hills aren't. Figure out what you can live with as the boss. If it's a health and safety matter then it's sacrosanct. But if it's just a generational preference, you might be able to find some way to compromise. Yes, we all know the robots are coming and I know folks who drool at the prospect of never having human employees again. But this mindset assumes that their business can utilize robots, they could afford robots, and that if the whole workforce were made up of robots, those same robots would become valued customers who would buy their product or service? Give some thought now about what you'll do with and for employees who are different than yourself. This issue is not going away.

## Natural Disaster Preparedness At Your Business

As you're working your way through your list of startup ideas or your list of policies or procedures you want to implement in your existing business, give some thought to natural disaster preparedness. I know it's anxiety producing to even have to think about such matters, but in business they're part of the landscape we chose to enter.

We're seeing more and more advice from government agencies about being able to survive for fourteen days or more in the event of a natural disaster. Do you have a plan in place for your employees in the event that a natural disaster should strand them at the workplace for even one, two, or three days?

I know the tendency is to think everybody would just go home, but even here in sunny California, I've lived through a dust storm so severe that it left people stranded miles from their homes for up to four days due to road closures. Are you able to provide your employees with even drinking water for four days if something similar happens?

Allow me to remind you that you have legal duties to your employees and even other legal duties to your customers who may be in your place of business when a natural disaster strikes. Minor efforts at planning for such an eventuality right now will pay big dividends later.

Simply knowing what you have on hand and how it could be utilized is a great starting point. The United States government has disaster preparedness information that's available through a simple web search. Why not make the decision right now to do the right thing by your customers, your employees, and yourself by planning ahead.

## Change Or Die

The skills I've developed over a lifetime are rapidly becoming obsolete. I don't think about this often, but sometimes the reality hits me in the face when I attend a trade show or other industry-oriented affair and see all the new ideas and technologies flooding in. More recently it's confronted me in the field when I've been asked to look at some new project that's being undertaken by a client. To digress for a minute, I spent the first half of my career in various crafts. To that end I spent periods of my life as a mechanic, machinist, welder, and electrician. I went from there to being a building contractor (i.e., remodeling and building homes), and later still a general engineering contractor (i.e., installing or building process equipment, refineries, oilfields, and chemical plants). Today, while I still recognize all of what's going on in each of those areas, the ideas, tools, and skill sets required in each has changed dramatically over the past forty years.

I understood in my thirties that even if my skill set stayed tip-top, if I didn't obtain a different way to live out my life and earn a living, my body would eventually be unable to keep pace. To that end I promised myself that if I ever had the chance I'd return to college and prepare for a more cerebral means of earning a living. When we're young, the physical rigors of making a blue-collar life, a no-collar life, or a pink-collar life don't seem all that daunting. But as we age, our bodies begin to teach us a new truth; to be able to compete we must continuously learn, adapt, and remain physically fit enough to keep up with younger and younger workers. While there's a great deal to be said positively for the knowledge and maturity of an older worker, there are corresponding positives to be noted in the raw physicality of the young. It's with those two perspectives in mind that we work to balance our own lives and those of the workforces we deal with as business owners and managers.

In recognition of the limitations of both the young and the old, technology has been developed that is able to overcome the inexperience of the young and the loss of youthful vigor of the old. It comes to us in the form of computers, computerized technology, and thinking machines our society long ago dubbed "robots." However, the purpose of this passage isn't going to go full-blown robotics. I'm more interested here in the changing skill sets and changing tools required in our society's quest to be faster, cheaper, and better than what came before. With each change there are corresponding changes required in what workers know and what ability they have to use the latest tools in their craft. At this point when I mention tools, don't just think screwdrivers and crescent wrenches. Here we should think of all technologies as tools. This certainly includes the hand tools common to craftsmen everywhere. But it also includes computers of all shapes, sizes, and designs and the equipment they're integrated into.

At age nineteen I began to learn pipefitting. By twenty-four I was highly proficient in it and could build and repair just about anything made out of pipe through cutting, threading, fitting, welding, or the use of chemical adhesives or heat for joining. All of these still exist, and yet the technologies have advanced to the degree that people working in these areas return to training classes regularly now to learn the properties of the new materials, how to design using the new materials, and new techniques in cutting and joinery. The same thing can be said for electricians, mechanics, machinists, carpenters, and so forth. Now you may be reading this and saying to yourself, "I don't have to worry about this because I'm not involved in any of the skilled trades, and it will never be an issue for me." Unfortunately that's a myopic view. I also visit factories, professional offices, refineries, chemical plants, mine sites, bowling alleys, restaurants, and cemeteries, and every single one of them is being affected by new ideas, new rules, new tools, and even a new mindset of the current generation of workers.

Whether you own a food truck or plan to build composite components for spaceships, as a business owner or manager, you're affected by all this, and you'll have to behave accordingly. The sooner you begin to consider this continuously emerging reality and plan for it, the better off you, your business, and the people who work for you or do business with you will be. You need to be asking yourself questions about where your industry is headed; what technologies are available or emerging that will make your business more viable; and how you can intersect all these concepts in a way that makes you more competitive, desirable to work for, and more profitable than others around you. Remember that the overall theme of this book is "Out Of Brains." These technologies give you the ability to leverage the brains and relationships you have on hand to your best advantage, but only if you can embrace and manage them well.

I want to end this passage by denoting the common phenomenon of coasting. My children used to say that I reinvented myself about every seven years. This came about because they saw me grow tired/bored with professions I was involved in. At about year five, I'd begin to look for something that challenged me. In the last two years, I'd mastered the skill set required and no longer had to work so hard to stay on top of the game. In essence, I was coasting. The momentum I'd built in the previous years was strong enough to carry me forward to new challenges. As the years have passed, I've experienced this with businesses I've owned or managed and, more recently, I saw the pace accelerating as I passed age sixty. I remain busy in the businesses my wife and I own and I continue to write daily, but I no longer get up at four a.m. to get to the field or the office before anyone else. I know my years are numbered, just as yours are. So unless you're ready to get out of business or retire, you can't afford to coast. For at least a while longer yet, you must change or die.

## Caution: Innovations Can Be Good Or Bad

Innovation is the key to the longevity of a business. There's a constant challenge to remain relevant to the times in which a business lives. It's always been this way, and I'm confident that it will remain so in the future. As a business-driven society, we find the need to innovate in design, manufacturing processes, sales methods, and employee training on a routine basis. Consequently, when I encounter a business that takes great pride in telling me nothing has changed at their firm in the last fifteen years, I hope they're making high-end single-malt Scotch whiskey and not cell phones. While innovation is best built on a solid foundation, it eschews being cast in stone.

You're going to continue to see the pace of change accelerate throughout your business life. Get used to it, or get out. I don't envy the next generation this pace of change because it seems to carry with it a sense of everything being more and more transitory and less and less stable. I think this mindset drifts over into other areas of our lives such as marriage, family, society, and religion. Some things can and should innovate and change, but there are other foundational pillars that humans have held on to for millennia; we discard them at our own peril.

Be cautious in your business and strive to identify and differentiate between innovations which are transitory and those which have long-term ability to sustain your business. Not every innovation which comes down the pike will be of use to your particular enterprise; don't needlessly contort your business to try benefit from an innovation. Resist the urge to do something purely because "everybody else is doing it." Innovation should only be embraced if it works for you; not every innovation is for every business.

Strive to be nimble enough in your business that you can make use of an innovation at the right time and to get out before the peak of opportunity has passed. This requires more than just your willingness to jump on board. It requires that your business is positioned to benefit from the innovative idea and not that the innovative undertaking will overwhelm your people, location, or financial resources. A great business innovation in the wrong hands may actually destroy the possessor. Learning when to move from innovation to innovation will be as much art as science.

## Business Doesn't Always Require A Public Showcase

Home-based businesses continue to pop up and flourish in this economy. In some cases, clients have come back to their home-based offices and sales sites after realizing they were wasting valuable financial resources on the office downtown in order to look like a business. Do you want to impress people or make money?

Sometimes image can be everything in an image-conscious line of business. But this is not always the case and needs to be carefully considered. I warn new business owners and managers constantly about how renting office or showroom space you don't need can eat up thousands of dollars a month in unnecessary rent, insurance, and utility costs alone.

Technology makes it increasingly easy and cheap to work in virtual settings from anywhere in the world at any time of the day or night. As I'm writing this passage, it's 11:32 p.m., and I'm home in my sweat pants. The key is to actually be in a successful business, not just look like you're in a successful business. Your goals must be to get into business, stay in business, and do so profitably. If you don't need a showcase for your business, why have one?

## Market Bubbles Are A Two-Edged Sword

One of the trickiest business situations to enter into is the launch of a business in a market bubble. Now, not everyone who reads this is an old business hand; some are entirely new to business or just thinking about going into business. I'm going to borrow a definition from Investopedia® and then expand on it a bit to add some specific clarity: "A bubble is an economic cycle characterized by rapid expansion followed by a contraction." A market bubble is a situation where a certain type of business is suddenly hot. The trailing reality is the contraction Investopedia speaks of, wherein there is usually just as rapid of a drop. Companies and individuals often become wealthy during the expansion phase. But if they don't get out before the rapid market contraction, they may lose everything they made and then some.

Market bubbles have been around since the beginning of commerce. I expect they'll be around for as long as humans do business with other humans. Some of them arise due to fads, new consumer cravings, and new technology. In my lifetime, they've just as often been created by legislation, where the government changes rules or regulations. This fuels a sudden rush to meet the new rules and regulations or to take advantage of some tax incentive. This often makes government a powerful and, in my opinion, dangerous player in the bubble marketplace. In a capitalistic system, it becomes problematic when the government gets to pick winner and loser industries and companies through legislation. A great deal of this problem arises from the fact that lobbyists drive so many of these agendas, even more so than market demand or actual regulatory need. It's often nothing more than a form of regulatory market manipulation by insiders.

In my lifetime, I've seen market bubbles created in the frozen yogurt business, hazardous waste cleanup, solar water heating, housing, wind energy, and more recently, solar power in general. My aim here is not to debate any specific goodness or badness in any of these business opportunities. What I want to make clear is how dangerous it can be to time your entry and exit. In the case of a fad, it's one of those "jump on board and hope this thing takes off" affairs. If you pick the right fad and your timing is good, you can become a millionaire in short order. If the fad fizzles or your timing isn't right, you can lose your life savings, your marriage, and your self-respect. In the case of a regulatory-driven market bubble, it may be of longer duration with a corresponding longer "get aboard" period. However, it seems to me the folks who lobbied for the regulation or legislation are often best positioned to know when and how to get onboard the bubble and exploit it fully.

If you're a business neophyte, market bubbles can be similar to lottery tickets; someone's going to win the lottery, but the odds are astronomically against it being you. Now, let me say I've known folks who hit market bubbles and became wealthy as a result. Sadly, I've known far more who tried to jump on board the train as it was already rolling and fell under the wheels. In the case of the latter, they were often convinced by the early riders to buy their seat on the train just as it crested the final hill. Experienced market bubble players know there's an end out there, and they also know if they don't time getting off the train perfectly, they not only won't maximize their profits, they may very well lose everything. I recall a salesman I knew who had a $400,000+ annual income. He and his wife saw a market bubble in a food business fad; people were becoming millionaires in less than a year, opening multiple outlets, and retiring to lives of leisure. Despite having a great life already, this man quit his job, burned his bridges with his employer, and sunk his life savings into the fad.

As you may have guessed by now, he bought in from one of the early riders who saw the end coming and wanted off the train. The business continued to boom for another six or eight months, and then the fad began to fade. To be clear, there was a steady and modestly profitable business that was going to be there forever, but the idea of making millions, franchising, and retiring to the South of France was no longer in the picture. In about a year, the former salesman saw the writing on the wall and went back to his old company and asked for his job back. After all, he'd been their best salesman, and surely they'd want to bring him back aboard their train. Alas, it was not to be. During the year he was gone, he'd been replaced by another salesman who was doing just fine and being paid far less. He ended up working for another company for about a quarter of what he'd previously made.

The lure of quick riches is the bait that takes the inexperienced businessperson almost every time. Yes, some do succeed. Conversely, the great majority don't. A potential neophyte business owner rarely has the connections, the market savvy, the business knowledge, or the required capital to tap one of these markets timely. It happens, but it's rare. I think the solar energy industry is a good lesson for the present in that there were companies who had lined up millions or even billions of dollars in investment, government loans, and government grants so that by the time the flag dropped and the race was on, they were well ahead of those people just realizing an opportunity existed. There were also those electric companies and electrical manufacturers who were already in the business, in possession of extra capital, and already tooled up to go. I'm sure if you think about it or research it, you can name other similar opportunities. Let me end this for now by saying be careful out there.

## Expect and Oppose Pirate Competitors

An ongoing frustration for those of us in all types of business is the problem of pirate operations run by unlicensed or non-permitted competition. They range from the unlicensed produce peddler, to the restaurants operating out of people's patios, to unlicensed contractors, and more recently, even people acting as hotel room plastic surgeons. They're not only costing consumers money and costing legitimate businesses sales, in some instances they're spreading food poisoning, performing substandard construction, and botching surgeries that leave people dead or disfigured.

On one hand I hear many people saying, "Leave them alone, they're just trying to make a living." On the other hand, I hear legitimate business owners ask, "Then why did I put my life savings into starting this business and why I am being asked to buy business licenses, construction permits, demonstrate competence, undergo and pay for health and safety inspections, comply with air and water quality regulations, and pay taxes on my operation?" You and I as business owners/managers need to support the latter position. I know that if you're new to business this seems mean-spirited. Very soon you're going to understand that it's a matter of your business survival.

Let's level the playing field here. Let's either go after all this kind of activity through heightened government enforcement and get it to pay its fair share and comply with each and every law applicable to the rest of us, or let's leave everybody alone and just let everyone do what they think is right in their own mind. As a business owner or manager, you've got to adopt a pro-business mindset going forward and ride your elected representatives to look after your interests. After all, you're being taxed and regulated to death by them—shouldn't they make it as easy as possible for you to generate tax revenue for them?

You are going to find that competing with legitimate businesses that are jumping over all the same hurdles that you are, is going to be tough enough. Businesses of all sorts can and do go under because the pirate competitors can sell the same product or service for 40-60% less than someone who is obeying all the rules and paying all the fees. In the worst recent case I recall, a business went under in a little less than three years, taking 100% of the owner's retirement savings with it. The cause was that this brick and mortar business couldn't compete with people operating illegally out of their garages or patios and advertising their products on Craigslist®.

# CHAPTER 7

## Money Is The Lifeblood Of Your Business

### Business Dreams And Business Money

I t's been my observation that if you truly want to succeed in a business startup, it's better to have more money than dream. While our business dreams often have no limits, the money we have to make them come true usually does.

### What Do Your True Costs Look Like?

Let's say you've done some of your homework and you have a great idea for a business that has every opportunity to survive, even in this toughest of economies. Have you fully explored your costs? Even successful businesses can take from eighteen to thirty-six months to break even. That means that for that same period, you need to have the cash on hand, a credit line, or a rich uncle that will allow you to keep paying the bills until the pump is primed and begins to pour out cash.

Far too many people going into business for the first time expect their income from the business to develop more quickly than it does. They envision cash flow equaling rent, utilities, insurance, telephones, advertising, and payroll in rapid fashion. The reality is, most business startups are money pits in their early weeks and months, and some are money pits until the day the doors close. Don't be foolishly optimistic about cash flow. Ignoring your true costs and not having emergency funding available is deadly.

## Entry Costs For Your Business

As I mentioned earlier in talking about business hurdles, when we talk about entry costs in this book for the business startup, the concept relates to what the costs are to get into a specific line of business. There are low entry cost businesses, medium entry cost businesses, and high entry cost businesses. So if you want to get into a high entry cost business, but you only have the capital for a low entry cost business, if you go ahead and jump into the fray thinking you are faster, smarter, or can run leaner than the other people you're going to compete with, you can pretty much guarantee a bankruptcy.

I had a client almost twenty years back who had $60,000 to go into business with, and the business plan we worked up showed it would cost a minimum of $84,000. These were the hard numbers to open the doors and survive for a year. This client was just certain if they launched the business, sales would be so brisk that the lack of capital could be overcome (if you build it, they will come). I conceded this was possible, but not at all probable. It took less than a year for the client to burn through the $60,000, lose the business, and in short order lose a marriage.

If it had been play money the client could have afforded to lose, it wouldn't have hurt so much. But it was life savings money from a husband and wife, and it devastated the client, spouse, and their marriage. You have to take the entry costs of the business you may be thinking about as seriously as you'd take a heart attack. Mishandling this important consideration can cost you money, your health, and your marriage or other personal relationships. You're not inventing business for the first time—taking the time to study, understand, or listen to other people's experiences will pay dividends and may save your nest egg.

## Where Will The Money Come From?

When talking with people who are planning to launch a business, I always ask them about their financing with a simple question: "Where will the money come from?" The range of responses I receive covers the spectrum from those who have a full business plan and full financing lined up, to those who are praying for cash flow and trusting God to send them customers. I never blatantly endorse or condemn either approach because the idea of the question was to get people talking and thinking about how they're going to pay for the cost of goods sold, utilities, payroll, taxes, insurance, equipment, miscellaneous supplies, unforeseen contingencies, and on and on and on.

New businesses for the most part are financed out of pocket. By that I mean that the new business owner or owners have either saved or borrowed the money necessary to finance their business out of their own pockets or those of family and friends who often act as reluctant investors. This approach assures that on several levels, the budding entrepreneurs have skin in the game and will suffer personal loss if they don't fight hard to make the business succeed. It also assures they'll have family and friends rooting for them, criticizing them, and cajoling them to make a go of it if only so they get their investment back. Consider the latter group to be a mixed blessing.

For those who've been in business a while and have a proven track record with verifiable accounting and bank records to back up their profitability in other business, more formalized means of financing through banks or investment groups comes into play. One of the fairy tales I often have to dispel is that if you have a great idea, a bomb-proof business plan, and a nice personality, then the friendly folks down at the local business bank will loan you money through a line of credit. Maybe, but no banker was ever fired for saying "NO" to this kind of loan request. Conversely, if you have assets such as a house or other real property that can be put up as collateral... maybe.

People who enter business or enter a new line of business for the first time walk into a financial minefield unless they've spent years in that business before in order to understand the ins and outs of that particular industry. If you've never owned a restaurant before, what makes you think you have adequate financing on hand to make a success of it? If you've never manufactured widgets on your own before, what makes you think you have adequate financing on hand to weather a year's financial ups and downs? I know this sounds harsh, and it's meant to be; business is a mercilessly rough-and-tumble full-contact sport.

The main reason a new business most often fails is inadequate financing. You not only have to have enough money on hand to make all the initial capital outlays required to get the ball rolling, you must also have adequate financial reserves in hand to deal with the million little vicissitudes that come along and the occasional gigantic financial catastrophe. The punch press dies; the industrial water heater heats no more; an uninsured drunk driver plows through the front of your donut shop; a federal agency sets new standards, forcing expensive environmental retooling; or your business is sued for some sort of tort and you need a $15,000 retainer for a first-class business lawyer.

## Business Plans Are A Necessity

I wrote my first business plan and my first business prospectus (not the same thing) for a business I worked for when I was a general manager of a small company. We were seeking loans and/

or investment from banks or investors in a small-scale industrial project. If memory serves me correctly, the total capitalization was less than $500,000. At the time I had no formal training in writing a business plan or a prospectus, and I simply went out and bought a book with a template and started working my way through it. It was a long and tedious process, filled with the need to do research, writing, more research, rewriting, and tons of related math for the required financial projections in the capital budget, the operating budget, and the projected cash flow with profits and losses. This is not a minor undertaking.

Then and now, investors and banks considering investing in any kind of a business are going to be looking for a business plan and/or a prospectus detailing the pros and cons of the investment. They're also going to be looking for a ton of support documents, which will include things like financials, resumes or curricula vitae of key personnel, equipment lists, technical specifications, and a dozen other obscure items that will be unique to each individual project. What I came away from that first experience with was 1) the rudimentary knowledge of how to write a business plan, 2) some understanding of how to create a prospectus, and 3) exactly how much hard work goes into creating a business plan and/or a good prospectus. As to whether or not your business plan is any good, the key measure is: Did you get funded?

My advice to you if you are absolutely new to business but want to try to pick up investors or get a business loan is to produce a business plan with full financials. I also think a business plan is a great tool to use to fully think through your business idea even if you have the financing in hand and don't plan to borrow a penny. The exercise of forcing yourself to think about even the minutest aspects of your proposed business will pay dividends once you get the business underway. So if you have some penchant for tedious writing and tedious math, then going out and buying a book and/or a template on writing a business plan may very well get you underway to finding an investor or bank. At the least it will surely help you gain a better handle on just what it is you're about to undertake. If that's not your cup of tea, hire a professional.

There is any number of great, good, and mediocre books, templates, and YouTube® videos around that will do an adequate job of educating you for startup purposes. What I want to touch on is my own experience with people approaching me to write a business plan for them. A business plan can be written by a professional like me, who'll spend considerable time getting to know your business idea, researching the concept, and then reducing what is discovered to writing. After this, the plan returns to the client for comment and any edits required. They may be rewritten one or more times, and in the process you will accumulate many billable hours. Cost is a matter that should be fully discussed in advance.

Business plans can also be written by any of the hundreds of folks on the Internet who have mastered a specific template and charge a package price for a package deal. I think for many startups, this package approach is an excellent option. Financially substantial companies who deal with lawyers, accountants, and business consultants routinely know why they pay us the rates they pay us to do the work we do for them. For lack of a better point in which to inject this thought, I'd like to add that professionals will sometimes accept an ownership interest, a percentage of future profits, or preferred or common stock in a venture in lieu of money. I know of instances where professionals bartered services for goods. I once agreed to take construction services in lieu of cash and it worked out well for both of us. Be creative here if you don't have excess cash.

It's worth noting that people in my line of work, similarly to physicians and lawyers, are routinely approached by friends, family, and casual acquaintances to see if we might "throw together a business plan" for free or for cheap. My answer over the years went from, "Let me take a look at it" to a resounding "No." The reason I won't undertake these kinds of efforts and neither will other professionals is that on a business plan of the sort we develop, you can easily amass $5,000 in billable fees, and on a major project for a large corporation, it could be ten or even twenty times as much. What these queries tell me is that the questioner has no idea what they're asking. I've had people become incensed when they pressed me for a price and then were stunned with the numbers.

Throughout this book, I hope I impress you with how much work goes into the ownership and/or management of a successful business. The business plan or a prospectus is hard labor to create. You have the option of creating your own, buying a cookie-cutter version, or hiring a professional to create them. But regardless of the course of action you choose, there'll be a price to be paid. Don't be lazy or cheap here in the infancy of your business. I'd go even further and say that if you sense laziness for the work or cheapness to pay in cash or sweat equity, then starting a business may not be your cup of tea. No one owes you or me or our businesses anything unless we pay for it or they gift it. When we fight and invest ourselves and our resources in a business, it assists to transform us into business owners.

## Hire A Professional Accountant

If you own or are launching a small business and you don't use a CPA (certified public accountant) or a CMA (certified management accountant) to help you handle your finances and prepare your taxes, you're fooling yourself with the idea that this saves you money. A few who read this will have strong accounting skills; most will not. You will need professional help.

Frequently, business owners think they'll save a lot of money by setting up and handling their own books, preparing taxes themselves, or getting the cheapest bookkeeping and tax services they can find. I've used the same CPA husband-wife team for many years now. They've saved me a fortune, walked me through tax places I didn't understand, and given me great financial advice; they worry so I don't have too.

## Underfunded

I see many little strip malls and other low-rent commercial properties routinely go vacant as they are abandoned by tenant after tenant. Often, if they sell a product that I can use, I will stop, make a purchase, and chat them up. This doesn't come from a morbid sense of curiosity as much as from the fact that as a scholar-practitioner, I'm genuinely curious about people who go into business, why they succeed, or why they fail. The vast majority of the times, the ones who fail are simply naive and underfunded!

Surprisingly, many people who have a great product and a great location go broke because they underestimated how much money they would have to have until the business began to pay for itself, much less provide any salary or profit. Often this is evidenced by the lack of product on the shelves or perhaps just one or two of each item. Sometimes it shows up as the store being hot in the summer or cold in the winter as they struggle to hold down utility costs. To the trained eye, the signs are unmistakable.

Regardless of the reason, after not having budgeted and secured enough money to make it for one year, two years, or maybe even three years, some event or crisis eventually comes along and sinks the underfunded enterprise. Here the proprietor will not only fail to become a success, but all of the money she saved or borrowed has now been lost as well. I will say here again, have literally begged clients not to go into business because while they felt they had plenty of money, I didn't think they had even half enough.

Over the years I've seen many would-be entrepreneurs lose their life savings, insurance settlements, bank loans, and even their children's college funds as they dove into a surefire business venture without really wanting to know the true costs. The end result is often that embittered people are forced to go back to square one in life and start all over again. Some of us learned from our first failure and corrected our mistakes in the other ventures that followed. Always carefully count the cost and know the necessary funding before you venture out.

## Beware The Angels

When you're starting or managing a business for someone else and you need serious cash to make serious steps toward either your business's growth or survival, you'll end up looking to friends, relatives, banks, hard money lenders, and perhaps angel investors. I'll get back to the wider field of how to capitalize your business venture on another essay, but here I want to share about the angels.

Some years back, a business associate and I had a great idea where we knew there was serious money to be made if we could act quickly, but we had to have much more serious money than either he or I had available at that moment. As fate would have it, he was in California beach town for the weekend, and while there he happened to be introduced to a retired lawyer that he described as an angel investor.

My associate took this meeting to be a fortuitous happenstance and shared with this man the business idea we had. To make a very long story short, he came back into the office on Monday and told me he thought our capitalization problems might be solved. I heard about the venture capitalist's career in law, his beautiful home, and his membership at the most fabulous country club. I was amazed at this turn of events and hopeful it wasn't some kind of hustle.

Now when I say I'm amazed at something like this, it doesn't mean I've jumped aboard the amazement train with both feet, it means I'm not certain how to take what I've just heard and need some time to digest it. Our conversation closed out with my associate telling me that the investor wanted to put up $250,000 immediately and wanted to make a larger long-term investment shortly thereafter. The investor told my associate that a contract would follow in a few days for us to look over.

We went on with our lives, and about four days later, a contract arrived in the mail. Actually, I need to restate that—half of a contract arrived in the mail, and that half was seventeen pages long. The former lawyer turned angel investor assured us the rest of the contract was forthcoming as quickly as possible, but in the meantime we could read this first part and agree to it right then and there if we wanted the $250,000 right away. Who out there looking for money doesn't want it right away?

When I began to talk about going to law school more than decade earlier, this same business associate came to me one day and said he'd like to pay my tuition if I was serious. I readily accepted, and I enrolled in a juris doctor program where business people like me were supposed to be able to get a real handle on the law for use in their own business/work life. In the first year, you study contract law, among other subjects. That knowledge has been worth its weight in hundred-dollar bills to me.

Those contracts classes were still solidly in my mind, and I told my associate I'd review this document line by line, but we shouldn't jump in until we saw the entire contract. When he passed this information along to the angel investor and told him I was the holdup, I received a phone call from the investor later that same day. On the phone he was effusive and sought to reassure me of his stellar reputation and good intent. For some reason, that worried me even more. I simply asked him for the rest of the contract.

On Saturday, the angel investor emailed me references and even had two of his borrowers call me to tell me what a great person and business partner we'd get. I responded that I was duly impressed with the investor's alma mater, successful law career, and references, but we'd still wait to see the rest of the contract. The following week, the other half of the contract arrived in my email, and a hard copy soon followed by U.S. Mail. I put the hard copy in my briefcase for a read the following weekend since the entire contract now totaled thirty-one single-spaced pages.

Life has taught me to be one of those people who read every word of a contract before I sign it or suggest anyone else signs it. In this case, it was one of the most instructive contracts I've ever read in my life, and I've read and worked on hundreds of contracts over the past forty years. This one could've been used as a textbook example of how to invest in a company with the intent that if it actually made any money, the investor ended up in control and with the lion's share of the profits. I read it three times to be sure I wasn't just being even more paranoid than usual.

The following Monday, I sat down with my associate and shared with him the bad news. At first he was incredulous because the investor had been so nice, so obviously well educated, and so obviously wealthy. Over the course of the next hour as we went through the contract line by line, he began to see why this investor was so nice, obviously well educated, and so wealthy. This wasn't a hundred-dollar grab; this was a minimum six-figure payday. The investor was someone who understood contract law very well, understood investing, and understood how dreams cause people to make rash decisions.

For the $250,000 investment and the promise of more money later, the angel investor would own controlling interest, become a paid consultant to the company, and be paid out of operational revenue. The angel investor had the right to appoint an operations team, which was also to be paid out of operational revenue. Finally, the angel investor had the right to purchase the company at any time for $500,000; and if the business failed, we'd owe the entire amount of any and all loans back.

Now this was a clear win-win situation...for the angel investor. For my associate and me, we'd take our idea, our months of labor, our risk, and our financial investment and hand it over with the hope we'd get a tiny piece of the pie later. We'd have the angel investor's handpicked experts acting as decision-makers and our bosses, and we'd get almost nothing but an experience in return. We'd also be liable for repaying this angel investor every dime invested, including those salaries for the investor and the handpicked team, if the business failed.

We decided to decline the generous offer. The angel investor of course continued to court us for weeks and wanted us to reconsider our decision. We declined each financial offer and assorted overtures of ongoing friendship. We also made it a point to do more research about the angel. We learned that the angel investor controlled several small companies. They were companies where he'd once only been an angel investor. The original owners had taken on minimized roles or had entirely disappeared from the picture.

I've kept the contract as both a business memento and one of the most instructive documents I've ever read. You should always read the fine print, and as the Scriptures suggest, you should always be on the lookout for and beware of angels of all sorts, especially angel investors. You could certainly run across a good angel investor if you're lucky. Honest investors of all sorts will realistically want to make money for their risk. But someone whose goal is actually to take your money and/or your business, is not your friend or savior.

## What Is Working Capital?

Working capital is the amount of money you will have personally saved, borrowed from a bank, or borrowed from some other lender (e.g., relatives, friends, private investors, etc.) that you will use in operating your new business. This money is meant to keep operations going and pay business expenses during the startup and operations period. The hope here being that eventually working capital can be replaced by profits and the freed-up capital made available for other uses. True working capital is never viewed as profit since it turns over continuously. Upon startup, business income is almost always less than business expense.

For businesses, especially new businesses, having inadequate working capital almost always means the difference between the success or failure of the business (a concept sometimes called undercapitalization). I've seen many businesses go under for lack of adequate working capital. So while a business may have money in the bank, even large sums of money in the bank, if the money in the bank (current assets) is less than the amount the business requires to stay ahead of the monthly bills (current liabilities), there's trouble and perhaps even a bankruptcy ahead.

People who don't pay more than passing attention to business finance will often hear talk of companies having operating reserves of millions, tens of millions, hundreds of millions, or even billions of dollars; they assume those companies are doing great. But if you peer beneath the surface into the day-to-day details, a company with billions in operating reserves could actually be on the verge of bankruptcy if the bills coming in are going to exhaust those reserves and no financially viable means exist to replenish them in a timely fashion. Sears® comes to mind at this moment in history.

For investors, managers, and economists, working capital is a liquidity concept: Can we meet our obligations as they arise? A business might show a profit in given months (e.g., April, June, July and September), but if it can't maintain a positive cash position by having more money in the bank than it needs to pay the bills in all twelve months, that business can't continue to operate due to an overall loss. Hence, a few profitable months in the summer doesn't guarantee a business will even be around come January.

Unfortunately it's very common to see new business owners (and even some old business owners) underestimate their working capital needs going forward. They (owner or owner's family) begin to see themselves as "rich" and begin to spend what should have been increased working capital, hence increasing reserves for those lean winter months. Later they find they can't meet their financial obligations in the months ahead. Think of business owners and corporations you've seen who were "living large" in August and out of business come February.

This myopic view is an unfortunate aspect of human nature, and I suspect it always will be. If you want to remain in business and not just to be able to say, "I used to be in business," then you have to treat working capital as sacrosanct to the life of your business. The people I've seen treat it as "mad money" are out of business when the hard times come along and the business slows to a crawl. Their splurge for a vacation, sports car, or season tickets to their favorite professional team later comes to be recognized as the torpedo that sunk their business dream.

## Creative Destruction
Upon considering going into business, some of you may have read the expression creative destruction (with regard to capitalism) for

the first time. I'm not going to write a dissertation here on the topic, but having been involved in some creative destruction myself, I will devote a few paragraphs here to what it is and why it is. It's not, as some have suggested, an evil plot to destroy jobs in a competing company or country. Furthermore, its primary goal is not to make corporate dismantlers richer, though it sometimes does.

Let's say that a company (big or small) has accumulated capital, launched a business, and has either floundered or perhaps been successful for decades and then suddenly comes to the end of its life; yes companies get old, experience failing economic health, and die, just as people do. The accumulated capital of the company can either be allowed to sit and dissipate (e.g., rust, be stolen, becomes outdated, etc.), or it can be sold off to release the capital to be used in another fresh business effort.

The business has failed or is failing. The owners, whether they are actual hands-on owners or stockholders, stand to lose all the capital they placed at risk. The new business, new jobs, and new opportunity to make a profit from the carcass/corpus of the old company will absolutely be lost if nothing is done to retrieve it. Losing a job or a business is a highly emotional experience. Nevertheless, if owners' emotions are allowed to rule the day here, EVERYTHING can be lost.

Not every failing business can be saved; some can, many can't. However, frequently a business finds itself in a place where there is no miraculous turnaround available. In these instances, some companies choose to ride it into the ground while others decide to cannibalize what they still have before they're forced to do so in bankruptcy. The best of companies practice creative destruction routinely within different divisions so they always have a phoenix rising from the ashes in one of their aging enterprises instead of seeing the whole place go under at once.

This same process happens all over the world and in every kind of political environment because no capitalist, socialist, or communist government can allow the means of production to fall completely apart and yet continue to survive. So, whether the economic planning is capitalistic (decentralized) or communistic (fully centralized), this life-from-the-ashes scenario I just painted takes place continuously, regardless of what name it is given. Failed economies around the world have often failed because they could not or would not grasp this reality.

Elsewhere in this book I talk a bit about bankruptcy and how it figures into creative destruction. But for now consider that some of you look at Craigslist®, eBay®, and legal filings every day searching for "great deals" from people or companies who find themselves in a place where they need to liquidate assets to recover their capital so they can survive to fight another day. Meanwhile, none of us hesitate to drive as hard a bargain as we can with those people selling off their assets; are you a creative destructionist or vulture capitalist—you decide.

## Three Important Business/Political Terms You Need To Understand

Miriam Webster offers us the following three classic definitions.

**Capitalism:** An economic system characterized by private or corporate ownership of capital goods, by investments that are determined by private decision, and by prices, production, and the distribution of goods that are determined mainly by competition in a free market.

**Socialism:** Any of the various economic and political theories advocating collective or governmental ownership and administration of the means of production and distribution of goods.

**Communism:** A theory advocating elimination of private property; a system in which goods are owned in common and are available to all as needed.

## Don't Spend A Dime Needlessly

Everything you buy to use in your new business doesn't have to be brand spanking new. If you're patient and look around the marketplace, you'll find other people had the same dreams you did, but couldn't keep them flying. This means there are bargains out there on everything from lathes to steam tables, from desks to software, and just about anything else you'll ever need. Buying anything at any time that doesn't increase your productivity enough to cover the additional costs and boost the bottom line is a waste of financial resources.

## Operate Like You're In A Turnaround

In the world of business people like me and companies like mine are sometimes brought into faltering businesses to figure out why they are faltering and to determine how best to turn their "business ship" in a more favorable direction. We call this effort a turnaround. If we're called early enough, a turnaround can often be accomplished. If we're called in when the ship is twenty feet from the rocks, it's far too late. If you remember nothing else out of this passage, remember to call for help early rather than late.

For me, turnarounds are one of the most interesting aspects of the business world, but not so much so for the company needing the turnaround. Turnarounds often become necessary due to business collapses or dramatic changes in the business environment. Some business collapses are related to quirks in the economy such as black swan events; most are not. I've never had a candid owner tell me they truly didn't see any problems coming; I have had them admit they didn't react quickly enough. Turnarounds always involve pain on several levels.

If business owners and managers scanned the horizon daily and operated more like they were trying to turn their company around continuously based on the feedback they pick up from the business world, they'd be better served than waiting until they have no other choice. Companies that operate in a constant state of introspection and are working regularly to identify problems on the horizon before they become fatal, may falter due to the truly unforeseen, but never due to having grown complacent. In my experience, complacency seems to frequently precede the need for turnarounds.

### Are They Keepers?

Your employees have a huge impact on your financial viability. Just fitting a body into a slot to get you by, may work for a short while. But if you have the wrong person in the wrong slot, or even in the wrong company, they are going to hurt your bottom line. I've seen individual employees slowly destroy the business they worked for. Sometimes it's been through embezzlement, but more often than not it's through bad attitude, poor work habits, or improper behavior with or against fellow employees. You'll need to revisit this concept regularly in your business; employees can change over time.

Finance must be taken into account with regard to those you employ. It's not enough that people are nice or trying hard. We often use serious quantitative analysis in business. However, you don't have to have a background in business economics to figure out if an employee is worth their keep. Determine what they gross for you, take away what they truly cost you (i.e., not just the dollars you pay them), and then see if that number makes them worth the money and the psychic effort they receive. Just the fact that they make you some money doesn't mean they're keepers.

### Give Credit Only Where Credit Is Due

One of the big questions you'll need to ask and answer early on is: Will your business extend credit, and if so, under what terms?

My very first thought on this is "Don't extend credit unless it's absolutely essential to the life of your business." Many businesses are essentially cash and carry or cash on delivery (COD), and the people doing business in those fields know and understand this already. From there on it gets murkier. The entire field of extending business credit is beyond the scope of this book. For our purposes I'm interested in companies getting underway or companies that have only been in business five years or less and are still feeling their way along the extending credit trail.

The first question you should ask yourself is: Must I extend credit in order to be able to compete in this line of business? If the answer is no, then you're free to go on with your business under a COD basis and life is good. If the answer is yes, then you have a much trickier set of issues to deal with, and they're all issues that deserve some serious consideration. 1) Who needs/wants credit? 2) How do you determine their creditworthiness? 3) How much credit will you extend overall? 4) How much credit will you extend to an individual account? 5) How will you track monies owed you? 6) How will you handle your slow receivables? 7) How will you deal with serious arrears and bad debt? Now I can assure you there are other credit issues you need to think about as well, but this isn't an MBA program; it's simply bits here and there that I hope will seed further thought and research on your part.

**Question 1:** Who needs or wants credit from your new business? If the answer is no one, then you're good to go and you can ignore this question. But if the answer is either some of your customers/clients or all of them, then we have to look at the other questions.

**Question 2** deals with how you'll determine their creditworthiness, but first I'd ask them if they have lines of credit with a bank or if they have credit cards they can use. We go down this road because you really don't want to be in the credit business.

Failing that approach, you'd want to use the starting point of having them fill out a credit application. You'd either personally need to spend time determining if they're a good credit risk, or, if you have no clue how this is done, you'd have to hire someone to do it for you. Whatever you do here, don't just give them credit because they seem like nice people.

**Question 3** may seem odd at first, but unless you have unlimited personal funds to loan to your customers/clients, you're going to have to know the limit to how much in total you can afford to offer everybody you deal with at one time. Your operating capital will be a finite number. Inside that finite number you not only carry customers, you have to keep the lights on, buy supplies, pay your employees, pay your taxes, and perhaps even take some money for your own work so you can continue to eat regularly. If you've been so generous to your clients/customers that you've left your operation financially penurious, you'll be in danger of starvation, a workers' walk-out, collections actions against you, or bankruptcy. If you've let your goods get out the door on credit, or you have thousands of dollars sitting on your books in service, or professional fees you can't collect, you'll die from negative cash flow issues that you created.

**Question 4** is determined by what you find out during their credit check and what they ask for as a line of credit. This would include the amount, any collateral, the term of the credit, and any interest or penalties you're going to assess for being late or defaulting. You're going to need to learn about the Uniform Commercial Code and small claims court. If you're new to business, you're going to be more prone to generous terms. That's because you haven't had anyone try to beat you out of thousands of dollars YET. Trust me, as the voice of experience, if you stay in business long enough, you're going to have this happen, and the difference between recovering the money and losing it forever may well be in how adeptly you handle these terms and conditions portions of a "written" agreement; get a lawyer to build you a template. These terms and conditions vary by industry and you need to learn whatever "usual and customary" is for your service, professional, manufacturing, or retail offerings.

**Question 5** seems fairly simple when you are getting started because you have no customers/clients, and as they begin to come in you can probably jot them down and track sales and debt on a notepad. However, if your business continues to grow, you're going to need some sort of an accounting system. When I started my first business that accounting was all on paper. It was single entry, and I could do it all myself. Later it was still paper; it evolved to double-entry, and I could still do it myself. In the early years of computer software, I worked with accounting software that cost a quarter of a million dollars. It was developed by a local university and required that a professor come on-site and tutor the staff and me. Eventually Peachtree®, QuickBooks®, Mind Your Own Business®, and a host of other inexpensive accounting programs came along. Today the QuickBooks® version I use has far more functionality than that quarter-million-dollar version ever did and costs less than $500.

**Question 6** deals with how you plan to handle gaining payment from your clients/customers. Now if you don't offer credit and only take credit cards, cashier's checks, money orders, or verified bank drafts, you can ignore this passage. But if you plan to offer lines of credit or accept personal/business checks, you're going to get into the collection business at some point. If you've read my other work or heard me speak, you know my feeling about money you can "collect" being much more important than money you can "book." In its least obtrusive mode, you'll need to send out statements and track payments. In its most unpleasant mode, someone has to make calls, send demands, threaten legal action, visit the client/customer, or appear in either small claims court or full-blown civil court to try and get your money. Have a plan before you need a plan.

**Question 7** is certainly not the last question you'll ever have in this subject, but it's the last one I'm addressing here. It's somewhat tied to question 6 because it deals with what you plan to do if all your statements, demands, visits, and threats of legal action have failed. If the amount is relatively small, you can pursue it in small claims court without a lawyer. If it exceeds your state's statutory limits for small claims, it will have to go into civil court. Now you're talking legal fees and court costs. Many of you who are reading this will have never been to a lawyer's office in your life on any matter, much less a civil matter. Let me say right up front that the numbers you're going to lose have to be balanced against the numbers you're going to put out with your attorney to obtain justice. If the amount is less than $10,000, I'd certainly ask the attorney to write a "demand letter" on your behalf. But I'd think long and hard about going into full-blown civil court.

The last issue has no number, but it comes from personal experience. You're going to get bad checks, counterfeit bills, fraudulent credit card charge-backs, outright grifters, deadbeats, and formerly valued customers who hit hard times and go broke. You're going to lose money in bankruptcies unless you demanded hard collateral up front for credit, have an iron-clad claim, and have a grizzly bear of an attorney going to bankruptcy court on your behalf. Get ready for these happenstances now if you plan to go into business. I had someone I'd trusted, gone to church with, and done business with for years burn me for $80,000 when the economy took a bad downturn. It almost took me and some other contractors he'd treated the same way under with him. I still recall the letter from the bankruptcy court telling me there were no assets and the bankruptcy was total and final. I've also won judgments I was never able to collect. Your mental health has value, and sometimes your best bet is to let some things go.

Most of you won't be able to let things go in your early business career; I say this from personal experience. If they cheat you badly enough, you may even be out hunting for them with a gun. Ask yourself if they really owe you enough money that you'd be willing to spend the rest of your days in prison for a clearly premeditated murder. Now as time goes by, if your business doesn't die off, you're going to get much smarter about the extension of credit and how you deal with people asking for credit. This would be a good time to remind you that the pricing you use for your goods or services must also have some factor in it for bad debt that you have to write off. Most people going into business have no idea how credit actually works or how pricing or credit finance rates are determined. I learned the methods and legalities in business school. You need to either make an intensive study and gain some expertise beforehand or get a CMA or CPA on your phone list.

## Collecting The Money Is The Problem

Booking revenue is not the problem in your new business. If you offer credit in any form, there will always be takers. Collecting the revenue once you have got it on the books is where the whole matter gets sticky. If you have little or no assurance going in that you are going to collect for your product or services, why not just stay home, make love, play golf, or enjoy your family. You will have more cash at the end of the day than you would have otherwise, because you will also have avoided giving away your money in the form of goods or services. Sometimes, you'll have a happier and more stress-free life if you didn't make the sale.

New businesses are notorious for taking extreme risks because they are so desperate to get some traction for their dream. More experienced business people know this and some of the unscrupulous ones make a routine practice of using this to their advantage.

It is a very frequent issue with contractors, caterers, or material suppliers. It's been such a problem that numerous laws have been put in place to protect the gullible or good-hearted. But this kind of financial abuse is certainly not limited to these industries I've mentioned. Do not get so excited over a potential big sale that you become sloppy about assuring you'll get paid.

## Eating The Seed

The following passage comes from Psalms 126:5-6. It holds something of a hidden message for many people but is extremely relevant to those people who plan to own or manage businesses. It's such a simple concept that one would think everybody in business would automatically understand it, and yet the number of people who lose their businesses or lose their management positions as a result of violating the concept revealed is staggering.

*"They that sow in tears shall reap in joy. He that goeth forth and weepeth, bearing precious seed, shall doubtless come again with rejoicing, bringing his sheaves with him."*

From my previous books and/or having heard me speak at one time or another, many of you know that in my early years I was a pastor of a small Christian church. During those years I amassed more than 3,000 sermons and God only knows how many lesson plans. The public-speaking experience and the feedback from live classes were invaluable in shaping my thinking, my speaking, and more recently, my writing. I spoke on this concept many times, and I've sung the song "Bringing In The Sheaves" countless times since I was a six-year-old, where I read it for the first time from the Broadman Hymnal. For you youngsters, that's way back in 1960. For the not-so-young, it was your childhood era as well.

There are two verses here that I see as clearly interrelated. The first talks about tears, planting, and joy. Or, more precisely it talks about tears, sowing, and joy. The second speaks of going, weeping, and bearing, or carrying, what the verse terms "precious seed." It's relevant to you business owners and business managers because it conveys the concept of working capital in a very down-to-earth and tangible way. It's more easily overlooked if you have no farming background. Farmers get this one almost immediately.

In ancient times, farmers would gather seed at the harvest to be set aside solely for the next planting in the spring. Since there were no patented seed stocks and everything that grew could be thought of as open seed stock, the farmer just collected his seed for the next year. No research labs, no custom-seed growers, no geneticists, no seed retailers. Just the farmer and his seed. Seed which, I might add, was now exceedingly critical to the survival of his farm, his family, and himself; without this seed, he and his family would eventually starve.

There's a middle piece to this story that is critical to your understanding. Research labs, custom-seed growers, crop scientists, and seed retailers are sometimes seen as evil in our era. But these same people keep assuring society that even if something happens to the seed a farmer has set aside, he can go to the seed retailer and there will be seed available; no one needs to die of starvation over the lack of set-aside seeds. This was not the case when this Scripture was written. There were fat harvests and lean harvests; there were issues of food insecurity after harvest (e.g., rot, mold, theft, rats, insects, etc.); there were even questions about seed germination rates due to poor rain and whether or not there was enough for a second planting.

Consider the possibility that the farmer had a lean year and had set aside the required seed to assure there would be a crop the next year so that life could go on. Consider then too that his family had struggled through the fall and winter months with hunger and perhaps malnourishment. Imagine the debates that would take place around that family table as mother, father, and several hungry little mouths debated eating the seed. I was once a young father with four children and a wife. I can picture all too clearly how that would have went down, especially if the parents were divided about using the seed to feed their babies.

Let's say they made it through the winter, and spring came with good rain and all the best weather they could have hoped for. That would not end the debate back at the table. You see, even then there was likely going to be a period of three or more months from the time the seed went in the ground until the time there was a harvest. Yes, there may have been things they could hunt or gather to survive, but never doubt that it would be just that, a matter of mere survival. The worst of the hunger and what ancients called "the starving time" often came after winter had passed.

When you read these two verses now, I hope you see them a little differently and why they are phrased as they are. *"They that sow in tears shall reap in joy. He that goeth forth and weepeth, bearing precious seed, shall doubtless come again with rejoicing, bringing his sheaves with him."* Now of course, what the farmer and any other businessperson is looking for is that harvest and that hoped-for profit. In the farmer's case, it would be sheaves, or bundles of grain. In your case, it will be something different entirely (unless you're subsistence farming). The seed and the harvest are inseparably intertwined; there cannot be one without the other.

Seed is working capital, because stored within the seed is a future convertibility to things that produce life and wealth. Just as surely as seed represented capital to that farmer, today such capital can be found stored in land, gold, silver, or federal reserve notes. Now many of you reading this will readily grasp that money is capital and that for your business to survive its winters and starving times, there must be adequate working capital available in some form to carry you through. Families who cave to their momentary hunger eventually starve or become indentured to someone who hasn't eaten their seed. That's a story as old as civilization.

If you're new to business, there will eventually be a temptation to eat the seed. The temptation doesn't always arise out of necessity. Often it arises because human beings want "things." We want cars, trucks, boats, planes, homes, nice clothes, fine foods, the latest electronic gadgets, weekend getaways, and month-long vacations in a warm, sunny place. If you work hard and you're successful at your work, all of those things can eventually be yours. But if you consume the seed and a time comes when the seed is needed to stay in business, you're going to go out of business, or return to the wage slavery you thought you'd escaped.

The good news here (and there is good news here) is in the part of the Scripture where it says, *"...shall doubtless come again with rejoicing, bringing his sheaves with him."* What that says to the man or woman who preserves their business capital, and reinvests it in their business in a wise and appropriate fashion, is that a time will eventually come where there is a harvest or a profit that is many hundreds or even many thousands of times a multiple of each seed. Hang on to your seed/working capital, and don't think for a moment that the Scripture doesn't have any practical business advice.

### Is It Time To Get Out?

I vaguely recall from an old business school case study that the owner of Rollerblades was quite unhappy when he sold out for $30,000,000 and the company went on to become a $300,000,000 entity. Sometimes we can only carry an idea so far with the resources we have before someone else has to come along who can take it to the next level. Some would think that the Rollerblade guy was fortunate he didn't hang on until it was a $3,000,000; $300,000; or $30,000 idea.

You'll need to be brutal in your self-assessments regarding you, your business, and its future prospects. If you can't be brutal, then hire someone that you'd listen to and allow them to give you any hard facts you might otherwise ignore. I've witnessed far too many viable businesses that should have been sold or new partners and management brought in, that later went into decline and died off completely. When that happens, all the potential value you once worked so hard to create is destroyed.

People move out of businesses they own for a myriad of reasons; not always by choice. It can be related health, age, family, politics, diminishing profits, a lucrative buyout offer, the death or divorce of a spouse, or the death or departure of a business partner. You don't need to be going broke to be thinking about when you and how want to exit your business. I believe that it is far better for you to be able to make a solid and well thought out business decision to get out in advance, rather than to wait so long that all your options have vanished.

Always be considering your exit strategy. Life in business is like a roller coaster ride on most days. Once you've been around the track a couple of times you'll start to see the patterns that you missed on the first cycle. Don't ignore your gut or your business experience here. You may be thirty years old or you may be sixty years old, business doesn't give you points for youth or age. Change sometimes creeps up on us and sometimes it simply jumps out before us. Always be asking yourself, "Is it time to get out?"

## Bankruptcy

I saved this part for last because it is such a painful concept for you to even have to consider, much less one to have to live through.

My hope here is that by talking to you about bankruptcy now, that it will enter into your business considerations all through the years and all along your way. I don't offer this information because I hope you go bankrupt, I offer this in the hope that having been warned what the definitions are, that you'll be able to spot potential economic problems long before they take you towards a bankruptcy.

Lawyers and accountants are taught at least three different definitions for what constitutes bankruptcy. I'm going to simplify that greatly and for our purposes say that it's a case of owing more than you can pay back during the agreed-upon terms and time available. It can happen to individuals and it can happen to businesses. However, not everyone who is technically bankrupt elects to or is forced into bankruptcy. Consequently there are a lot more people and businesses that are technically bankrupt who never actually go bankrupt.

Individuals and businesses avoid filing for bankruptcy because financial systems have deliberately made that action costly. Bankruptcy has heavy consequences for all parties involved. The costs to the bankrupt include loss of assets, loss of favorable credit, and a heavy risk premium is attached to any financial actions taken by the bankrupt individual or entity for many, many years to come. The costs to the lenders/investors range from a partial to a total loss of the capital, goods, or services they put at risk.

Digressing for a moment, it's good to recall here that both the lender/investor and the now bankrupt individual or business both enter their financial relationship knowing this can happen. At least we assume they know. New business owners are often the least informed and the most ill-informed. Financial institutions, manufacturers, and others on the lender/investor side of this equation generally go to great efforts to assure the creditworthiness of the individual or business they are lending or selling too.

Even then, finances may falter or outright fail, and bankruptcy ensues. Also, don't discount the danger of false information on the credit application or loan contract. Trust but verify.

The several types of bankruptcy are based on chapters within bankruptcy law. They range from types that allow creditors and debtors to try to work out some way to restructure the debt so that all parties salvage some or all of their capital, to total bankruptcy, where the court judges there are no assets or almost no assets remaining and the carcass/corpus must be liquidated in order to get some of the capital back for creditors. At this extreme end, that often amounts to pennies on the dollar. If you ever wondered why creditors don't like to needlessly force debtors into bankruptcy, this is the reason.

It's pertinent to mention here that not all creditors of a bankrupt entity are created equal. There is a hierarchy of creditors that determines who gets to come to the trough to feed first. These tiers are again determined by various laws and/or contracted agreements. The tiers of creditors can be numerous, and often it's only the first one or two tiers that even see pennies on the dollar come back to them. Many of us have received letters from the courts telling us that someone we gave credit to has been determined to have no assets and their bankruptcy is complete; no pennies on the dollar are available.

I know this seems like a brutal system, but when you compare it to the debtor's prisons that existed a couple of centuries back, it looks a little less brutal. In the United States, because we hear so much talk about democracy, we automatically assume credit is a democratic principle and everybody should be given credit. Wrong! Credit is and should be extended based on credit worthiness, and only after both parties have had an opportunity to sit down, check one another out, and negotiate some kind of contract with terms that carry a level of risk that is acceptable to both parties.

Without credit, our current economic system would grind to a halt. That's true whether you're financing that new seventy-five inch curved panel television for $4,000, selling $20,000 worth of fertilizer, or financing the equipment for a new $20,000,000 factory. So even in harsh economic times, credit remains important. When credit doesn't flow, it leads to economic stagnation and unemployment. Bankruptcy is an integral part of our credit system. It works as a kind of forced creative destruction to keep capital at work within our system. It further keeps that system healthy and turning over the same capital again and again, as money, goods, or services are borrowed and paid back.

Where we can get in real trouble is when third parties, with little or no skin in the game, begin to make demands on either creditors or debtors that violate good financial principles. This often brings potential debtors/borrowers to the table when they have no legitimate business being there. When this happens, we enter territory outside the acceptably risk-laden boundaries of finance, and we enter an economic wilderness whose boundaries have been established by the bones of those who've perished there over millennia. If you're going to be in business, you have to begin to study the ideas behind credit and debt. It doesn't work in the simple, even childish manner many think. This naiveté leads to bad business deals, bad debt, and failed companies.

# CHAPTER 8

## SURVIVAL TERMS IN LAW, REGULATIONS, AND FINANCE

### What You Don't Know Can Cost You

I was talking to a client recently about new safety regulations that went into effect last January and how they affect his business. He was stunned because 1) he hadn't heard about the regulation I was reading to him, and 2) it was going to be expensive to implement at his business.

As a general rule, the phrase "ignorance of the law is no excuse" is a law school mantra. As for being expensive, it's the cost of doing business, and we all have the choice to stay in business or go out of business in these instances. There is also that third group, the one that ignores the law until they get caught.

As a business owner or manager, you need to stay on top of safety trends, business laws, and administrative regulations that affect your industry. If you don't, it's going to cost you. For instance, OSHA is not the tiger it once was, but one of the reasons tort law exists is to correct wrongs where laws or administrative regulations fall down.

I get new regulations from different industries flowing across my desk weekly; they fill my email on a regular basis. If you as an owner/manager aren't getting this kind of information regularly,

I can guarantee you are simply out of the loop. Get into your industry's trade publications and start catching up today.

Most new small businesses do not have the money for professional staff to look over these matters. As a new business owner or manager it falls to you to become at least semi-professional in areas of business, finance, human resources, contract law, tort law, and the myriad of administrative regulations that over lay your industry.

The essays that follow this one are a mix of items that I think you have to be thinking about and developing a working awareness of. In areas where you are in over your head, you have to ask for help. That can be professional help or just the help of another fellow business person.

Remaining ignorant on laws and regulations guarantees business failure.


## Words And Leases Have Consequences

When entering into a lease for a business property, be sure to read every single word. Each word or phrase has the power to modify the meaning of other words or phrases. If you don't fully comprehend the lease in its entirety and without any lingering doubts, then don't sign it until you can consult a lawyer or at least an experienced business consultant.

I know a business where the owners didn't grasp the concept of CAM (Common Area Maintenance) and soon discovered that their rent each month was actually about 50% more than they'd budgeted for. Sometimes this is purely an oversight and sometimes it happens because of business neophytes being too embarrassed to admit a lack of business knowledge and asking more pointed questions.

Some leasing agents are no doubt disreputable and try to obfuscate. But far more often I find that it's a matter of people in business speaking the language of business and people new to business failing to understand it. If there are terms or words that are Greek to you, then say so and ask for an explanation. If none is forthcoming or details remain unclear, then seek out an explanation before you sign anything.

CAM refers to fees paid by lessees (renter) to lessors (landlord) for the use and upkeep of common areas used by multiple business tenants. This includes common bathrooms, patios, parking lots, signage, lighting, kitchens, conference rooms, landscaping, irrigation, and pest control. The possible list of items affected by CAM can be nearly limitless depending on where you're leasing and what class of business property it is. Ignorance is always expensive.

## He Who Has The Best Paper Wins

I can say with a high degree of confidence that the party with the most accurate and complete set of detailed records does better in the business world. When I work through files with clients to help them be sure they have all their ducks in order as they try to land or maintain a contract, I sometimes come away from those sessions amazed that people don't take notes, get details down in writing, or insist on highly detailed contracts when money, careers, and companies are at stake.

If you end up in a contract dispute, every single letter, email, text message, and even your handwritten records of the times of phone calls you made to the other party can end up in front of a judge and/or jury. Business novices are so excited to be doing business that they don't consider, or perhaps have no clue, that deals can blow up and destroy a dream. This is where the tedious recordkeeping side of owning or managing a business pays dividends. You do this as a form of insurance and you pray that you never have to use it.

When deals are being negotiated, it's a heady time. It's often like an engagement to be married; everybody involved is lovey-dovey. A little later, the contract details get worked out, and that's like planning a wedding. Both sides want the wedding to go forward, but suddenly they're confronted with the fact that one party wants five hundred people at the wedding and the full sit-down dinner, and the other party wants to make a quick trip to a Las Vegas wedding chapel and then hit the buffets.

Finally, there's the actual marriage, where both parties begin to see that they didn't understand what the other person wanted at all. This is the point where you realize neither of you is going to get everything you wanted out of the deal. Sometimes folks can live with this and sometimes they can't. This is also the point where divorces come or contracts are breached. Both are painful and involve lawyers. Better records with better details equates to better outcomes for the party diligent enough to do the tedious work and compile the paper.

## Forms Of Business Ownership

Much of this book can be applied around the world; this topic will only hold true in the United States. One of the very first issues you're going to need to resolve if you're launching a business is what form the business will take. For those new to business, this usually happens when you go down to your city clerk's office or your county clerk's office to get whatever sort of business license it is your local government requires of you. I live in California, and it wouldn't be uncommon to have both county business licenses and multiple city business licenses in order to do business in multiple municipalities or jurisdictions. Let's say you're at the county clerk's office filling out the necessary forms, and you come to an area that asks you to choose the form your business is going to operate under; there will be several options.

In general, you are going to see 1) sole proprietor, 2) husband and wife, 3) partnership, 4) limited liability company, 5) limited liability partnership, and 6) corporation.

This list is not intended to be definitive or exhaustive; it's here to give you some idea of the options. In some states, counties, or municipalities, there may be hybrids of these six, and there may be others not even mentioned here. Your challenge will be to wade through them and make a pick. If the moment you see these options for the first time is as you're filling in the blanks, I urge you to STOP. That's right, you should stop the process, take the forms in paper format or go home and download them from a computer, and educate yourself on what each of these mean. If you are then in any way unclear, call your business consultant or your business lawyer if you have one.

Your business consultant doesn't have to be a hired professional like me. It can easily be a friend or family member who has been successful in business for years and whose judgment you trust. But if you need a business lawyer, then get a real one. There are tons of people around like me who went to law school but ARE NOT lawyers. If they'd wanted to be lawyers, they'd have hung on through their state bars and went out and learned real lawyering and not just what they read in textbooks and heard in lectures. In any event, you're going to need some help considering the implications for you of the business type you choose. If you choose right, life will be smooth and your assets will be safe. If you choose wrong, life will be tumultuous and you could lose everything you have, even your home.

Below I offer some brief explanations of each of the business types I've listed above, but I would add that most people starting a small business start out as either a sole proprietor or a husband and wife. The other forms that are named usually can't be thrown together on the spur of the moment as you apply for your license; they require serious forethought. There are pros and cons for each business type. You and your spouse, investors, or partners need to sit down and come to an agreement on this early in the game. The impact of your selection will ripple forward through everything you're about to undertake. Many business plans go through rewrites due to the parties involved changing their minds on business type. I genuinely don't mind this because I charge for that rewrite.

*Let me offer a quick warning here. The laws are different in each of the fifty states, and I'm not even going to claim expertise on business entity law in California where I live. You need to delve into your own state and local laws to be certain you pick the best form of business entity for you. Consult a lawyer...*

**Sole Proprietor:** A sole proprietorship is the simplest form of business startup. It does not require the formation of a legal entity (e.g., Limited Liability Company, Corporation, Partnership, etc.). The license you receive to operate references you as that sole owner and lets the world know you own that business and are personally responsible for its debts. It's estimated that 70% of U.S. businesses operate as sole proprietorships.

**Husband And Wife:** First off, let me say that if you live in one of the nine community property states, the rules governing you as a husband and wife will be different than the other forty-one states. In the forty-one non-community property states, the IRS will likely view you as partners (see IRS Form 1065, Publication 334, and Publication 541) or partners in a joint venture, and you'll need to consult an attorney to make sure you're on track.

In the nine other states, such as California, the husband and wife are partners by virtue of all they own together being community property. This holds true unless there was some sort of legal agreement prior to the marriage (i.e., prenuptial agreement). The IRS will treat the income as common to both. The license they receive to operate references both the husband and the wife and lets the world know they both own that business and are both personally responsible for its debts.

**Partnership:** A partnership is a form of business where two or more people share ownership. Each partner will contribute money, property, labor, skills, etc. to the business. For those contributions, each party is entitled to a share of the profits or losses sustained by the business.

Partnerships have a couple of peccadillos I want to alert you to. I mention in another passage in this book that partners have liability for their partner's negligence or misconduct (unless it's a Limited Liability Partnership). Partners must also maintain their percentage of the partnership when infusions of cash are required; poor partners can find themselves being squeezed out or enduring a forced sale to leave the partnership.

**Limited Liability Company (LLC):** In the U.S., this is a specific form of a privately held company. It provides the benefits of "pass-through" taxation similar to a sole proprietorship or partnership and also provides the "members" (in California they are not called partners) of the LLC with limited personal liability, like a corporation. As a general rule, liability in an LLC is limited to the assets of the LLC and protects the members of the LLC from having their own assets seized to satisfy a judgment.

**Limited Liability Partnership (LLP):** In LLPs, some or all of the partners have limited liability; you'll need to consult a lawyer on how this works in your state. LLPs look somewhat like corporations and partnerships. In LLPs, the party receives their share of untaxed profits and must pay taxes themselves. One of the major advantages in an LLP is that a partner is not liable for another partner's negligence or misconduct.

**Corporation:** Corporations are legal entities (legal persons) that are considered separate and legally distinct from their owners. In general, corporations have many of the rights that individual people do. They also have responsibilities just as individual people do. Corporations have the right to enter into contracts, borrow money, loan money, sue and be sued, hire employees, own assets, and of course pay taxes. Corporations come in several forms, and you'd be wise to hire a lawyer to guide you in a corporate formation. Corporations can have one owner or they can have thousands of owners. Corporations are the chosen mode of business entity for companies both great and small. I've worked for two-shareholder corporations and other corporations with thousands of shareholders.

Allow me to close this out by saying that business law pertinent to partnerships, business entities, and agency are serious classes in law school and require serious effort just to gain a basic grasp. Yes, if you are very smart, you could self-educate with one of the hundreds of books out there of the DIY nature. The problem with self-education, based on my experience and the lessons I've learned, is that it can often be the most expensive form of education. The school of hard knocks is brutal when it teaches you that you missed a lesson or misunderstood what you thought you knew. I'd been in business as a sole proprietor, husband and wife, LLC, and corporation by the time I hit law school; I was stunned by my own legal ignorance on several matters in each of them as we studied there.

If you're desperate to get underway, you'll likely rush down and create a sole proprietorship or a husband and wife entity. Remember the risk each entity type carries or protects you from, and when you've calmed down, consider your other options. You can go back tomorrow morning and start the change necessary to take on a different business form if you find yourself panicking over the possibility of losing everything you've worked for and being faced with living in your car or under a bridge. The bad news is that liabilities that arose under a prior business form are adjudicated under that business form. Filing for recognition by your state as a corporation won't eliminate responsibilities (e.g., finances, negligence, misconduct, etc.) incurred during years as a sole proprietorship or husband and wife.

## Partnerships

In addressing the concept of business partnerships, I want to be careful to not get too technical, and yet I need to remain technical enough that you have a good grasp of both the benefits and dangers of business partnerships. When I attended law school, we had a four-unit course entitled "Agency and Partnership," which included a textbook, a book of case studies in agency and partnerships, and an outline of more than two hundred pages depicting the legal ins and outs of agency and partnership. While I found it to be one of the most interesting courses I took there, I also understand that people who aren't deeply enamored with the ideas of business don't get all teary-eyed with joy when topics of this sort arise. Despite general apathy toward these concepts on the part of law students, as well as most people who plan to enter business, a fundamental knowledge of how partnerships (and to a lesser degree agency) works could save you a great deal of time, money, and legal fees later on. I say later on because partnerships are like marriages…no one enters into either marriage or a business partnership with plans for a divorce, and yet it happens.

Simply stated, a partnership is the joining together of two or more people conducting business with the intent to make a profit. Partners share profits, and they share common interests. With that in mind, a partnership can have hundreds of partners, thousands of partners, and even tens of thousands of partners if those involved are so inclined. More often than not, the partnerships I've had dealings with had less than a dozen people involved and most frequently only two or three. Some were formed to conduct a retail business, some were formed to conduct a wholesale business, some were formed to conduct a construction business, and some were formed to conduct a professional business (e.g., law, medicine, accounting, engineering, etc.). I would have to say that with the exception of the lawyers, most of the people I've known who jumped into partnerships had no real idea of how they functioned; some of the partners paid a very steep price for their on-the-job training. One of the most dangerous aspects of partnership is unlimited liability for the actions of a partner.

Partnerships can take on several forms, and the wisest partners make sure to get the conditions of the partnership in a writing. They don't enter into a legal partnership simply because they bragged to some third party that "Me and Bob are business partners." The reason I say "enter into a legal partnership" is that by your boast that you and Bob are partners, you've planted in the mind of the hearer that you and Bob are indeed business partners. Now perhaps to a business and legal novice, that's just casual conversation over a drink. But to people in business and to their lawyers, it's a declaration that you have a partnership relationship with old Bob that could put you on the hook for Bob's ongoing business actions. They can now assume things like you being Bob's business agent and Bob being your business agent. They can also assume that you and Bob have some responsibility for one another's business acts and debts.

Since I'm not writing a textbook here, but do hope to raise your curiosity, I want to offer several headings that you could enter into a Google® search and get a fair amount of information. This research could at the very least raise your degree of wariness and at most completely terrify you out of ever entering into any sort of partnership. Here are a few: 1) partnerships, 2) limited partnerships, 3) partnership property, 4) partner's interest, and 5) a partner's personal property stake in the business.

The issue of how a partnership gets underway is generally covered under another heading: partnership formation. I alluded earlier to how a partnership can be casually created in the minds of other business people and potential creditors. If you're fortunate, it will have been better thought out and more formal than bragging over drinks. Partnerships are formed either by contract or by what the law calls estoppel. Estoppel is the principle that the law precludes a person from asserting something contrary to what they've already implied by a previous action or statement of that person or by a previous pertinent judicial determination. Now you might be beginning to understand how legally and financially loaded that phrase, "Me and Bob are business partners" actually is. It doesn't take a written contract, and ill-advised bragging is more than enough to put your neck in the partnership responsibility noose.

Here are a few more headings for your Google research: 1) partnerships formed by contract, 2) partnerships formed by estoppel, 3) factors that indicate a partnership exists, 4) forming a limited partnership, and 5) dangers of third-party claims of partnership by either a third party or one of the existing partners.

I previously mentioned marriage and partnerships in the same sentence; they do share far more in common than we understand at first blush. Partners can own property together, go into debt together, operate in legal concert, and they can be held liable for the actions of the other partner. It's in these areas of overlap that many of the problems arise in a partnership. Some of you who read this will have been married or are perhaps still married and have had a joint checking account. Now that arrangement can work out very nicely if both partners in the marriage have common goals, motivations, and self-control. You already see where I'm headed with this, so let's get there. One marriage partner can spend all the money in the joint checking account, indebt the other partner, and in general create havoc in a marriage if bad decision-making reigns. It's no different in a business partnership.

Here are several more headings where you could conduct a Google search and get a good amount of information. Topics of importance in this area include: 1) partners and their fiduciary duties to other partners, 2) partners and their abilities to bind other partners in a contract with third parties, 3) partners' ability to buy or sell real property of the partnership, and 4) partners' "joint and several liability" in tort claims.

Terminating a partnership is again a lot like a marriage. I have a long-time business associate who likes to say that when he was a young man, fifty years ago, "Marriage cost $30 to get into and $300,000 to get out of." If you've been through the termination of a partnership or a marriage, you know there's a lot of sad truth in that statement and you also know that there's frequently acrimony and bitterness in the process. In this era I see more and more people, even those without great personal wealth and perhaps bringing to the marriage great personal debt, who opt for prenuptial agreements. A good partnership contract will have many of those same elements. The lack of a good partnership contract at dissolution will take on the air of a contested divorce. Relationships are torn apart forever, friends pick sides, and the lawyers just rack up those pesky hourly charges.

Let me once again offer a few more useful search terms for Google: 1) creating a partnership, 2) dissolving a partnership, 3) reasons partnerships are dissolved, 4) partners' rights to damage resulting from dissolution, 5) partnership dissolution resulting from a partner's death, and 6) partners' liability for debt after the partnership is dissolved.

This little essay weighs in at approximately 1,500 words. That's 1,500 more words than I knew the first two or three times I entered into partnerships forty years ago. I was ignorant, my partners were ignorant, and in the end, friendships were tragically destroyed because none of us had a clue about business partnerships, or about one another for that matter. In the years since, I've had some good partnerships and some bad partnerships, but none of which I entered into as blindly as I did in those early days. I'm going to beg you here to really think hard about entering into any kind of a partnership unless you've got your eyes wide open, know the potential partner(s) like you know yourself, and have some good legal counsel to help you and your partner(s) draft a solid partnership agreement (contract) that protects all your interests. In the absence of those elements, you'll lose money, sleep, and most likely, partners who once were friends.

## Your Government Business Partners

Here's another kind of partner. I've mentioned this partner throughout this book and even more so in this chapter. I tried to hit it from multiple directions. When you go into business, even as a sole proprietor, you will still have one or more partners. This is true because whether you live in the USA or you live in the PRC, one or more governmental entities are going to partner with you.

These partners will help you make decisions about almost every issue related to your business, and they'll expect a share of the monies your partnership earns for all their help. You need to get used to it. You do not have to like it, but you do have to learn to work with it and take it into every calculation. If you cannot or will not, they'll eventually help you see the error of your ways.

## Your Government Business Partners' Record Keeper

Many of you will find yourself rushing around each year at year's end to get your W-2s, 1099s, and a handful of other records ready and the info out to the IRS by the yearly deadline. You'll go through smaller and less traumatic versions of this monthly and/or quarterly with other government tax collecting agencies. For those of you who are starting up or in your early years in business, you likely didn't realize that when it all started you'd spend so much of your time performing recordkeeping efforts for your government partner, did you? If you haven't yet launched your new business effort, you need to look at this aspect of being a business owner and take it into consideration before you launch.

## Handling The Red Tape Associated With Your Business

Having owned or managed several businesses over the years, I've found the number of forms, fees, and communications I'm forced to provide to government agencies has grown exponentially since my first experiences back in 1973. Because of advanced degrees and law school, I can now do 90% of them myself. I wonder how a new entrepreneur with a small dream manages to launch and sustain a business these days without drowning in forms, fees, and communications they barely comprehend.

When I first became a licensed contractor thirty years ago, it cost me about $500 to get my license, bonding, and insurance in place. Today it runs at least ten times that much. Craftsmen I've known who had a dream, some hand tools, and a little bit of money have built multi-million dollar construction companies and now employ hundreds. I don't see the same possibilities for young people now unless they have a lot of financial backing. This simple work-hard-and-make-something-of-yourself opportunity seems to have dried up greatly.

So you ask me, "As a business consultant, why would you complain?" The truth is a small business can't afford me. So you then ask, "Why do you care?" I care for some existential reasons, but I also have purely selfish reasons. The big companies who can afford to pay people like me with a string of initials behind their names all started out as an entrepreneur with a dream and a little money. When the small business incubator ceases to function, at some point there are no baby companies around to become big companies who can afford me.

## Politics Doesn't Affect Me

Back in the early eighties, when I was a foreman in the oil business, I was assigned to work with my machinist to select and order all the equipment to completely retool an old machine shop we had at the company garage. As I recall, we had about $80,000 to spend on the effort, and both of us wanted to get it right. The machinist certainly knew a whole lot more about the task than I did, and I liked everything he picked. Most of the stuff we bought was gently used, but one piece was brand new. It was a very large Tarnow® lathe made in Poland. When it arrived and was unpackaged, I thought it was one of the most magnificent pieces of equipment I'd ever seen. When that machinist later left the company, I taught myself to run it and spent more than two thousand hours standing by it in the early mornings over the next four years.

Now let me back up. After the lathe arrived and after we'd got it all set up, the owner of the company came to me one morning a couple of months later with a newspaper in his hand to show me the headline. There'd been political upheaval in Poland between the Poles and the USSR, and there was talk of embargoes, revolution, invasion, and all sorts of other political upheaval in Central Europe. "What do we do now, Farrell, if we need parts for this lathe?" he asked. This was an early example of anxiety working in my favor because we'd also made the deal include all the change gears and the most common parts to fail on this lathe; truth be told, there weren't many weak parts in these lathes. Until that day, I'd never given much thought to how international politics can invade a business or a career thousands of miles away.

Most of us would just like to be allowed to live out our lives without political influences affecting us. It's irritating enough to have to deal with the problems that our own local, state, and federal governments can bring upon us; we definitely don't want international issues as well. As a business owner or manager or just one of the people being asked to buy a truckload of widgets for the company you work for, you must think globally and you must think of the potential impact of political upheaval in those global markets as you make your decisions. International shortages, crop or business failures, and foreign elections can affect you. Revolutions in countries that send you your raw materials can devastate your business and cause you to close the doors. Here are two important matters you need to address: 1) the reliability of your supply lines, and 2) having an alternate plan if your supply lines are cut.

Fortunately for me, the lathe never faltered during the period when it would have been most difficult to get parts. However, I've never again failed to fully examine the company I was buying from, where it was located, and the reliability of their supply lines. As my momma would've said, "The experience threw a scare into me." Throughout this book, I have hoped to do the same with you. This is not because I like to scare people, but because human beings, at least smart human beings, learn from the things that have a strong emotional impact on them; fear is a strong emotion. If you're new to business or management, you should think of it as "taking a run through the jungle." While jungles are filled with beauty, they're also filled with potential dangers for the uninitiated. Tread cautiously and be prepared.

## Twenty-six Useful Terms Of Business And Law

The following several thousand words are added here as a resource to you. They are the terms that I feel are most important for a new business owner or manager to have a working knowledge of. I'm not a lawyer, and you're not a lawyer. But having said that, each of us is better able to operate in a legally complicated environment if we have some grasp of the vernacular. I don't suggest you try to digest this all at once, and it may be best just to thumb through this section to familiarize yourself with the headings initially. Later on, as the need arises, you can come back here for some guidance, and based on that you could seek more formal definitions or legal assistance. Business law is complex. Even lawyers specializing in business law will often have pursued an advanced law degree within specific areas (e.g., contracts, business tort, taxes, etc.)

Concepts of business law will be different for you than they would be for a lawyer. In fact, if you went to a university and took a course entitled "Business Law" and then you went to law school and took a course entitled "Business Law," you'd show up for that law school class thinking you had some grasp of what you were about to study. In fact, you'd actually be at a disadvantage over members of your class that had no presuppositions. You'd be forced to un-learn some of what your university professor taught you unless he or she was an attorney and shaped the class in that direction. Lawyers think of business law as a series of sectors where they might wish to focus their practices (e.g., business formation, banking and finance, taxation, human resources, industrial relations, intellectual property, Internet, environment, contracts, torts, etc.). Business owners and managers don't think that way.

Each of these areas of law and a dozen lesser ones comprise business law and will play a role in your life as a business owner/manager at different points in your career. In the past year I've spent significant time involved in contract law, employment law, environmental law, intellectual property law, business formation law, real property law, Internet law, and marketing law. When I was twenty-three years old, I could have never imagined the turn my life has taken because law was of very little interest to me then, just as it's currently of very little interest to some of you who'll read this. But as my career advanced and my business exposure grew, I realized that the world of business hangs tenuously on threads of the law. So I made the decision to go to law school when I was age fifty-four because I was spending more and more of my business time with lawyers and in legal proceedings.

Let's come up with a workable definition then for *business law* as it will pertain to you initially in your early business life or your early management career. Business law takes in all of the laws that determine how you're going to form and run your business. This means that all of the laws that pertain to how to start, buy, manage, close, or dispose of any type of business is business law. Business law sets the rules that all businesses are supposed to obey. Once upon a time, business law would have been limited to those state and federal laws enacted by elected government bodies, but in the present time, administrative laws (i.e., those laws promulgated by unelected bureaucrats at agencies of the government) are an equally vast third prong of the body of laws that grow every year. It's no longer enough to know your state or federal law; you now must also consider vast compendiums of administrative regulations.

I don't want to write a book on business law; there are far better qualified people out there to do that, and I really don't think that people who will buy my book are part of that audience. What I want to do in the following definitions is offer you some important basics. I hope that by seeing your ignorance of the laws (as I one day saw mine), you'll be motivated to begin to take business law just as seriously as you take gross margins, net profits, and income taxes. I do recommend that you take a business law class at your local community college, four-year college, or university. It can't help but further open your eyes and inform the way you go about the conduct of your business. Again, there are thousands of self-help books devoted entirely to business and business law out there on the shelves.

I considered using the definitions as they appeared in *Black's Law Dictionary*, and after starting to actually read them again, I thought better of that idea. Legal language is long, verbose, stilted, and often tough to comprehend until you immerse yourself in it. So I'll do my best here to break this handful of legal terms down into short definitions meaningful for a layperson. I believe if you're reading this book you're just trying to get a better understanding of the law so you can survive in business and not launch a law career. Again, if you need more formal definitions, I'd guide you to some of the fine legal dictionaries out there, *Black's Law Dictionary* if you can stand it, or a local attorney familiar with your state's laws.

**Administrative Law:** That body of public law which deals with issues such as collection of revenue, sanitation, public safety, water laws, police services, fire services, environmental regulations, etc. You'll most likely encounter these laws when getting business licenses, health permits, environmental issues, air pollution issues, storm water runoff permits, fire department inspections, and local business licensing and taxes.

You'll likely encounter this in your business on a daily basis while others among you may never encounter these kinds of laws as a part of your business. Do get to know the administrative agencies and their laws that impact your business. I need to add here once again that these laws can seriously outnumber and be far more onerous upon your enterprise than statutory laws will be.

Most of these administrative agencies will also have their own staff of administrative law judges or administrative hearing officers who'll conduct legal hearings and hand out verdicts with the power of a court; they're not to be taken lightly. You're going to face these judges or officers in labor issues, environmental issues, planning and development issues, and many more.

**Alternate Dispute Resolution:** Procedures developed to settle legal disputes through some means other than litigation. These are primarily limited to arbitration or mediation. You'll most likely encounter this in your business in issues where a suit has in fact been brought by either yourself or a plaintiff and you wish to settle it without the time and expense of going to court.

**Arbitration:** The investigation and a decision on matters disputed between two adversarial parties. Voluntary arbitrations are entered into at the consent of both parties. Compulsory arbitration occurs when one of the parties is forced to take part by statutory rules. While arbitration has become a broad general term encompassing the entire process, its original meaning was all about the submission of evidence and the subsequent hearing of that evidence. The decision was thought of as a separate issue and is termed an "award." You'll most likely encounter arbitration in your business in labor disputes, contract disputes, or disputes over some damage or "property right" one party asserts against another.

**Assault:** The threat or application of force on or toward another which causes that person to have a reasonable apprehension that an imminent harmful or offensive touching is about to take place. It's also simply putting another person in fear that they are about to experience battery. You'll most likely encounter this in your business when you, your manager, or another employee either threatens or is threatened by you, your manager, employee, or someone they come in contact with while in your employ. The threat can take the shape of being in someone's face, yelling threats or insults at people, or just approaching them in a rapid manner as if you intend to strike them. Waving a gun or some other weapon around would also fall into this area.

In my career, I've seen assaults committed by everybody from manual laborers, to physicians, to lawyers, to bankers, to engineers, and every other job or profession you can imagine. It's so common and so often ignored that people come to take it for granted as being acceptable behavior. The wake-up call comes when the person who was victimized either calls law enforcement or an attorney. All the talk in the world about how this is "normal behavior in our line of business" will not overcome the fact that if a crime has been committed, someone (or multiple someones) is going to pay a penalty. This can include criminal and civil action. It is a major factor in many labor litigation settlements.

**Battery:** Battery occurs when, against someone's will, there is a harmful or offensive touching, such as an unlawful beating (i.e., not an act of self-defense or some consensual act of sadomasochism). It can be a simple touch by putting your hand on someone, a shove, a slap, or a kick. You'll most likely experience this in your business when you, your manager, or an employee physically attacks you, your manager, your employee, or a customer. Once again, all the talk in the world about how this is "normal behavior in our line of business" will not overcome the fact that if a crime has been committed, someone (or multiple someones) is going to pay a penalty. This can include criminal and civil action. It is a major factor in many labor litigation settlements.

**Bankruptcy Law:** The body of law that deals exclusively with bankruptcy. In the United States, bankruptcy laws are federal laws and not state laws.

**Bankruptcy:** The condition of a person (legal or corporeal) who is bankrupt and therefore subject to bankruptcy laws. Once someone has committed bankruptcy, they become subject to legal action by their creditors to recover what they can of the money, the services, or the goods the bankrupt has received from them. Insolvency is another term with nearly similar meaning. You'll most likely encounter this in your business if you or one of your creditors becomes insolvent, resulting in a filing for bankruptcy.

I might add that this is one of the reasons you need to have a good process in place for granting credit because it is inherent in any relationship where you choose to extend credit that you also have agreed to be governed by federal bankruptcy proceedings. Creditors gain a ranking for disbursement of any funds based on their legal standing. There are secured creditors and unsecured creditors, and if you don't have solid credit processes in place, you will be left holding an empty bag when the court makes its decision.

**Civil Law:** The system of law that deals with the relationships between private individuals; this system does not concern itself with criminal law, military law, or matters of religion. The American system of law is based on English common law.

**Commerce Clause:** The Commerce Clause derives from Article 1, Section 8, Clause 3 of The United States Constitution. It grants to Congress incredibly broad powers to regulate commerce with foreign nations, among the several states, and with the Indian tribes. I cannot overstate how broadly this law has been interpreted to allow Congress to touch on every area of commerce and almost every area of your life and your business.

You'll likely encounter this in your business in ways you never even knew existed as it affects what can be sold, how it can be sold, and where it can be sold. If you do business in other states or other nations, you'll become much more aware of its reach and the laws and statutes which have been promulgated. You'd have to read a good deal of case law just to get a small grasp. I suggest being aware of this power but not that you attempt to become an expert.

You will need to educate yourself fully if you should decide to engage in interstate commerce or importing or exporting goods.

**Compensatory Damages:** Monies awarded by civil courts to indemnify a person (corporate or corporeal) for a loss, injury, or a detriment that arose from the illegal conduct of another. The myth in the legal realm is that these monies will make whole the person suffering the loss. Realistically there are some injuries, losses, or detriments so egregious that there are no true means to make the damaged party whole.

You'll likely encounter this in your business in the form of either paying or receiving monies for events such as harassment, breach of contract, assault, adhesion contracts, interference with a contract of another, patent law violations, discrimination, labor law violations, unfair competition, false advertising, breach of a fiduciary duty, and tort claims against you or your business; the list is nearly endless.

**Contract:** While the concept of a contract seems fairly simple (i.e., offer, acceptance, and consideration) and straightforward, how you can end up in a legally binding contract situation is not. A simple definition would be an agreement between two or more parties that involves the exchange of "promises," which are enforceable by law.

As a simple example in a sales contract: "I'll buy 200 of your widgets for $6 a piece." "I accept your offer to buy 200 of my widgets for $6 a piece." This is a classic offer, acceptance, and consideration (money) example. Going into counteroffers and other more convoluted aspects of contracts is beyond the scope of this writing.

You'll likely encounter this in your business on a daily basis. We all make thousands of minor contracts in the course of our lives without even realizing it. Your problems arise when you don't understand that the words or writings of a business are given much heavier weight in courts than your casual offers of, "Bring me some grapes and I'll buy you a beer the next time we meet."

**Contract Law:** Contract law is a massive body of law concerned with the many aspects of legally binding contracts: how they're negotiated, how they're accepted or rejected, and how they're adjudicated in the event of a disagreement or breach at a later date. This is a legal specialty, and its technical difficulty eats new entrepreneurs alive. Get a good contract lawyer on your team to review your contracts.

You'll likely encounter this in your business on a daily basis. Even the fact that you put a sign on your bakery case to sell muffins for $2 a piece is an effort to initiate a contract. You don't have to be making deals with foreign countries for $20,000,000 to be dealing with contracts. A warning here, they can be made verbally, in writing, or simply by the nod of your head at an auction.

**Contract, Breach Of:** Breach of contract occurs when one or both parties to a contract fail to live up to its terms. Such failure usually brings on a lawsuit or lawsuits wherein any of the aggrieved parties can petition the court to force the breaching party to compensate them for any contractually covered loss brought on by the breach.

It's considered a cause for such legal action when any binding agreement or a "bargained-for exchange" has been met with non-performance, interference, the delivery of substandard goods, substandard services, etc.

Breach is not always made known by an actual acknowledgement (i.e., I'm not going to meet the deadline) by the defendant. It occurs whether or not there has been such an acknowledgment as well as if the breaching party informs the other party of intent to breach through non-performance or by their actions or conduct (i.e., they closed their doors and left town).

You'll likely encounter this in your business at some point, and when you do, I would encourage you to get all the facts first before proceeding with legal action and see if there is some way available which allows the breaching party to heal the breach. If you're successful in this act, it will save you and/or your creditor/lender a lot of heartache and attorney fees. That's not how it is on television; that's how it is in the real world.

**Default Judgment:** This is a binding judgment of the court or administrative officer, which comes about as a direct result of one party failing to take some required action resulting in a verdict for the other party.

You'll likely encounter this in your business when either you or someone you've brought legal proceedings against fails to respond to a legal summons or fails to show up for a legal proceeding. Ignoring legal problems won't make them go away.

Don't ignore a summons of any sort; get a lawyer involved early so they can guide you through the process. The court dislikes people who fail to take the legal system seriously, fail to respond, or fail to appear.

**Jurisdiction:** Jurisdiction refers to the power of a legal agency (e.g., civil, criminal, political, administrative, etc.) to exercise legal authority over a person, subject matter, or territory. In law, this is a critical power, as it determines which set of laws and rules will be involved.

You'll likely encounter this in your business with regard to local, state, and federal business ordinances and laws. You'll definitely become subject to the laws of some jurisdiction in business contracts. You'll also find you are subject to various jurisdictions of the web of state and federal agencies you'll deal with regularly.

This is the place where I encourage you to do your homework and learn about the various jurisdictions that will have power over you and your business. I do business in multiple states and learned years ago that the civil and criminal laws of Texas, California, Oregon, New Mexico, and Delaware are all different; so are the other forty-five.

**Law, Statutory:** Statutory law refers to law that is enacted by an elected legislative body such as a state legislature or the Congress of the United States.

You'll likely encounter this in your business on a daily basis for as long as you chose to remain in business. Get to know the statutory laws that impact your business.

**Law, Regulatory:** Regulatory laws are laws enacted by administrative agencies of the government and are empowered by delegation of an elected legislative body.

You'll likely encounter this in your business on a daily basis for as long as you chose to remain in business. Get to know the regulatory laws that impact your business. I need to add here that these laws can seriously outnumber and be far more onerous upon your enterprise than statutory laws will be.

**Mediation:** Mediation is a form of alternative dispute resolution where a third-party known as a mediator works with two or more parties to settle their dispute without litigation. The goal of mediation is to reach a mutually agreeable settlement. You'll most likely encounter mediation in your business in either a labor dispute or in some dispute with a vendor, customer, or client. I've also seen mediation utilized where there was a dispute between two tenants of a shopping center to settle questions of property rights to parking spaces, signage, or common areas.

**Ordinance:** An ordinance is a legally binding piece of legislation enacted by some recognized governmental body. Usually these bodies are going to be local and can include a board of supervisors, city councils, park and recreation districts, and other special districts. In California, we have thousands of special districts with ordinance power.

You'll likely encounter ordinances in your business as you navigate the web of rules in the local area or region that will regulate how you conduct your business. Historically, this has included ordinances as diverse as blue laws, dry counties, planning and development, zoning, health permits, hours of operation, architectural features, and even headstones on graves; the list is nearly endless.

**Punitive Damages:** Punitive damages are meant to punish the defendant. These are damages awarded by a court that go beyond just compensating the plaintiff for loss or injuries. In some instances, the court is empowered to treble punitive damages set by statute or a jury to make the punishment of the defendant more severe. Such damages are meant to be a lesson to the defendant and the community at large that such behavior will not be tolerated by the courts.

You'll likely encounter this in your business when either you as a plaintiff or you as a defendant enter into a lawsuit over a civil matter such as breach of contract, patent right violation, or some other injurious action that caused loss of property, bodily injury, or loss of some financial right or benefit. Punitive damages can destroy a business by wiping it out financially.

**Remedy:** In law school, you spend a full semester on the study of remedies. That should give you some indication of how complex the concept can be. A simple definition holds that remedies are the means with which a court of law enforces a legal right, imposes a legal penalty, or makes a court order to impose the will of the court or a person (corporate or corporeal). Judges often have great leeway in this area and can get very creative in crafting their remedies.

You'll likely encounter this in your business if you are either the plaintiff or the defendant in a civil action. In some cases, the law is very specific about what the plaintiff can receive as compensation for some wrong. Remedies drift off into the area of Solomonic wisdom at times as judges are asked to craft remedies for which there are few, if any, precedents. Sometimes this works out well and sometimes the remedies border on the bizarre.

**Small Claims Court:** Small claims courts are courts whose jurisdiction is limited to certain financial amounts; they seem to vary from state to state. In California, an individual or a sole proprietor can sue for up to $10,000, and a corporation or other similar entity can sue for up to $5,000. The laws of other states vary.

This is a special court where the rules of order are simplified and the proceedings, while not casual, are less formal than in a full-blown civil court. There are restrictions on how many actions one can take in small claims court in a single year. Lawyers are generally not allowed in small claims courts, and the parties or claimants represent themselves.

You'll likely encounter this in your business if you are suing or being sued for the types of amounts of money listed above. You should check your local small claims court to determine the limits in your state. Even though the court is less formal, be sure to take the matter seriously, prepare well in advance, and while you can't have a lawyer in the court with you, in most cases you can certainly hire one to help you prepare.

**Statute Of Limitations:** A statute of limitations is a law that establishes a specific timeframe within which legal actions must take place. There are both civil and criminal statutes of limitations in effect in some states. You need to be aware of the statutes of limitations relevant to your business in your state or the states you conduct business in.

You'll likely encounter this in your business with regard to torts, either by you or against you. It can also involve acts such as embezzlement, fraud, misrepresentation, misuse of company property or assets, and, once again, the list can be endless. In many cases, the ticking clock of the statute of limitations does not start until the tort or the crime is discovered. This works to your advantage when a crime against your business comes to light months or years later.

"Sleeping on your tort" is a term used by lawyers to denote those instances where claimants have failed to file an action with the courts in a timely manner. Here the relevant time limits placed by the ruling statute have expired and the claimant loses the right to pursue the action. As I was writing this book, I had a client come to me with such an issue, which involved $30,000. I referred the client to a lawyer, but the outcome was that the clock had tolled and the client could no longer pursue the claim.

**Tort:** The word "tort" comes from the Latin *torquere*, meaning "twisted or wrong." A tort occurs whenever a civil wrong or wrongful act injures another party. The act can be deliberate or it can be unintentional. As a general rule, your ignorance of the law is no excuse and is not an acceptable defense when a tort has been committed.

**Tort Law:** Tort law is massive and involves all the rights, obligations, and remedies that a court utilizes to provide relief to plaintiffs who have suffered some sort of harm due to the acts of others. The plaintiff is the party claiming the harm has been done to them, and the tortfeasor is the party accused of the harming. This is not reality television, and these cases usually involve mundane business issues.

In every tort action, three things must be proved: 1) the plaintiff must prove that the tortfeasor was under a duty to act or perform in a certain way, 2) the plaintiff has to show that the tortfeasor breached this duty by failing to act in accordance with the terms or conditions of the duty, and 3) the plaintiff must prove s/he suffered actual damage, injury, or loss that resulted directly form the tortfeasor's breach of that duty.

**Tort, Business:** The most common business torts involve economic relationships, negligence, intentionally wronging another party, interference with a business, passing off inferior goods or services, injurious falsehoods, trade libel, conspiracy, inducement to breach a contract, tortious interference, and misrepresentation.

At one time or another you'll likely experience one or more of these in your business. It would be good to know what the terms above mean, but defining them completely here is beyond the scope of this writing. I'd suggest you Google® any of those terms that are confusing to you and be certain you grasp their significance. It's a good way to know if you've been wronged and an even better way to make sure you or your employees don't wrong another party.

Allow me to repeat this because it's very important and might save you some heartache in the years ahead. As a general rule, your ignorance of the law is no excuse and is not an acceptable defense when a tort has been committed. Many business owners that I've worked with have lamented to me when they called or we sat together that they had no idea they or one of their employees were breaking a law in something they had done.

## AUTHOR'S AFTERWARD

All the while we were editing this book I continued writing, despite the fact that I was thirty thousand words over the needed volume to begin with. I'm now about fifty thousand over and I was asked by one of my editors if I shouldn't just plan another book. I ended up with less than I wrote, but more than was suggested to me. What I find is that much of this writing about business has helped me to see my own beliefs in black and white. This in turn forced me to examine those beliefs and see if they still held up after all these years. We're in a unique period in history where huge changes to business and the way business is conducted are starting to break on the shoreline of our civilization.

Artificial intelligence and its progeny, Automation, are having an impact on businesses as never before. They will continue to have an increasing impact in the next forty years. Some of my colleagues believe that as much as one-third of the human race could find itself unemployable over that same coming forty year period. This is troubling to me on many levels, and it should be troubling to you. If you own or manage a business, or you plan to own or manage a business, this will be the environment of business you will have to navigate. These changes will create issues in regulations, human resources, finance, marketing, laws, and the entire business landscape in ways we can't yet imagine.

Yet despite all the changes it will create for those of us in business, the greater challenges are more likely to be societal. Massive populations of people around the world who are unemployed or unemployable have always been a recipe for political upheaval. If we accept that there could be nine billion people on the plant in 2050, my colleagues' dire prediction would mean as many as three billion people here with no means to provide for themselves or their offspring. If we as business people, and fellow human beings, consider these issues now, there may still be time to avert catastrophe. A dystopian future would be in no one's best interest.

I want to close by thanking you for taking the time to look this book over and for considering some of the issues I raise here. I hope that it will provide you food for thought, and even for debate with your stakeholders. The goal in all this is to go into business, stay in business, and succeed in business. If you liked *Out Of Brains*, please share it with another would-be business owner or current business owner. In addition to writing, teaching, corporate training, and occasional public lectures, I'm on Facebook® at *Farrell Neeley & Associates*. I don't post there daily, but I do post useful business information throughout the week.

Farrell F. Neeley, PhD
December 28, 2017

www.ingramcontent.com/pod-product-compliance
Lightning Source LLC
Chambersburg PA
CBHW031953190326
41520CB00007B/235